The Operated Heart at Autopsy

Stuart L. Houser

The Operated Heart
at Autopsy

 Springer

Stuart L. Houser
Boston MA 02114
USA
shouserl@verizon.net

ISBN 978-1-60327-807-2   e-ISBN 978-1-60327-808-9
DOI 10.1007/978-1-60327-808-9
Springer Dordrecht Heidelberg London New York

Library of Congress Control Number: 2009928015

Printed on acid-free paper

Springer is part of Springer Science+Business Media (www.springer.com)

Preface

After 17 years of private practice as a cardiovascular surgeon, my partners questioned the rationality of my decision to leave the clinical practice behind and become a cardiovascular pathologist. In fact, their disbelief of my intention to make the "leap of faith" was understandable. For a surgeon, the operating room is where the action is. It is as simple as that. And when a cardiac surgeon can hold in his hand a beating heart, now off-bypass and improved by an operation just completed, satisfaction is real and profound.

However, life is complex. Throughout my surgical career, questions regarding the pathogenesis of atherosclerotic cardiovascular disease arose; curiosities of various phenotypes of the disease piqued my interest. I became aware of the power of investigative techniques that might address these questions. I then began to realize that my career in the operating room left me little time to address them. I needed to study the disease full time in order to contribute to my understanding of it.

Ironically, my first autopsy as a pathology resident was on an individual with a past history of coronary artery bypass surgery. When it came to examining the heart, the dissection, as all pathologists know, was complex. However, I found it to be straightforward and enjoyable. But I subsequently learned that my fellow residents and mentors did not share my intrigue and comfort in defining the nuances of the operated heart. In fact, after my first autopsy in training, calls soon began coming from frustrated fellow residents who were facing, with significant wonder and trepidation, similar cardiac dissections at autopsy. To this day, twelve years later, the calls continue to come.

My motivation to write this monograph came one evening when, as a first-year resident attending a New England Pathology Society meeting, I was sitting next to a pathologist in private practice. I introduced myself to him, told him my story, and informed him that I was currently rotating on the hematopathology service and that I was finding it surprisingly interesting. He told me that I should forget about hemepath and focus on writing a book that would expedite his approach to the operated heart at autopsy.

Herein my focus is so directed. By drawing on lessons learned as a cardiac surgeon, I will strive to offer reasonable guidelines to the pathologist who, at autopsy, faces the challenge of evaluating a heart that had previously undergone surgical treatment of one kind or another. Such previous surgery may have been construction of coronary artery bypass grafts (CABG), replacement or repair of one or more heart valves, repair of one or more congenital heart anomalies, or some other procedure. Questions will arise at such an autopsy. When a past medical history is lacking, what is the best way to determine exactly what operation was done? Was the cause of death heart-related? What was the impact of the heart surgery on the cause of death? What is the importance of technical issues of the heart surgery in a given autopsy? What steps should be taken in the actual dissection of the heart. . .and in what order? What are the anatomic landmarks, i.e., "footprints" of a surgeon, to look for when examining the operated heart? Importantly, as the pathologist in charge of an autopsy of an individual who died during or following open-heart surgery, what do I, the pathologist, tell the cardiac surgeon who **needs to know** what happened? The goal of this monograph is to assist the pathologist in addressing these and other related questions, whether he or she is a resident in training or a professional in academic or private practice.

Acknowledgment

The author is grateful to Michelle Forrestall Lee for her expertise and gracious assistance in photographing the cardiac specimens illustrated in this manuscript. Thanks also to Dr. H. Tom Aretz for his tutorial guidance in the author's transition from a cardiac surgeon to a "card-carrying" cardiac pathologist, while astutely recognizing that "once a surgeon. . .always a surgeon."

Contents

Chapter 1
External Evidence of Open-Heart Surgery

Abstract Specific external findings at autopsy can provide important clues relating to adverse perioperative circumstances when death occurs during a hospital admission in which heart surgery was performed. An open sternotomy found at autopsy should trigger in the pathologist's mind a sequence of possible scenarios leading to the demise of the patient in the peri- or postoperative hospital course. Careful examination of the chest wall may reflect a variety of minimally invasive approaches to heart surgery used for technical and/or esthetic indications. The skin of the extremities may reveal evidence of the harvest of tissue used for bypass conduits. It is important to look for tubes, wires, and lines in the early postoperative period. Importantly, at the time of autopsy, there may be external evidence of an intraoperative and/or postoperative low cardiac output state.

Keywords External examination · Chest wall · Extremities · Chest tubes · Hemodynamic monitoring · Mechanical support

External examination of a body at autopsy will reveal specific findings relating to previous cardiac surgery. These findings will vary somewhat depending on what procedure was done and how long prior to autopsy the surgery was performed. If the pathologist lacks knowledge of a past history of heart surgery and/or the details of the operation(s) done on the heart of the deceased, a major clue, viz., the presence of a scar over the middle of the sternum, should prompt an eager search for other external clues relating to the previous heart surgery. Are there scars on the lower extremities from where greater and/or lesser saphenous veins were harvested for use as conduits for aortocoronary artery bypass grafts? Are there scars on the upper extremities reflecting an extended search for suitable bypass conduits? Is there a scar in the inguinal area marking the possible site of femoral arterial and/or venous canulation to establish cardiopulmonary bypass? If so, why was such a procedure done? These questions would prompt one to start thinking about a strategy of focusing on the subsequent internal examination of the body.

Most of the external findings are straightforward and easily documented. In addition, as has been already hinted above, some of these findings can be strikingly informative and provocative, particularly when death occurred during the hospital admission in which the heart surgery was performed. They can provide important clues relating to adverse perioperative circumstances prior to death. Some reflections of such occurrences include the presence of an intraaortic balloon pump (IABP), a ventricular assist device, and/or dialysis catheters dwelling in large veins or intraperitoneally. In short, such findings are evidence that ventricular failure had been a serious clinical issue in the patient's hospital course. If so, it is up to the pathologist to analyze the autopsy findings and explain why the heart had failed. An understanding of scenarios leading to poor surgical outcomes will increase the pathologist's perspective in assessing the heart at autopsy.

Look at the Skin of the Chest Wall

Most, but not all, open-heart surgery is performed through a median sternotomy. Therefore, the most common external finding relating to previous cardiac surgery is a vertical scar or fresh skin closure over the sternum. A pale scar will be found if the cardiac surgery was performed months to years prior to autopsy. A darkly pink scar is consistent with a postoperative period of a few weeks. A fresh skin closure usually signifies that death occurred during the admission in which the surgery was performed. In the latter case, the prosector may or may not see skin sutures, depending on the skin closure technique used by the surgeon. If the surgeon used a subcuticular technique, i.e., a running, usually absorbable suture in a deep layer of the epidermis, the skin closure will not reveal "stitches" superficially.

An open sternotomy found at autopsy (Fig. 1.1) should trigger in the pathologist's mind a sequence of possible scenarios leading to the demise of the patient in the peri- or postoperative hospital course. Perhaps the patient developed right

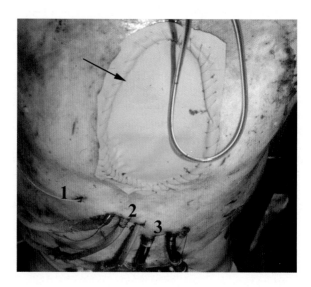

Fig. 1.1 An Eschmark bandage is sutured to the skin (*arrow*) to cover an underlying open sternotomy and protect the mediastinum

ventricular failure following cardiopulmonary bypass (CBP), or "pump run," and the surgeon was unable to safely close the sternotomy without causing tamponade of the dilated right heart. If so, subsequent internal examination of the block may focus on finding a cause of right heart failure, such as ischemia of the right and/or left ventricle, mechanical obstruction (acute pulmonary embolus), or pulmonary hypertension. Perhaps the patient had "crashed" hemodynamically in the intensive care unit following surgery, and efforts of open-heart resuscitation failed. In this case, the sternal wound would usually be left open when the body is transferred to the morgue. A less common complication includes a postoperative mediastinitis, which was treated by sternectomy [1] and open drainage of the wound. Here, little if any sternal bone would be found, and the wound would show granulation tissue with or without a purulent exudate. Any purulence should be cultured, even though the effort would very likely duplicate previous clinical data.

As mentioned above, not all open-heart surgery is performed through a median sternotomy. In the past decade, cardiac surgeons have used so-called minimally invasive approaches to operate on the heart. Three such approaches include partial median sternotomy, anterolateral minor thoracotomy, and a parasternal approach [2]. Coronary artery bypass surgery and procedures on the mitral and aortic valves have been performed through upper, mid, or inferior partial sternotomies [3]. For technical or cosmetic reasons, operations on the mitral valve are sometimes done through a right thoracotomy. This approach has also been used for operations on the tricuspid valve and atrial septal defects. Operations through mini-thoracotomies can allow endoscopically supported surgery but may require cannulation of a femoral artery and vein to achieve cardiopulmonary bypass [4], access that would leave an inguinal wound closure or scar on external examination. Pericardial resections, so-called pericardial windows, are performed through a subxyphoid approach or left anterior or anterolateral thoracotomy, usually to drain large pericardial effusions. A left thoracotomy approach has also been used in reoperative and minimally invasive coronary artery bypass grafting (CABG), aortic arch and descending aortic aneurysm repair, and aortic valve replacement [5]. It may be indicated if patent grafts are vulnerable to injury by a re-do sternotomy, if there were prior sternal wound complications or mediastinitis or anterior thoracic radiation therapy, if there is a retrosternal gastric conduit, or if there is a tracheostomy [5]. It is the approach of choice for repairing a descending thoracic aortic aneurysm, a traumatic tear of the aortic isthmus, and repair of certain congenital anomalies, such as patent ductus arteriosus and coarctation of the descending thoracic aorta. Therefore, in the current era of minimally invasive heart surgery, scars may be found over only a part of the sternum as well as on the adjacent anterior and/or lateral chest wall.

Look at the Skin of the Extremities

Following surgical placement of CABG, scars or fresh wound closures on one or more extremities will reflect the harvest of tissue used for bypass conduits. Historically, the greater saphenous vein has been commonly used for conduit tissue. Evidence of its use may be represented by one or more long scars or multiple short scars over the medial aspect of one or both lower extremities. In the past ten years in some centers, the greater saphenous vein has been harvested by an endoscopic technique, leaving a single short scar over the distal medial aspect of the thigh. One or more scars over one or both legs posteriorly might reflect the harvest of one or both lesser saphenous veins, which are the veins of choice for use as conduits if there is an insufficient supply of greater saphenous veins. An insufficiency of greater saphenous vein may be due to inadequate quality of vein, such as small size or varicosities, to inadequate quantity of vein, in the setting of a re-do CABG when the greater saphenous vein had been used in a previous operation, or to a combination of both. Scars over sites of basilic and/or cephalic veins in one or both upper extremities may reflect a somewhat desperate need for conduit tissue for bypass surgery. More recently, a scar over the ventral aspect of the forearm might reflect the use of a radial artery as a bypass conduit. Any inflammation of a wound should be documented and, if there is a purulent exudate, it should be cultured. Finally, the absence of cutaneous scars on the extremities does not necessarily mean that a CABG procedure was not performed. It is important to recognize that some coronary bypass operations are completed with the use of one or both internal mammary arteries alone, leaving no surgical scars on the extremities.

Look for Tubes, Wires, and Lines in the Early Postoperative Period

After closure of the sternum or chest wall following cardiac surgery, minor or major bleeding may occur. Bleeding can result from an insecure suture placement, breakdown of a particularly friable tissue, or a significant coagulopathy. It is because of this risk of bleeding, that the pericardium is left open after heart surgery to reduce the incidence of pericardial tamponade. Plastic chest tubes are placed routinely by the cardiac surgeon to drain postoperative accumulations of blood in the mediastinum (Fig. 1.1) and pleural spaces (Fig. 1.1 to Fig. 1.2). If an autopsy is performed before removal of the drains, two or more tubes will be found exiting the mediastinum through 1–2 cm skin incisions below the xyphoid process of the sternum. In addition, one or more lateral chest tubes may be found draining one or both pleural spaces. The sites and apparent effectiveness of these drainage tubes should be documented. Ineffective drainage would be reflected by residual collections of fluid or blood clot. After this documentation, the tubes should be removed from the body. Remote from the operation, scars at the time of autopsy will reflect the use of these drainage tubes.

Before closing the sternum, the surgeon also routinely puts temporary pacer wires on the right atrium and right ventricle. These wires are brought out through the skin usually just below the ribs to the right of the midline and sutured to the skin. The purpose of these wires is to expedite the use of a temporary pacemaker in the event of a postoperative bradycardia or heart block. If they are still in place at the time of autopsy, it should be so noted by the pathologist. They should be left in place until the status of the epicardial placement of the wires can be confirmed by subsequent examination of the heart.

For hemodynamic monitoring, the surgeon will sometimes place a left atrial pressure line (Fig. 1.1) through the right superior pulmonary vein and bring the other end out through the skin below the ribs to the right of the midline. Left atrial pressure is a measure of left ventricular preload [6]. Monitoring it can be very helpful in patient management during and after heart surgery, since it serves as an important means of assessing intravascular volume and left ventricular function. Similarly, a pulmonary artery, or Swan-Ganz, catheter may have been used to monitor hemodynamic data, such as pulmonary artery pressure, pulmonary artery wedge pressure (which correlates with left atrial pressure and left ventricular end-diastolic pressure), and cardiac output. This pressure line may be found exiting the skin of the neck, arm, or inguinal area depending on which central vein insertion was used. If present at the time of autopsy, the position of a left atrial catheter (Fig. 1.2) or a Swan-Ganz catheter (Fig. 4.10, catheter in SVC) should be documented.

Fig. 1.2 A left atrial catheter exits the right superior pulmonary vein and, as it passes between the right side of the heart and right lung, it underlies a chest tube placed to drain the right pleural space postoperatively

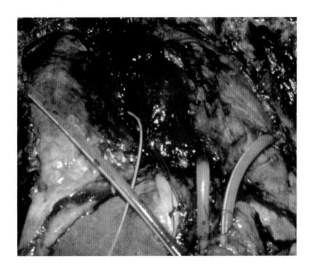

Look for Evidence of Preterminal Mechical Ventricular Support

At the time of autopsy, there may be external evidence of an intraoperative and/or postoperative low cardiac output state. An IABP will appear as a plastic catheter exiting the skin in an inguinal area. Deep to the skin, the balloon catheter enters the femoral artery and should extend to the level of the aortic isthmus, which can be documented on subsequent internal examination of the aorta. At this end of the intraaortic portion of the catheter is a balloon, which inflates in diastole and deflates in systole, the timing of which is triggered by arterial pressure or ECG signal. The hemodynamic benefit of the device is an increase in coronary artery perfusion with balloon inflation and a decreased left ventricular afterload with deflation of the balloon. The pathologist should define the external position of the balloon pump and record any evidence of lower limb ischemia, which might be attributable to compromise of femoral arterial flow by the intraluminal shaft of the balloon pump [7]. If there is evidence of lower limb ischemia, which can range from reddish discoloration to frank gangrene of a toe, foot, or leg, the pathologist will be prompted to search for significant peripheral arterial atherosclerotic occlusive disease on subsequent internal examination, particularly of the iliofemoral arteries. Lower limb ischemia due to IABP insertion can result in edema and elevated intracompartmental pressure in the leg, which can threaten viability of the leg and foot. Open surgical wounds on the leg may reflect an effort to relieve this pressure by performing a fasciotomy [8]. One or two drive lines exiting the skin of the upper abdomen laterally indicate the use of one or two ventricular assist devices during the clinical course of the deceased. Use of a ventricular assist device usually represents treatment of persistent ventricular failure, which has been treated unsuccessfully with an IABP or when placement of an IABP is precluded by arterial atherosclerotic disease.

Look for Evidence of Acute Renal Failure

A common result of a low cardiac output state is renal failure, usually due to acute tubular necrosis. The renal failure may have been present prior to heart surgery and accentuated by the physiologic stress of the surgical procedure. Alternatively, loss of renal function may have resulted anew from a maloccurrence of surgery, which caused profound ventricular failure. On the other hand, the patient might have had end-stage renal disease, which was unrelated to heart disease, going into cardiac surgery, and revealing a bulging subcutaneous linear or U-shaped tubular subcutaneous mass in an upper extremity, consistent with an arteriovenous fistula used for chronic hemodialysis. At any rate, management of renal failure in a patient following heart surgery may necessitate peritoneal dialysis or hemodialysis [9]. Consequently, at autopsy, the pathologist may find a peritoneal catheter exiting the skin of the abdominal wall or a hemodialysis catheter exiting the skin over a femoral, subclavian, or jugular vein. It would not be surprising in this situation to also find an additional line exiting the skin over a femoral or radial artery, indicating a need to monitor arterial pressure prior to the patient's demise. Recording the presence of any of these external lines at the time of autopsy is an appropriate routine. When the abdomen is opened, the position of the peritoneal catheter should be noted before the catheter is removed.

Miscellaneous External Findings Are Notable

There is a variety of findings on external examination of the body that are nonspecific but frequently found at autopsy following recent open-heart surgery and a catastophic postoperative course. Anasarca, or massive whole-body edema may be obvious to the observer at autopsy. It may in part relect fluid overload following a long pump run [10]. It can reflect massive extravasation of fluid following allergic and anaphyllactic reactions to transfusion of blood products necessitated by severe bleeding due to inadequate hemostasis and/or marked coagulopathy following surgery [11]. Multiple cutaneous ecchymoses may reflect successful or failed attempts in times of stress to place percutaneous central venous catheters to restore serious losses of blood volume or maintenance intravenous fluids. These bluish-red patches of discoloration of the skin are commonly seen in the neck (overlying internal and external jugular veins), clavicular areas (associated with subclavian vein "sticks"), and groins (overlying femoral veins). Similarly, hematomas overlying percutaneous punctures of radial, carotid, and femoral arteries may be small or large, resulting either from errant efforts to make venapunctures or from attempts to draw arterial blood to measure oxygen saturation or to place a catheter for monitoring arterial blood pressure. Subsequent deep, internal hematomas may be associated with these superficial findings and reveal evidence of iatrogenic hemorrhage that would otherwise be difficult to explain. Furthermore, when the internal block is later examined, a hemorrhagic accumulation of blood may be found that is not associated with an external ecchymosis or hematoma, presenting a problem regarding its origin. For example, blood that has dissected the adventitia of part of the aortic arch and descending aorta without evidence of a true aortic dissection may be difficult to explain until close examination of the left supra- or infraclavicular area shows a puncture site in the skin made by a large-bore needle.

References

1. d'Udekem Y, Lengele B, Noirhomme P, El Khoury G, Vanwijck R, Rubay JE, Dion R. Radical debridement and omental transposition for post sternotomy mediastinitis. Cardiovasc Surg 1998;6:415–8.
2. Wang WL, Cai KC, Zeng WS, Jiang RC. Experience in using three different minimally invasive approaches in cardiac operations. Med Sci Monit 2003;9:CR109-13.
3. Farhat F, Metton O, Jegaden O. Benefits and complications of total sternotomy and ministernotomy in cardiac surgery. Surg Technol Int 2004;13:199–205. Review.
4. Gulbins H, Pritisanac A, Hannekum A. Minimally invasive heart valve surgery: already established in clinical routine? Expert Rev Cardiovasc Ther 2004;2:837–43. Review.
5. Pratt JW, Williams TE, Michler RE, Brown DA. Current indications for left thoracotomy in coronary revascularization and valvular procedures. Ann Thorac Surg 2000;70:1366–70.
6. Daughters GT, Frist WH, Alderman EL, Derby GC, Ingels NB Jr, Miller DC. Effects of the pericardium on left ventricular diastolic filling and systolic performance early after cardiac operations. J Thorac Cardiovasc Surg 1992;104:1084–91.
7. Erdogan HB, Goksedef D, Erentug V, Polat A, Bozbuga N, Mansuroglu D, Guler M, Akinci E, Yakut C. In which patients should sheathless IABP be used? An analysis of vascular complications in 1211 cases. J Card Surg 2006;21:342–6.
8. Barnett MG, Swartz MT, Peterson GJ, Naunheim KS, Pennington DG, Vaca KJ, Fiore AC, McBride LR, Peigh P, Willman VL et al. Vascular complications from intraaortic balloons: risk analysis. J Vasc Surg 1994;19:81–7; discussion 87–9.
9. Bahar I, Akgul A, Ozatik MA, Vural KM, Demirbag AE, Boran M, Tasdemir O. Acute renal failure following open heart surgery: risk factors and prognosis. Perfusion 2005;20: 317–22.

10. Runge TM, McGinity JW, Frisbee SE, Briceno JC, Ottmers SE, Calhoon JH, Hantler CB, Korvick DL, Ybarra JR. Enhancement of brain p0(2) during cardiopulmonary bypass using a hyperosmolar oxygen carrying solution. Artif Cells Blood Substit Immobil Biotechnol 1997;25:297–308.
11. Vamvakas ED. Allergic and anaphyllactic reactions. In: Papovsky MA (ed.) Transfusion Reactions. Bethesda, MD: American Association of Blood Banks. 1996;81–124.

Chapter 2
Exposing the Cardiopulmonary Block

Abstract The pathologist performing an autopsy on the body of an individual who had undergone open-heart surgery weeks to years previously needs to be aware that the heart may be adherent to the posterior surface of the chest plate. The chest plate should be removed without injuring the heart and then examined for clues regarding coronary artery reconstruction. Before removing the cardiopulmonary block from the body, any tubes exiting the heart and sewn to large vessels should be cut a few centimeters away from the anastomoses to facilitate isolation of the heart. When the organ block has been removed from the body, the heart should be isolated. If a coronary injection is planned, and particularly if there is one or more bypass grafts on the heart, no attempt should be made to remove a densely adherent parietal pericardium from the heart until after the injection is completed. Instead, the aorta should be prepared for the coronary injection.

Keywords Adhesions · Chest plate · Assist device · Cardiopulmonary block

Adhesions Happen

The space between the heart and the anterior chest wall (chest plate) varies in depth from one person to another. The pathologist performing an autopsy on the body of an individual who had undergone open-heart surgery weeks to years previously needs to be aware that the heart may be adherent to the posterior surface of the chest plate. Normally, the parietal pericardium would serve as a protective barrier between the heart and the chest wall. Following open-heart surgery, however, the surgeon leaves the parietal pericardium open in order to minimize the risk of tamponade due to postoperative bleeding. If the heart subsequently becomes adherent to the chest plate, hasty removal of the chest plate at autopsy may result in tearing of the anterior surface of the heart (Fig. 2.1) and partial avulsion of anterior bypass grafts [1]. Surgeons are well aware of the potentially distrastrous complication of sawing into the heart with a re-do sternotomy, and try to avoid it if possible by using approaches other than median sternotomies, as mentioned in Chapter 1. At autopsy, the prosector, after cutting the ribs laterally, should carefully lift the inferior aspect

S.L. Hosuer, *The Operated Heart at Autopsy*, DOI 10.1007/978-1-60327-808-9_2,
© Humana Press, a part of Springer Science+Business Media, LLC 2009

Fig. 2.1 The posterior
surface of a chest plate
reveals adherent muscle
avulsed from the right
ventricular wall (*arrow*) and
diaphragm (*arrowhead*) at the
time of removal of the plate at
autopsy

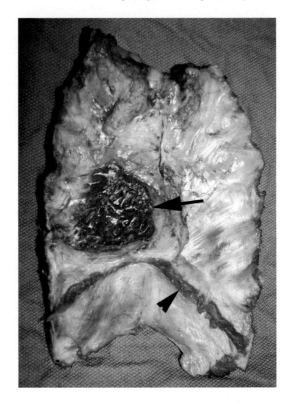

of the chest plate and look at the distance between it and the heart. If the heart and
chest plate are free from each other, the chest plate can be removed in a routine
fashion. If the heart is adherent to the chest plate, the adhesion should be lysed with
a scalpel, shaving the blade as close to the chest plate as possible. (Let the reader
be advised that when this author refers to sharp dissection, he is referring the use
of a scalpel. . .not scissors.) This technique will preserve the integrity of the anterior
wall of the right ventricle and avoid injury to vein grafts on the right and internal
mammary artery grafts to the left anterior descending artery (LAD), which will be
a distinct advantage if a postmortem injection of bypass grafts and coronary arteries
is indicated (discussed in Chapter 3).

The Chest Plate Has Information

After its removal from the body, the chest plate should be examined. The sternal
closure should normally be solidly healed if surgery had been performed more than
twelve weeks previously; if it is not, then incomplete healing has occurred, resulting
in a pseudoarthrosis [2]. Next, one should examine the posterior aspect of the chest
plate to see if both internal mammary arteries are present. If one is missing, usually
the left one (Fig. 2.2), it was probably used as a coronary artery bypass conduit,

Fig. 2.2 The posterior surface of a chest plate shows a scarred site remaining (*asterisk*) after a pedicle of tissue containing the left internal mammary vessels was harvested intraoperatively. The in situ right internal mammary artery (*arrow*) and adjacent medial vein are clearly seen

usually to the left anterior descending artery (LAD). This observation is particularly helpful if the pathologist lacks information regarding details of the open-heart surgery. Alas, operative notes are not always available at the time of autopsy.

In coronary artery bypass surgery, an internal mammary artery is dissected off the chest wall usually as a pedicle, including the artery, both accompanying veins, and surrounding fibromuscular tissue. It has traditionally not been "skeletonized" in the dissection in order to minimize the risk of injury to the artery. Intercostal branches are cut between small hemoclips, which the surgeon applies to control bleeding. Therefore, when the pathologist at autopsy examines the posterior aspect of the chest plate from which an internal mammary has been removed, he usually finds a one-centimeter wide bare or scarred path traveling parasternally most of the distance of the plate. It is fair to note, however, that the absence of an internal mammary artery from the chest plate means that it was surgically dissected off the chest wall with the apparent intention of using it as a conduit for coronary artery bypass, but not necessarily used as a bypass conduit. It may not, in fact, have been used for one of a variety of reasons. Perhaps, when the surgeon examined flow from the distal end of the mobilized artery, it was deemed insufficient because of small size and/or spasm of the artery, injury to the artery during mobilization of the pedicle from the chest wall, or possible atherosclerotic disease in the subclavian artery proximal to the take-off of the internal mammary artery. Whatever the scenario, if the surgeon is unhappy with the vessel and chooses not to use it, he will ligate it proximally and dispose of it. The message to the pathologist at autopsy is that even though an internal mammary artery is missing from the chest plate, none may be found when the heart is examined.

Assist Devices Are Meaningful

Ventricular assist devices are used in efforts to treat heart failure [3] that is refractory to medical regimens and intraaortic balloon pump therapy, or when attempts to place an IABP fail. They can provide three therapeutic functions. One benefit of an assist device is to rest a failing heart until it recovers from an acute injury, such as myocardial ischemia secondary to an acute coronary occlusion, or inadequate myocardial preservation during a complex operative procedure. Another goal of assist devices is to serve as bridges to heart transplantation, that is, to support cardiac output until a suitable allograft can be used to replace a recipient's own heart with end-stage failure. A third and more recently accepted treatment is to insert ventricular assist devices to allow them to function as destination therapy, i.e., when no further interventional therapy is planned [4].

If a left ventricular assist device is in place at autopsy, a large tube will be coming out of either the left atrium or the apex of the left ventricle (Fig. 2.3 B) and will connect to the inflow arm of the pump apparatus. A tube graft attached to the outflow arm of the pump will be found sewn to the ascending aorta (Fig. 2.3D). The pump (Fig. 2.3C) attached to the tubes will usually be buried in the anterior abdominal wall (Fig. 2.3A–b), and a driveline from the pump will be exteriorized through the abdominal wall laterally. If a right ventricular assist device was placed prior to the death of a patient, a large tube will extend from the right atrium to the pump, and a tube graft will connect the pump to the pulmonary artery trunk by an end-to-side anastomosis. Fig. 2.4 shows an alternative means of cannulation to establish biventricular assistance. Before removing the organ block from the body, the tubes exiting the heart and the tubes sewn to large vessels should be cut a few centimeters away from the anastomoses to facilitate isolation of the heart. Any internal pump device should be removed from the body and set aside for later detailed evaluation, i.e., a careful search for thrombi (Fig. 2.3C), infection, or evidence of mechanical failure. Whenever an IABP or ventricular assist device is found at autopsy, it is important for the pathologist to understand that, after careful description of the location and status of the hardware, the challenge remains to be able to apply subsequent gross and histological findings of the heart to a clear and logical analysis that explains why the hardware was necessary in the first place. Only then does assessment of the operated heart at autopsy start to make sense.

Isolate the Heart with Care

When the organ block has been removed from the body, the heart should be isolated. This initial dissection is expedited by positioning the organ block posterior, or

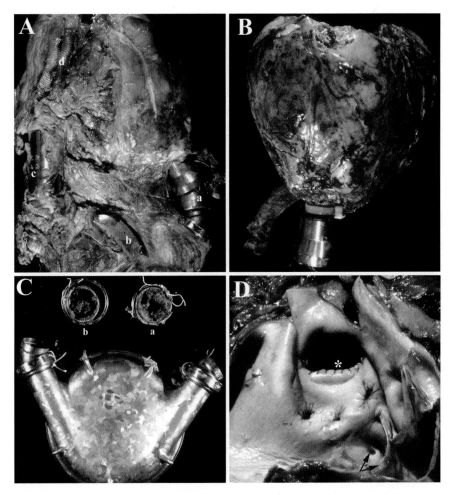

Fig. 2.3 A mediastinal block of tissue contains a left ventricular assist device found at autopsy. (**A**) An *inflow line* (*a*) exits the apex of the left ventricle and feeds blood into the mechanical pump (*b*). An *outflow line* (*c*) receives blood from the pump and delivers it into a Dacron tube graft (*d*), which is sutured to the ascending aorta. (**B**) The heart is exposed, revealing the large metallic tube inserted into the apex of the left ventricle. A strip of Teflon used to buttress sutures closing the myocardium around the cannula is seen falling away from the specimen. (**C**) The mechanical pump is cleanly illustrated. Note the thrombus found at the connecting points between the pump and the *inflow* (*a*) and *outflow* (*b*) *lines*. (**D**) The ascending aorta is opened longitudinally. Cephalad, the anastomosis (asterisk) of the tube graft to the aorta is widely patent. The right coronary ostium and adjacent leaflet of the aortic valve (*arrows*) are caudal to three proximal anastomses of vein grafts to the aorta

dorsal, side up. The aorta should be severed at a level just above the diaphragm. The descending thoracic aorta is then separated from the esophagus by sharp dissection, mobilizing the distal aspect of the aortic arch. The esophagus is then mobilized from surrounding soft tissue from the diaphragm to the larynx. It is then detached from

Fig. 2.4 A cross-section of
the heart reveals cannulation
of the *right* and *left* ventricles
placed surgically to achieve
biventricular assistance

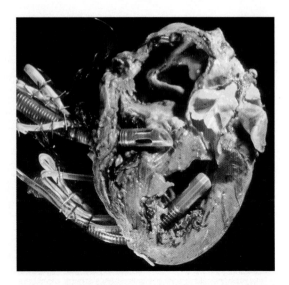

the larynx, and reflected caudally, still attached at the gastroesophageal junction. The main stem bronchi are then severed 1–2 cm below the carina, allowing removal of the trachea and larynx from the surrounding mediastinal tissue.

The lungs may be adherent to the diaphragm and/or the parietal pericardium and to the exposed surface of the heart. These adhesions should be broken by blunt dissection if possible, i.e., by carefully sweeping a hand through the adhesions or by pinching fibrous adhesions focally between fingers and thumb. If sharp dissection is necessary, care should be taken not to violate the parietal pericardium. Furthermore, the left lung may be overlying an internal mammary artery graft to the LAD. Lysis of this adhesion must be done with care to avoid injury to the graft. Less commonly, similar care is needed to avoid injuring a right internal mammary graft. When the lungs are free of the heart, they are removed by mobilizing the bronchial stumps and severing the pulmonary vessels close to the hila outside the parietal pericardium.

The inferior vena cava should then be severed just above the diaphragm. The heart is then separated from the diaphragm by blunt and/or sharp dissection, staying outside the parietal pericardium. If a coronary injection is not necessary, the parietal pericardium is removed at this time (see Chapter 4). If a coronary injection is planned, and particularly if there is one or more bypass grafts on the heart, no attempt should be made to remove a densely adherent parietal pericardium from the heart until after the injection is completed. The reason for leaving the pericardium on the heart until after the injection is to avoid inadvertent injury to the underlying bypass grafts and/or coronary arteries. The examiner in this case will feel much more comfortable removing the adherent parietal pericardium after the injection, when coronary reconstruction is defined on X-rays in front of him/her, than before an injection is performed, when no comparable "pretty picture" is likely to be available.

Assess the Need for Coronary Artery Injection

The following circumstances may be considered indications for performing post-mortem coronary artery injections:

1. Suspicion that the cause of death was an acute myocardial infarction.
2. Occurrence of death during a hospital admission in which cardiac surgery was performed.
3. Past history of placement of a coronary arterial stent.
4. Question of a congenital coronary artery anomaly.

The injection is therefore carried out with the purpose of achieving one or more of the following goals:

1. To assess the coronary arterial tree for in situ evidence of anomalous vessels, atherosclerotic occlusive disease, and/or acute thrombosis.
2. To define the anatomic location and patency of coronary artery bypass grafts and/or coronary artery stents.
3. To guide the prosector in the dissection of the coronary vessels, correlating the appropriate focus of the dissection with pertinent angiographic findings.
4. To aid in the prosector's understanding of coronary anatomy as it relates to individual cases of cardiovascular disease.

Prepare the Aorta for Coronary Artery Injection

In preparation for the coronary injection, the descending thoracic aorta is detached at the level of the isthmus and set aside. A posterior aortotomy is then directed with scissors in a retrograde fashion through the aortic arch and into the ascending aorta. As one passes the take-off of the innominate artery, a common surgical landmark, the pledgets of the sutured closure of the previous aortic cannulation site can usually be palpated anteriorly on the surface of the ascending aorta. An intimal "dimple" may also be visible at this site (Fig. 2.5) inside the aorta.

The aortotomy is continued posteriorly down the ascending aorta to avoid injury to any vein grafts sewn to the anterior wall. As the aortotomy approaches the aortic valve, proximal anastomoses of bypass grafts to the aorta will be visualized (Fig. 2.6). These proximal anastomoses will usually connect aorta to vein grafts. Less commonly, one encounters proximal anastomoses between aorta and radial artery grafts and/or internal mammary arteries used as what are called free grafts, i.e., internal mammary arteries that are detached from their subclavian artery origins. By convention, the number of bypass grafts done in any given coronary artery reconstruction equals the number of distal anastomoses. Hence, if three proximal anastomoses are encountered at autopsy, the prosector knows that at least a triple

Fig. 2.5 The aortic arch has been opened posteriorly, exposing the take-offs of the innominate artery (*arrowhead*), the right common carotid artery, and the left subclavian artery. An intimal dimple (*arrow*) marks the site of aortic cannulation during a previous open-heart operation. The site has not re-endothelialized, which is characteristic of an early postoperative time frame

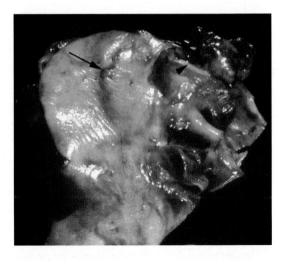

Fig. 2.6 Two proximal bypass graft anastomoses (*arrows*) are found on the anterior wall of the ascending aorta as visualized through a posterior aortotomy being extended in a retrograde fashion from the aortic arch

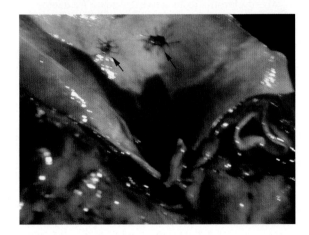

CABG had been performed. However, if one or more of the venous conduits had been grafted in sequence to more than one coronary artery, or if an internal mammary artery graft had been constructed in the usual fashion, the CABG would have been more than a triple. The injection can help the pathologist who is lacking knowledge of specific operative details determine the number of grafts constructed.

Preliminary Injection Is Instructive

The aortotomy is extended into the noncoronary cusp of the aortic valve to allow easy visualization of the native coronary ostia. If one veers off to the left or right with the scissors, the left or right coronary ostium, respectively, could be violated.

Fig. 2.7 Supplies used by the author to inject contrast material into the coronary arterial tree at the time of postmortem injection. (**A**) A tapered tip large syringe expedites injection of native coronary ostia and relatively large proximal vein bypass graft anastomoses. (**B**) A needle adapter, which is useful to engage comparatively small vessels, attaches easily to the end of a plastic luer lock syringe (**C**)

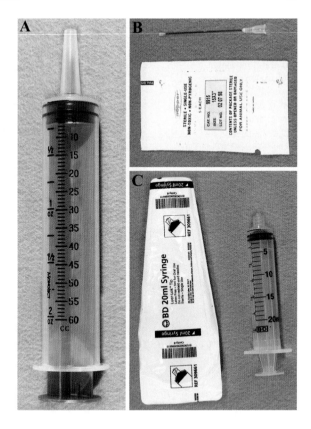

Adjacent left atrial wall posteriorly should be incised to expedite this exposure of the ostia. At this point, each of the proximal anastomoses and native coronary ostia should be injected with saline. The purpose of these preliminary injections is to determine the optimal syringe and needle adapter size needed for subsequent injection of contrast material (Fig. 2.7). This preliminary injection will also afford the prosector a sense of the patency of the vessels. Furthermore, if one of the grafts or proximal coronary arteries is obviously occluded, time will not be lost trying to inject these occluded vessels with contrast material in the radiology suite. A policy of minimizing the time that the radiology technician has to spend to accommodate the pathologist's need to complete these postmortem injections will enhance one's ability to gain the technician's cooperation and willingness to continue to support the exercise as future need arises.

Finally, if there is a left internal mammary artery (LIMA) graft in place, it will usually be sewn to the LAD (Fig. 2.8). If it is easily identified, it should be opened proximally by incising it transversely with a scalpel and injected with saline. If it is obscured by adherent surrounding tissue, a transverse, anterior incision with a scalpel into this soft tissue at the level of or just above the pulmonary valve will usually expose the internal mammary artery. Sometimes one or more small

Fig. 2.8 A heart is retrieved at autopsy with three coronary bypass grafts. A vein graft to the right coronary artery is seen proximally in the right A–V groove. A second vein graft (*arrow*) is directed to an obtuse marginal branch of the circumflex coronary artery. The distal anastomosis (*arrowhead*) of a left internal mammary artery to the LAD completes this coronary reconstruction

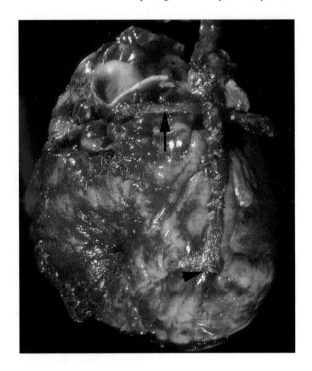

hemoclips will help one identify the pedicle containing the artery. The surgeon places these hemoclips on intercostal branches of the artery so that he can safely sever the branches and mobilize the pedicle off the chest wall at the time of surgery. The lumen of an internal mammary artery is usually too small to accommodate needle adapters used to inject larger vein grafts. However, internal mammary arteries can be easily injected by using small plastic "angiocaths," which this author recommends (Fig. 2.9).

When the preliminary injections with saline have been completed as above, the logistics and timing of the angiographic injections must be coordinated with the appropriate radiographic technician. When an agreed upon time is reached, the heart can be placed into a plastic container, covered with a towel, and transported to the radiology unit for injection. It is suggested that another box-like container in which one can store contrast material, adapter needles, angiocaths, and syringes, and carry them to the radiology unit, be dedicated to this effort. If the injection cannot be accommodated into the X-ray technician's agenda the day of autopsy, the heart can be fixed in formalin or stored in a wet towel at 4°C overnight and injected the following day. Collaborating early the following day with the X-ray technician may expedite completion of the injection before the technician is faced with the stresses of the

Fig. 2.9 A 22-gauge angiocatheter fits most internal mammary arteries satisfactorily for postmortem injection. After removing the catheter assembly from the wrapper (**A**), the plastic catheter (**B**, short component), which is the only component needed for engaging the internal mammary artery, is removed from the rest of the assembly (**B**, long component with needle), which can be discarded with other sharp disposable equipment

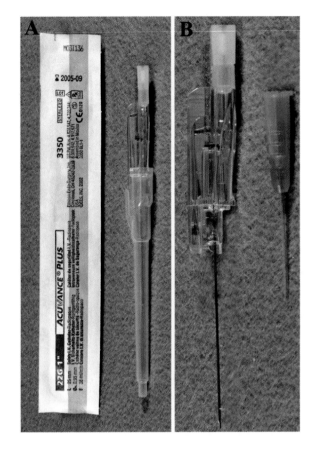

day's clinical demands. Once again, polite and gentle assertiveness frequently wins the day when one depends on the voluntary assistance of others to get things done.

References

1. Zehr KJ, Lee PC, Poston RS, Gillinov AM, Hruban RH, Cameron DE. Protection of the internal mammary artery pedicle with polytetrafluoroethylene membrane. J Card Surg 1993;8:650–5.
2. Angelini GD, el-Ghamari FA, Butchart EG. Poststernotomy pseudo-arthrosis due to foreign body reaction to bone wax. Eur J Cardiothorac Surg 1987;1:129–30.
3. Rose AG, Park SJ. Pathology in patients with ventricular assist devices: a study of 21 autopsies, 24 ventricular apical core biopsies and 24 explanted hearts. Cardiovasc Pathol 2005;14:19–23.
4. Selzman CH, Oberlandwer J. The price of progress: destination left ventricular assist device therapy for terminal heart failure. N C Med J 2006;67:116–7.

Chapter 3
The Postmortem Coronary Injection

Abstract The logistics and timing of the angiographic injections must be coordinated with the appropriate radiographic technician. Much can be learned from an initial scout film of the heart. Following the scout film, a meticulous injection protocol is recommended for consistency and accuracy in the angiographic analysis. Regarding the sequence of injections, the complexity of interpretation of the postmortem angiogram increases with the number of vessels and/or grafts injected because of overlap of vessels filled with contrast material. In cases of CABG, injection of the native coronary ostia may not be necessary, depending on the amount of information gathered after injection of the grafts. Postmortem injection of the heart should be viewed, if not embraced, as a means of expediting clinical-pathologic correlation in cardiovascular-related deaths.

Keywords Coronary artery injection · Scout film · Protocol

Remember the Scout Film

At the determined time, proceed to the radiology department with the heart in a covered container and a box containing contrast material and the necessary syringes for injecting the heart. Upon arrival in the imaging room, place the heart with posterior surface down onto a paper chuck on the X-ray table and ask for a scout film, i.e., an X-ray of the heart prior to injecting contrast material (Fig. 3.1). Much can be learned from a scout film of the operated heart. This baseline X-ray might demonstrate coronary artery calcification (Fig. 3.1A), which would otherwise be obscured by contrast material. It will also serve as a screen for the presence of intracoronary stents (Fig. 3.1B), the presence of which may not otherwise be known by the pathologist. If an internal mammary artery has been used as a coronary artery bypass conduit, a line of hemoclips on its intercostal branches, which were severed as the pedicle was mobilized from the chest wall intraoperatively, will provide an informative map of its course on X-ray. In addition, the scout film may reveal valve prostheses, valvuloplasty rings, as well as permanent pacemaker wires and

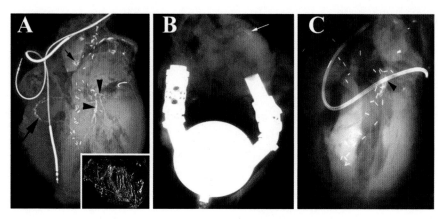

Fig. 3.1 A scout film of the heart can reveal important findings prior to injecting contrast material. (**A**) Prominent calcification is seen here in much of the RCA (*large arrow*), as well as in the LAD and proximal circumflex arteries (*arrowheads*). A metallic proximal anastomosis of a bypass graft to the ascending aorta (*small arrow*) may be subtle evidence of a previously performed off-pump CABG or at least of an atherosclerotic ascending aorta that defied safe manipulation with a side-biting clamp. The "chain" of metallic hemoclips marks the path of a LIMA to the LAD, and the sequential pacemaker wires in the right side of the heart are documented there before the heart is opened. (**B**) A stent (*arrow*) in the proximal circumflex coronary artery is found radiologically in a heart that required a left ventricular assist device clinically. (**C**) A pulmonary artery catheter (*arrowhead*) is documented by X-ray to have been well-positioned at the time of autopsy

pulmonary artery catheters (Fig. 3.1C), the presence of which may or may not have been known prior to the X-ray study. After the scout film is completed and the intracardiac positions of indwelling catheters documented, any intracardiac catheters should be removed prior to starting the protocol of injecting coronary arteries and/or bypass grafts, to avoid overlapping of the catheters with subsequent injected contrast material. Such overlap can interfere with accurate interpretation of angiographic images.

Follow the Injection Protocol

After the scout film is acquired, perform each injection of contrast material by *slow, gentle* injection of 3 cc into each vessel. The author uses MD-76R, a clear, slightly viscous solution of diatrizoate meglumine and diatrizoate sodium, a product of Mallinckrodt (Fig. 3.2). Injecting in a slow and gentle fashion will prevent disturbing intramyocardial accumulation of contrast material (Fig. 3.3) that will obscure vascular morphology and interfere with the interpretation of the study. During each injection, position the nozzle of the syringe or tip of the needle adapter in such a manner that avoids retrograde leakage of contrast material during injection. Avoidance of leakage can usually be accomplished by pushing the tip of the urologic ("snout nose") syringe firmly into the take-off of a native coronary ostium

Fig. 3.2 MD-76R, a clear, slightly viscous solution of diatrizoate meglumine and diatrizoate sodium, a product of Mallinckrodt, can be used effectively without dilution as a contrast material in postmortem coronary artery injections

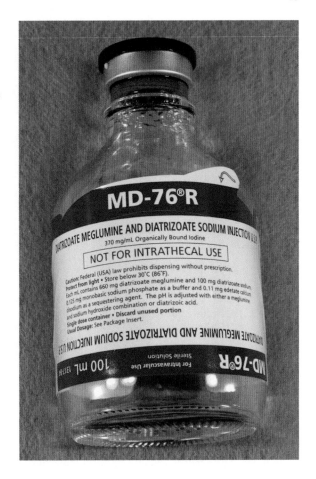

or into the proximal anastomosis of a conduit sewn to the ascending aorta. If a smaller needle adapter is used, it can be pushed into a vessel 4 or 5 mm so that tissue around the tip of the adapter can be pinched with finger and thumb or compressed with a string wrapped around that part of the vessel to avoid retrograde flow of contrast material. Maneuvers to prevent leakage of contrast material are particularly relevant to successful injection of an internal mammary artery graft. Such retrograde leakage can result in dye in ventricular chambers or, in case of an internal mammary artery, contrast material on the anterior surface of the heart, which will also interfere with the interpretation of vascular morphology (Fig. 3.4). Ask the technician to acquire one anteroposterior X-ray, i.e., with the posterior surface of the heart down, after *each* injection. This methodology is preferable to injecting multiple vessels prior to taking any X-ray since the complexity of interpretation of the angiogram may increase significantly as the number of injected vessels increases.

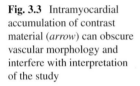

Fig. 3.3 Intramyocardial accumulation of contrast material (*arrow*) can obscure vascular morphology and interfere with interpretation of the study

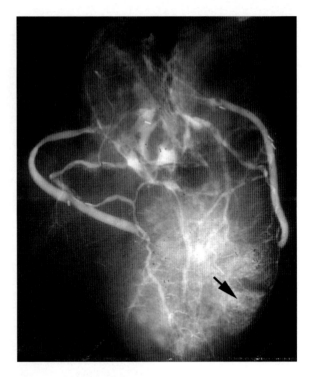

The following injection protocol is recommended for consistency and accuracy:

- If no bypass grafts are present, inject first the left coronary ostium and then the right coronary ostium. Finally, position the heart onto its obtuse margin and ask the technician to acquire a lateral view.
- If bypass grafts are in place, perform each injection in the following sequence:
  - Left internal mammary graft, which is usually to the LAD (Fig. 3.5), or right internal mammary artery graft if it goes to the LAD (uncommon occurrence)
  - Vein grafts (proximal anastomoses of vein grafts on the left side of the heart will be to the left of those going to the right coronary artery; proximal anastomoses of vein grafts to obtuse marginal branches of the circumflex coronary artery will be cephalad, or above, proximal anastomoses of grafts to the diagonal branches and LAD):
    - First, those going to the left side of the heart (LAD, diagonal, ramus medialis, and circumflex vessels. . .in that order) (Fig. 3.6)
    - Then, any graft going to the right coronary artery (the right internal mammary artery will sometimes be grafted to the right coronary artery)
  - Native left coronary ostium (unless proximal left-sided vessels have by this time filled by retrograde flow, in which case move on to the next step)

Fig. 3.4 Inadvertent leakage
of contrast material into the
right ventricle (*arrow*) can
complicate angiographic
interpretation

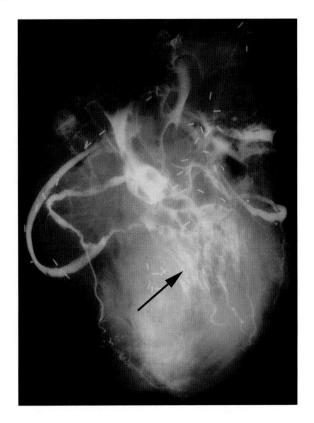

- Native right coronary ostium (unless proximal right-sided vessels have by this time filled by retrograde flow, in which case move on to the next step)
- Finally, position the heart onto its obtuse margin and ask the technician to acquire a lateral view.

Understand the Injection Protocol

Certain considerations are relevant to one's understanding of the injection protocol outlined above:

- As mentioned above, opening the aorta on its posterior wall will avoid injury of vein grafts, which are almost always sewn to the anterior or anterolateral aspects of the ascending aorta. Rarely, because of severe atherosclerosis of the ascending aorta, a vein graft to the left side of the heart may be sewn to the right side of the aorta and pass posterior to the aorta through the aortopulmonary sinus. In this situation, injury to the graft might be avoided by careful observation of

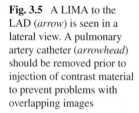

Fig. 3.5 A LIMA to the
LAD (*arrow*) is seen in a
lateral view. A pulmonary
artery catheter (*arrowhead*)
should be removed prior to
injection of contrast material
to prevent problems with
overlapping images

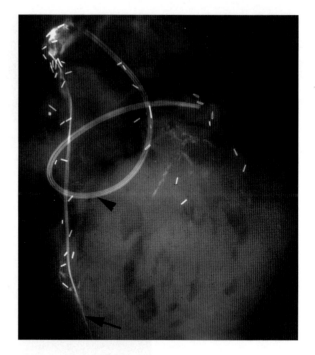

the intimal and adventitial surfaces of the aorta just ahead of the scissors as the
posterior aortotomy is extended toward the aortic valve. If the proximal end of
the graft is violated, the vein can be injected at the site where it was cut, and little
should be lost in the process.

- Regarding the sequence of injections, the complexity of interpretation of the postmortem angiogram increases with the number of vessels and/or grafts injected
  because of overlap of vessels filled with contrast material. The injection therefore begins with the left coronary ostium or, in the case of bypass surgery, the
  graft to the LAD, because the left main coronary artery and LAD or the graft to
  the LAD generally represents the most important source of data relating to a fatal
  myocardial infarction [1].
- For similar reasons, an X-ray is taken after each vessel or graft is injected rather
  than waiting until all vessels have been injected.
- The lateral view at the end of the injections provides an additional image with
  an alternative perspective, which will show vessels and anastomoses at different
  angles and often facilitate the interpretation of the study (Fig. 3.7).
- In cases of CABG, injection of the native coronary ostia may not be necessary,
  depending on the amount of information gathered after injection of the grafts.
  In a training program, consultation between the prosector and attending staff or
  assisting resident is useful regarding this decision.
- Postmortem angiography can illustrate evidence of established collateral flow
  (Fig. 3.8), which is pertinent to the understanding of the pathophysiology relating
  to individual cases of coronary artery disease [2].

Fig. 3.6 A postmortem study shows a LIMA (*small arrow*) nicely filling the distal LAD. A patent sequential vein graft fills a large ramus medialis through a side-to-side anastomosis (asterisk) and a large obtuse marginal branch of the circumflex through an end-to-side anastomosis (*large arrow*). An air bubble causes a filling defect at the latter anastomosis, an artifact that can be difficult to prevent while injecting the vessels. White arrowheads mark the metallic struts of an aortic valve prosthesis

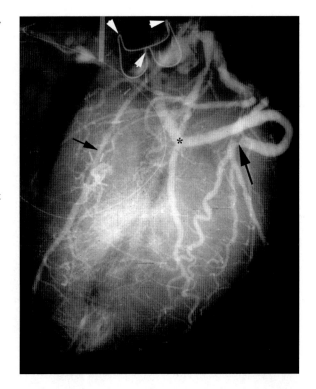

- Postmortem angiography can define anomalous coronary arteries [3, 4], which might not be recognized (at least without embarrassing frustration) by gross dissection alone.
- Postmortem injection of the heart should be viewed, if not embraced, as a means of expediting clinical-pathologic correlation in cardiovascular-related deaths. If an indication for the procedure is there, proceed with vigor.

A Story in Print Has Value

After completion of the injection, return the heart to a covered container for transport back to the autopsy suite, clean up the X-ray table of disposable materials, and ask the technician to print all X-ray images acquired. These prints will document the findings of the multiple injections and provide a means of studying the vascular tree and presenting the data at an autopsy conference. In an academic environment, the angiographic prints can serve as an effective medium for conveying pertinent didactic instruction regarding morphologic and pathologic points of interest in a given coronary arterial tree, and, if present, a coronary artery reconstruction with bypass grafts. Importantly, the information will prepare the prosector for

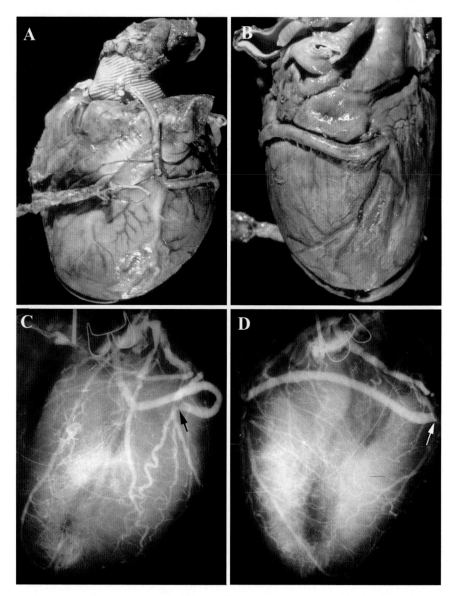

Fig. 3.7 Images correlate gross (**A** and **B**) and radiological (**C** and **D**) findings relating to a sequential vein graft to the left side of the heart. The distal anastomosis (*black arrow*) in an anteroposterior view (**C**) is depicted with additional perspective (*white arrow*) in a lateral view (**D**)

applying appropriate focus in the subsequent cardiac dissection. It will alert the prosector to focal areas of interest regarding removal of a tightly adherent parietal pericardium. It will provide valuable information regarding one or more sites of significant atherosclerotic plaque or thrombus in coronary arteries and/or vein bypass

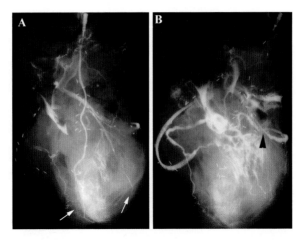

Fig. 3.8 A postmortem coronary angiogram shows evidence of collateral blood flow in the presence of CAD. (**A**) An injection of a LIMA fills the distal LAD. Retrograde flow of contrast material is limited apparently by obstructive disease. Furthermore, tiny vessels (*arrows*) distribute contrast material into the RCA and ramus medialis by collateral flow. (**B**) Subsequent injection of the vein grafts helps to confirm the anatomic pattern of the collateral vessels. A vein graft to an obtuse marginal branch crosses the circumflex (*arrowhead*) just distal to an apparent distal in-stent stenosis

grafts. Furthermore, the angiogram can easily and quickly document patency or occlusion of intracoronary artery stents, data which may in fact contribute information regarding a cause of death that would have otherwise been either missed or revealed only by tedious techniques of gross dissection.

References

1. Elsman P, van 't Hof AW, Hoorntje JC, de Boer MJ, Borm GF, Suryapranata H, Ottervanger JP, Gosselink AT, Dambrink JH, Zijlstra F. Effect of coronary occlusion site on angiographic and clinical outcome in acute myocardial infarction patients treated with early coronary intervention. Am J Cardiol 2006;97:1137–41.
2. Lim M, Ziaee A, Kern MJ. Collateral vessel physiology and functional impact-in vivo assessment of collateral channels. Coron Artery Dis 2004;15:379–88. Review.
3. Kim SY, Seo JB, Do K-H, Heo J-N, Lee JS, Song J-W, Choe YH, Kim TH, Yong HS, Choi SI, Song K-S, Lim T-H. Coronary artery anomalies: classification and ECG-gated multidetector row CT findings with angiographic correlation. Radiographics 2006;26:317–33.
4. Angelini P, Velasco JA, Flamm S. Coronary anomalies: incidence, pathophysiology, and clinical relevance. Circulation 2002;105:2449–54.

Chapter 4
The Cardiac Dissection

Abstract An approach is offered here to assist the pathologist with the actual dissection of the operated heart at autopsy. The challenge to the pathologist is to define any underlying cardiac pathology, recognize changes in morphology brought about by prior surgical intervention, and correlate the gross cardiac findings with the hemodynamic status of the deceased prior to death. Even without detailed clinical records, one can still perform the dissection in a consistent and careful manner that allows an accurate assessment of the heart regardless of postoperative adhesions and complex surgical reconstructions. Developing the plane of dissection between the heart and adherent parietal pericardium should be done with a scalpel, using a methodical technique. As one examines the external surface of the heart, one may observe clues that the surgeon had used cardiopulmonary bypass to rest the heart during surgery and that specific surgical procedures had been performed. By removal of the coronary arteries with any bypass grafts off the heart and subsequent careful examination of the chambers and great vessels of the heart, the pathologist can then begin to understand the "real story."

Keywords Dissection · Pericardium · Heart surgery · Coronary arteries · Surgical footprints · Cardiopulmonary bypass · Sharp dissection

In this chapter, an approach is offered to assist the pathologist with the actual dissection of the operated heart at autopsy. This dissection, depending on what operation was done and how long prior to autopsy the operation was performed, may range in complexity from a simple procedure to quite a daunting task. The challenge to the pathologist is to define any underlying cardiac pathology, recognize changes in morphology brought about by prior surgical intervention, and correlate the gross cardiac findings with the hemodynamic status of the deceased prior to death. In short, to what extent did failure of cardiac function contribute to the person's death, and how did the previous heart surgery affect the outcome of the case?

Having a detailed knowledge of the deceased's past surgical history, as provided by operative notes, hospital discharge summaries, and available informed clinicians is an obvious advantage to the pathologist at autopsy. However, even without this

S.L. Houser, *The Operated Heart at Autopsy*, DOI 10.1007/978-1-60327-808-9_4,   31
© Humana Press, a part of Springer Science+Business Media, LLC 2009

information, one can still perform the dissection in a consistent and careful manner that allows an accurate assessment of the heart regardless of postoperative adhesions and complex surgical reconstructions. Furthermore, armed with the information provided by a postmortem coronary artery injection and that all-important pre-injection scout film, the pathologist is able to focus attention on details of the dissection even if there is no past medical history available.

The Parietal Pericardium May Be "Socked In"

The first task in the dissection is to remove the parietal pericardium from around the heart. If death occurred in the early hospital course following heart surgery, this step will be as simple as breaking through minor soft adhesions by bluntly dissecting around the heart and lifting the heart out of the pericardial sac (Fig. 4.1). If the cardiac surgery was performed weeks to years prior to autopsy, the parietal pericardium will frequently be tightly adherent to the heart either multifocally or diffusely (Fig. 4.2). In the former situation, begin the lysis of adhesions in an area where the plane of sharp dissection is easily identified. When the parietal pericardium is diffusely adherent to the heart, one may have to search for a starting point. Surgical experience teaches that a good place to start looking for that plane of dissection is in the area of the inferior wall of the right ventricle. For some reason

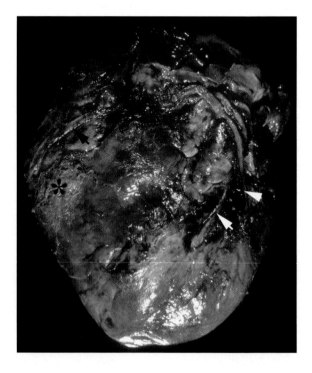

Fig. 4.1 Cardiac specimen harvested at autopsy in the early period following CABG surgery. Fibrinous epicardial exudates (*asterisk*) are a characteristic finding a few days after surgery. Vein grafts to the right (*black arrowhead*) and left (*white arrowheads*) sides of the heart are lightly adherent to the epicardial surface. Their flat appearance indicates clinical patency at the time of death

Fig. 4.2 Cardiac morphology is masked by dense adhesion of pericardial soft tissue weeks to years after open heart surgery

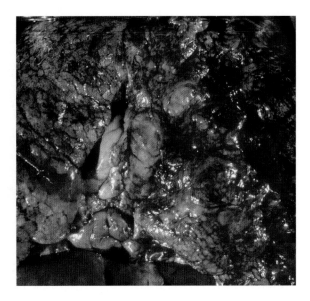

unknown to this author, one can usually find a focus in that area where the heart is free of adjacent pericardium. Finding that focus by carefully incising the parietal pericardium (Fig. 4.3) will allow the prosector to begin mobilizing the plane of dissection, proceeding from known (where the plain is exposed) to unknown (where the plane is yet to be exposed) in a deliberate manner.

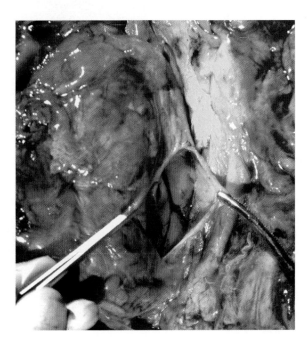

Fig. 4.3 Parietal pericardium is opened in an area where it is not densely adherent to the epicardial surface of the heart

Fig. 4.4 Retraction of
pericardium with a clamp
exposes a plane of adhesion
between the pericardium and
heart which can then be
developed safely by sharp
dissection

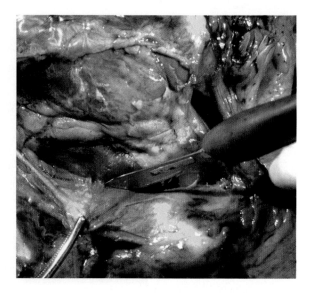

Developing the plane of dissection between the heart and adherent parietal pericardium should be done with a fresh scalpel, holding the back of the scalpel on
the heart (or any structure that the prosector does not want to injure) and the sharp

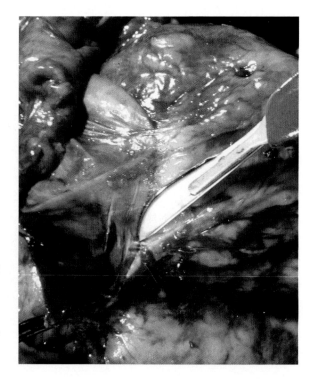

Fig. 4.5 Keeping the back of
the knife to the heart and the
sharp edge in the plane of
dissection exposes a vein
graft (*arrowhead*) without
injury, even if the presence of
the graft was unknown prior
to its exposure

edge of the knife directed into the plane of dissection (Fig. 4.4). By placing one or more clamps on a freed-up portion or edge of pericardium and retracting the pericardium away from the heart, one can sharply mobilize the plane of dissection with relative ease. One stays in the correct plane by avoiding leaving any epicardial fat or myocardial muscle on the freed-up pericardium. If fat remains on freed-up pericardium, the dissection is too deep; if parietal pericardium remains on the heart, the dissection is not deep enough. Following these guidelines will help one avoid injury to bypass grafts even when their locations are uncertain early in the dissection (Fig. 4.5). When the parietal pericardium has been removed from the heart, the dissection is continued in a cephalad direction until the ascending aorta and arch are cleanly exposed. The importance of traction and countertraction in the mobilization of adherent pericardium cannot be overemphasized. If a prosector is alone, the weight of the heart suspended from the retracted pericardium can serve as favorable countertraction. If an assistant is available to offer a pair of hands to apply traction by lifting the clamps on the pericardium, the prosector can easily apply the necessary countertraction on the heart by pressing on a towel or piece of gauze on the heart and creating tension at the plain of dissection. The value of a thoughtful assistant is real. . .in an autopsy suite as well as in an operating room.

Look at the External Surface of the Heart and Great Vessels

After the pericardial sac is removed, the ascending aorta should be severed in its proximal to mid-third portion, or just above the proximal anastomoses of any bypass graft(s). The heart should then be weighed to document any cardiomegaly. One should then assess the external surface of the heart and vessels. Evidence that the surgeon had used cardiopulmonary bypass to rest the heart during surgery includes suture material in the right atrium, typically in the right atrial appendage, and ascending aorta; unless, for technical reasons, such as a calcified aorta or aortic dissection [1], the pump run was established by placing catheters in a femoral artery and vein or other peripheral vessels. For drainage of venous blood to the pump, a double lumen catheter is commonly placed through an incision in the right atrial appendage. Alternatively, separate superior and inferior venous catheters may have been placed through an incision in the right atrial appendage and an inferior right atriotomy (Fig. 4.6), respectively, or in the venae cavae themselves adjacent to the confluence of each with the right atrium. In the operating room, as blood passes through the pump (heart-lung machine), it is oxygenated and filtered (Fig. 4.7). It is then returned to the body usually through an aortic cannula placed just below the take-off of the innominate artery. At the end of the pump run, when the heart is sustaining adequate systemic flow, these cannulas are removed. The defects in the atrium and aorta are closed with suture, which is evident at autopsy. As indicated above, the aortic cannulation site is closed with suture that is buttressed by Teflon pledgets (Fig. 4.6 inset) to prevent tearing of the aortic tissue as the sutures are tied down. (This author firmly believes that all pathologists doing autopsies should know what a Teflon pledget looks like and why it is used in a surgical procedure.) Another

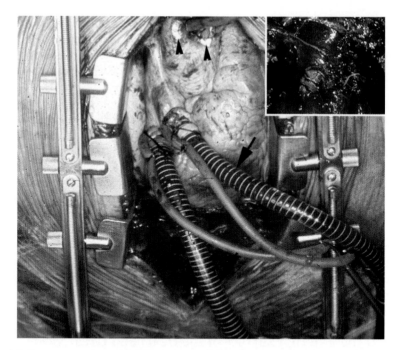

Fig. 4.6 Separate superior and inferior venous catheters (*arrows*) placed through incisions in the right atrial appendage and an inferior right atriotomy, respectively, drain blood from the right side of the heart into a heart-lung machine. Oxygenated blood is returned from the machine to an aortic cannula, which is inserted into the ascending aorta and secured by sutures that are buttressed by Teflon pledgets (*arrowheads*). After removal of the aortic cannula, the buttressed sutures are tied down (insert) to close the hole in the aortic wall

suture with or without pledgets may be found in the lateral right atrial wall. Still another suture with pledgets may be found on the anterior wall of the ascending aorta near its midportion. These points represent sites of catheters placed by the surgeon to administer cardioplegic solution retrograde or antegrade (Fig. 4.8), respectively, during the aortic cross-clamp time. A catheter for administration of retrograde cardioplegic solution passes through a small right atriotomy into the coronary sinus. Antegrade flow of cardioplegic solution into the native coronary ostia depends on a competent aortic valve for effective administration. By either route, the purpose of administering the cardioplegic solution is to establish rapid cardiac arrest and, depending on the surgeon's preference [2], myocardial cooling to preserve myocardial stores of adenosine triphosphate, hence maintain integrity of myocardial function, while the aortic cross-clamp is in place (usually just below the aortic cannula in the ascending aorta).

As mentioned above, if an autopsy occurs within the first week after heart surgery, temporary pacemaker wires may be noted on external examination of the body. If left intact until the heart is isolated, the ends opposite the externalized portions will be found embedded in the epicardial surface (Fig. 4.9), usually on the ante-

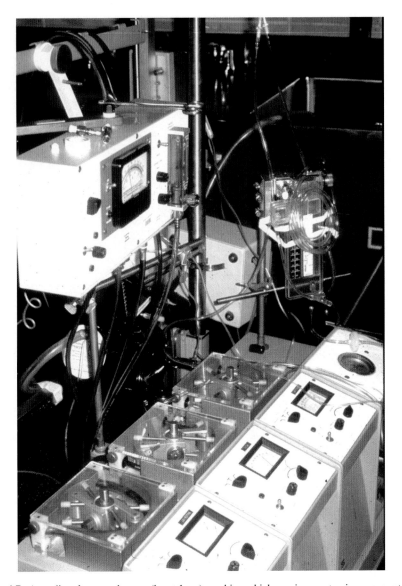

Fig. 4.7 A cardiopulmonary bypass (heart-lung) machine which receives systemic venous return from the body and returns filtered, oxygenated, and, as needed, temperature-regulated blood to the arterial circulation

rior wall of the right ventricle and the lateral right atrium near the appendage. If one or more permanent pacemaker wires are in place, they will be found "screwed" onto the epimyocardium. The opposite ends of permanent epicardial wires may be enclosed in plastic caps (capped) and buried subcutaneously or attached to a pacemaker battery in a subcutaneous pocket in the adjacent abdominal wall. When their location is documented, these wires should be removed.

Fig. 4.8 In the *upper* panel, the distal anastomosis of a vein bypass graft has been completed by the surgeon while the heart is arrested. Myocardial preservation is maintained by a cardioplegic solution infused into a catheter (*arrow*) in the ascending aorta between a cross-clamp above and the coronary ostia below. After removal of the catheter, the site of its previous entrance into the aorta is closed by tying sutures buttressed by Teflon pledgets (*arrowhead*, *lower* panel)

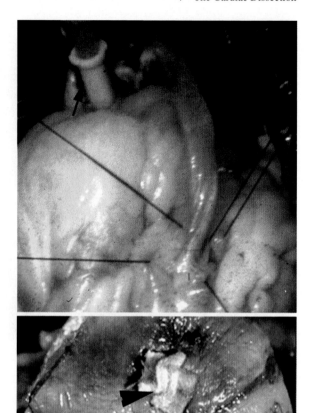

As one continues to examine the external surface of the heart, one may observe clues that specific surgical procedures had been performed. Some common findings are mentioned here. A suture line across the lateral wall of the right atrium should alert the pathologist to the possible closure of an interatrial septal defect or patent foramen ovale, tricuspid valve repair or replacement, closure of a ventricular septal defect, or resection of an atrial neoplasm, such as a myxoma. A suture line parallel and posterior to the interatrial groove might be a closure of a left atriotomy done to gain surgical access needed to perform a previous mitral valve repair or replacement, or resection of a left atrial neoplasm, such as a myxoma. A patch closure of a right ventriculotomy overlying the outflow tract is a common finding in a heart with Tetralogy of Fallot that has required surgical resection of hypertrophic myocardium that was obstructing the outflow tract. A suture line in the main pulmonary artery may have been placed after pulmonary valve replacement or exploration for a pulmonary embolus. A conduit extending from the right ventricle to the pulmonary arteries usually signifies surgical treatment of one or more congenital anomalies which compromise adequate blood flow to the lungs, such as pulmonary

Fig. 4.9 Temporary epicardial pacemaker wires (*arrows*) are placed routinely before surgical closure of the chest wall. In this specimen, temporary pacemaker wires and blood clots on the surface of the heart at autopsy characterize findings following a perioperative death

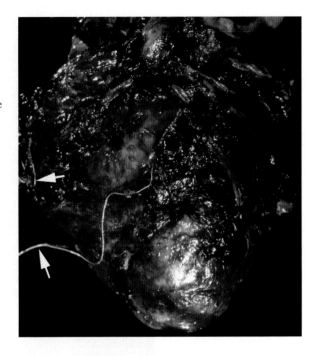

valve stenosis, tetralogy of Fallot, or truncus arteriosus. A suture closure buttressed by large Teflon strips over the apex of the heart (Fig. 4.10) could be explained by previous surgical repair of an apical left ventricular aneurysm or closure of a postinfarction ventricular septal defect (VSD), in which case the pathologist should look for proximal LAD disease or acute thrombosis of a dominant right coronary artery, respectively, and not be surprised to find one or more coronary artery bypass grafts on the heart. A suture line closure of the left atrial appendage may have been done at the time of mitral valve replacement to reduce the incidence of mural thrombus formation associated with chronic atrial fibrillation. It may alternatively indicate the use of left atrium to femoral artery bypass used by a surgeon to repair a traumatic tear or aneurysm of the descending thoracic aorta. An obliquely transverse suture line in the proximal ascending aorta usually represents closure of surgical access to replace the aortic valve. It may be associated with a previous septal myomectomy or resection of a diaphragm-like obstruction in the left ventricular outflow tract causing a hemodynamically significant subaortic stenosis.

Next, if one or more coronary bypass grafts are in place, they should be examined. It is gratifying to be able to correlate angiographic images obtained at the postmortem coronary artery injection with findings at the time of gross dissection. Thrombosed vein grafts will appear distended and firm to palpation, whereas patent vein grafts will be flat and soft. The presence of two vein grafts lying one on top of the other and having distal anastomoses to the same coronary artery is typically found after re-do CABG procedures. In re-do CABG operations, the surgeon usually resects a few centimeters of the end of the vein that is sewn to the aorta and ties

Fig. 4.10 A left apical
ventriculotomy has been
closed surgically by using
sutures buttressed by strips
of Teflon cloth (*arrow*). A
LIMA to the LAD
(*arrowhead*) is a finding
consistent with occlusive
disease commonly associated
with myocardial infarction
complicated by a left
ventricular aneurysm or VSD
necessitating repair through
an apical ventriculotomy

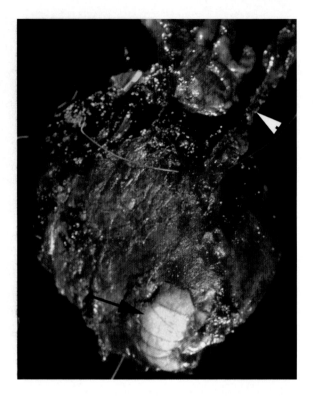

off the remaining proximal end. He will then construct the proximal anastomosis
of the new vein graft to the same hole in the aortic wall that had been occupied by
the resected old graft. If the new vein graft is significantly smaller in diameter than
the old graft, the proximal end of the old vein graft might be left in place, allowing the new vein to be sewn to a proportionately sized hole punched in the hood
of the old vein at its proximal anastomosis. This technique avoids stretching the
proximal end of the new vein graft by sewing it to an undesirably large hold in the
aortic wall.

The patency of each distal anastomosis can be documented by incising the graft
over it and passing a 1 mm probe through it. This maneuver should be done if the
postmortem injection is not performed or is inconclusive. Because an internal mammary artery graft is mobilized off the chest wall as a pedicle, which includes fibromuscular tissue and adjacent veins, a bread-loafing of the pedicle can be done to
document arterial patency (again, the postmortem injection is very helpful with this
documentation). The internal mammary artery and its pedicle should then be mobilized and reflected down to the distal anastomosis by severing the pedicle proximally
if necessary. Vein grafts are mobilized by cutting out each proximal anastomosis
with a "collar or button" of ascending aortic wall and swinging them down to their
distal anastomoses using sharp dissection, if necessary, to mobilize them away from
the surface of the heart.

Take the Coronary Arteries Off the Heart

One is now ready to take the native coronary arteries with intact distal graft anasto-moses (if grafts are present) off the heart. It is suggested that a good place to start this dissection is in the right atrioventricular (AV) groove inferiorly. With a scalpel, one can easily find a dominant right coronary artery by incising the fat in the groove and proceeding to mobilize the rest of the artery going from known to unknown. Usually, anterior muscular and acute marginal branches can be ignored and cut a few mil-limeters from their take-offs. When the artery is mobilized, it can be removed from the heart by cutting a collar of aortic wall around the right coronary ostium. The left main coronary artery can readily be found posterior to the main pulmonary artery trunk. It is easily palpated if atherosclerotic and/or calcific. Sharp dissection of epi-cardial fat will then reveal the proximal LAD. If the LAD is largely superficial, it is quickly "outlined" by cutting into the myocardium on either side of it and extending these incisions to the apex of the heart. Diagonal branches, unless large and possi-bly atherosclerotic, can usually be ignored. The LAD is then mobilized by incising myocardium deep to the artery. Care should be taken not to injure the vessel by cut-ting too superficially through an intramyocardial segment of LAD. A large ramus medialis branch, originating between the origins of the LAD and circumflex arteries, might be worth isolating and saving. The circumflex coronary artery is then exposed by incising epicardial fat in the left AV groove while lifting the left atrial appendage away from the groove. Obtuse marginal branches are usually superficial on the sur-face of the heart and can be mobilized by the same technique that was used to mobi-lize the LAD. If the right system is dominant, the distal circumflex will taper quickly in the AV groove after one or two obtuse marginal branches. In a left dominant or codominant system, the distal circumflex may send a large branch across the crux of the heart or parallel and to the left of the interventricular groove, respectively [3].

At this point, the pathologist is able to demonstrate ex vivo the configuration of the native coronary arteries and, if applicable, the pattern of coronary artery reconstruction. This exercise is instructive for the pathologist as well as for teaching residents, fellows, and physician assistants. If calcification of native vessels and/or bypass conduits is identified either by the postmortem scout film or by palpation, the coronary arteries and grafts should be fixed and decalcified. After decalcifi-cation, the vessels should be carefully bread-loafed at 2–3 mm intervals to docu-ment patency, determine evidence of acute thrombosis or dissection, and to quantify severity of atherosclerotic disease (Fig. 4.11). Correlation of these findings with angiographic data and clinical acute coronary artery syndromes [4] can be particu-larly instructive. Representative sections of pertinent gross findings should be sub-mitted for histological study.

Stain with Tetrazolium

Before fully opening the heart, it is frequently instructive to bread-loaf the apex of the heart transversely in three or four 1 cm-thick slabs. This maneuver will allow one to look for evidence of acute myocardial infarction, myocardial scarring, and

Fig. 4.11 The RCA (*asterisk*), LAD (*double asterisk*), and circumflex (*triple asterisk*) are sectioned in the fashion of a bread loaf in order to grossly quantify their involvement by atherosclerosis. Severe disease in the LAD is apparent (*inset*)

ventricular dilatation. If ischemic myocardial injury is a consideration, the section of tissue farthest from the apex should be tested for tetrazolium staining. Nitro-blue tetrazolium (NBT) and 2,3,5-triphenyltetrazolium chloride (TTC) will both nicely demonstrate a recent infarction in fresh myocardial tissue. This author uses the latter tetrazolium salt according to a well-documented staining procedure [5].

Open the Heart

Right Atrium

Opening of the heart is begun by incising the wall of the *right atrium* from the confluence of the inferior vena cava through the right atrial appendage. Right atrial dilatation might reflect a history of atrial fibrillation, various congenital heart defects causing left-to-right shunts, as well as primary or secondary tricuspid insufficiency. Relevant postmortem surgical "footprints" would include a pledgeted suture closure of a patent foramen ovale, a pericardial patch closure of a secundum, primum, or sinus venosus type of atrial septal defect, a valvuloplasty ring sutured to the annulus of a tricuspid valve that was regurgitant because of annular dilatation, or a tricuspid valve prosthesis perhaps placed to treat valvular endocarditis or tricuspid insufficiency associated with Ebstein's anomaly. Remnants of the Chiari complex (Fig. 4.12) manifested as either a Eustachian valve or Thebesian valve [6] may explain why the cardiac surgeon may have had difficulty passing the venous cannula [7] into the superior vena cava or a retrograde cardioplegia catheter into the coronary sinus [8], respectively.

Fig. 4.12 A Thebesian valve (*arrow*) overlies the coronary sinus above the posterior annulus of the tricuspid valve (*arrowhead*)

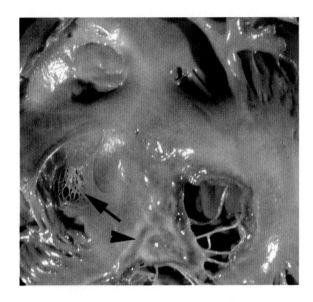

Right Ventricle

The *right ventricle* is opened by incising the lateral free wall through the plane of the commissure between the anterior and posterior leaflets of the tricuspid valve. A second incision opens the plane that joins the anterior wall and interventricular septum. The latter incision should be extended through the pulmonary valve and trunk of the pulmonary artery. Closure of a VSD frequently appears as an endothelialized patch, usually behind the septal leaflet of the tricuspid valve. In a heart operated on for treatment of tetralogy of Fallot, a defect in the thickened and anteriorly displaced subvalvular interventricular septum, representing a previous myocardial resection to open an outflow tract obstruction, may or may not reveal scar. A pulmonary valve prosthesis usually represents treatment of a congenital valvular stenosis.

Left Atrium

The *left atrium* can be opened by incising the posterior wall between the two superior or inferior pulmonary veins. The incision should then be extended through the left atrial appendage, looking for a mural thrombus. A greatly dilated left atrium, especially when associated with the finding of a mitral valve prosthesis or valvu-loplasty ring, is consistent with a history of atrial fibrillation. Resection or ligation of the left atrial appendage and, less commonly, multiple suture lines or endocar-dial scars isolating the pulmonary veins emptying into the left atrium (a so-called Cox-Maze procedure) [9] are confirmatory evidence of chronic atrial fibrillation. A valvuloplasty ring (Fig. 4.13) is a clue to a history of mitral valve prolapse, annu-lar dilatation due to left ventricular myocardial remodeling, or, less commonly, coro-nary artery disease causing an ischemic papillary muscle dysfunction. The presence of a mitral valve prosthesis is consistent with a past history of an irreparable mitral valve prolapse (perhaps a floppy anterior leaflet), postinflammatory (rheumatic) mitral valve disease (look for a concomitant aortic valve prosthesis), infectious endocarditis, congenital mitral valve anomalies, or ischemic papillary muscle dys-function treated by replacement versus repair. As mentioned above, a patch (usually endothelialized) in the interatrial septum may reflect previous resection of a myx-oma or surgical treatment of an atrial septal defect, either secundum type (fossa ovalis) or, less commonly, a primum type (inferior, or caudad, to the fossa ovalis), as associated with an endocardial cushion defect.

Fig. 4.13
A Carpentier-Edwards ring is seated on the mitral annulus by interrupted sutures. The underlying valvular suspension apparatus remains intact

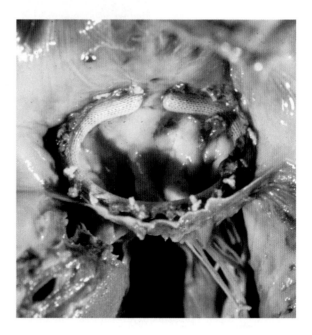

Left Ventricle

The *left ventricle* can be opened laterally through the obtuse margin in the plane of the lateral commissure of the mitral valve. If a mitral prosthesis is in place, it is worth noting how much of the native mitral valve and suspension apparatus had been preserved. This observation may be relevant to the maintenance (if at least the posterior leaflet and chordae remain intact) or deterioration (if both leaflets had been resected) of left ventricular function clinically [10]. The left ventricular outflow tract can be exposed by cutting through the anterior leaflet of the mitral valve. A surgical defect in the interventricular septum just below the aortic valve will indicate

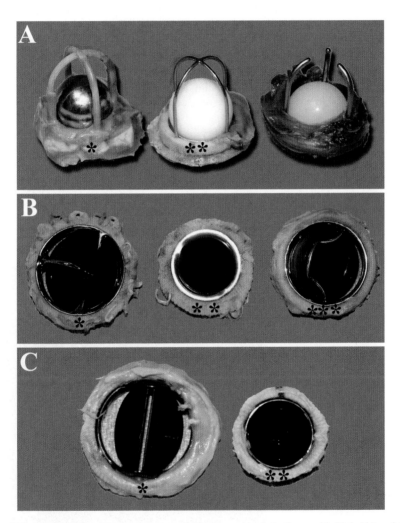

Fig. 4.14 Mechanical valve prostheses available for use include those with high (**A**) and low (**B** and **C**) profiles. (**A**) Variants of the Starr-Edwards valve prosthesis have included those with a metallic ball inside a cage (*struts*) covered with Dacron (*asterisk*), a plastic ball inside bare metallic struts (*double asterisk*), and a ball inside a partially open cage (Smeloff-Cutter valve). (**B**) Tilting disk valves include the Medtronic-Hall valve (*asterisk*), Omniscience (*double asterisk*), and Bjork-Shiley (*triple asterisk*) valves. (**C**) The St. Jude prosthesis is shown in the open (*asterisk*) and closed (*double asterisk*) position of its bi-leaflet configuration

that a myomectomy was done to relieve an outflow tract obstruction associated with an asymmetric hypertrophic cardiomyopathy or, uncommonly, a congenital subaortic stenosis. In the case of the former, look for endocardial thickening around the myomectomy site, which would be evidence of clinical obstruction by systolic anterior motion (SAM) of the anterior leaflet of the mitral valve [11]. Next, is there an aortic valve prosthesis? If so, what kind? If it is a mechanical valve (Fig. 4.14), does it open and close easily (a question to ask with a mechanical valve in any position)? If not, why not...thrombus (Fig. 4.15), pannus (Fig. 4.16), or vegetation [12]? If the prosthesis is biological, what kind is it (Fig. 4.17), and is there evidence of degeneration, a question to ask with a biologic valve in any position (Fig. 4.18). For routine valve replacement in an elderly patient, the bovine pericardial valve prosthesis is favored by surgeons over the porcine valve because the former appears to be more durable than the latter [13]. If the valve replacement is a homograft, it was probably placed because of the presence or history of infectious endocarditis at the time of surgery. If so, is there evidence of a previous root abscess or fistula between chambers, e.g., left ventricle and right atrium, as shown in Fig. 4.19? Also, if present, check the integrity of reimplantation of the native coronary ostia into the homograft aorta (Fig. 4.20).

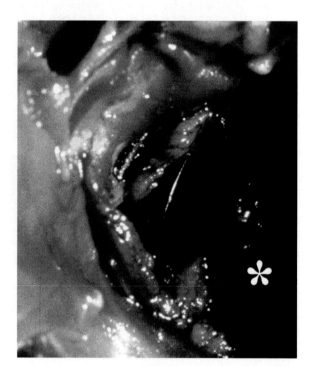

Fig. 4.15 A St. Jude aortic valve prosthesis is fixed in the open position by an occluding thrombus (*asterisk*)

Fig. 4.16 Movement of the tilting disk of a Medtronic-Hall valve is blocked by fibrous tissue (pannus) proliferating across the prosthesis from the annulus

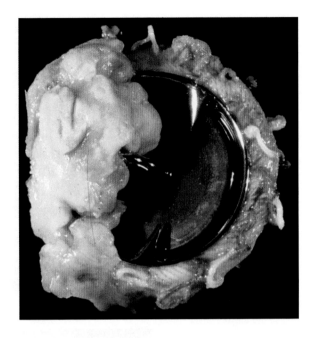

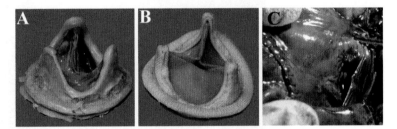

Fig. 4.17 Bioprosthetic valves found at autopsy may include a (**A**) Carpentier-Edwards porcine valve, (**B**) bovine pericardial valve, or (**C**) human aortic allograft valve

Aortic Valve

An *aortic valve* prosthesis may be in association with a tube graft reconstruction of the ascending aorta. If the valve prosthesis is within the end of the tube graft, a so-called composite graft, the surgery had been performed to treat either an ascending aortic aneurysm associated with a dilated aortic annulus causing significant aortic regurgitation, or an acute aortic dissection involving the native aortic valve to the extent that valvular competence could not be restored by suspending the prolapsed commissure with a suture technique. In either case, because the tube graft covers

Fig. 4.18 A degenerated
porcine valve prosthesis has
tears in two of its leaflets

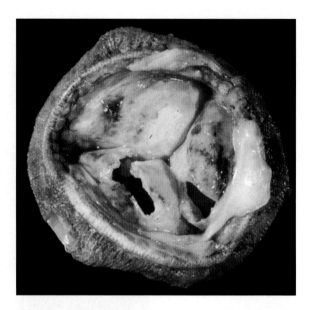

Fig. 4.19 An aortic root
abscess resulted in a fistula
between the left ventricle and
right atrium, which is traced
by a white ribbon

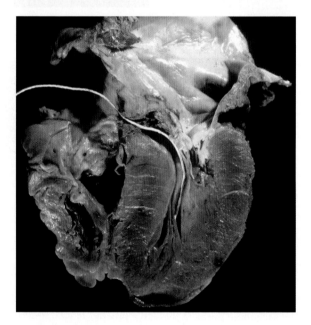

the native coronary ostia, the coronary ostia must be reimplanted into the tube graft
or a coronary artery reconstruction using bypass grafts is required (Fig. 4.21).

Finally, does the type of valve prosthesis correlate with the patient's age at the
time of valve replacement. A mechanical valve replacement is usually preferred

Fig. 4.20 When an aortic valve replacement is done with a human allograft, the allograft is sewn to the native LVOT proximally and native ascending aorta (*arrowhead*) distally. In the process, the graft covers over the native coronary ostia, requiring their reimplantation into the homograft (*arrow*) or reconstruction by CABG

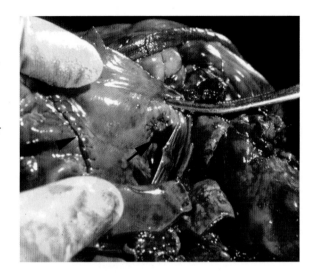

Fig. 4.21 CABG (*arrow*) has been done to establish coronary arterial flow following reconstruction of an ascending aorta with a composite tube graft. The composite graft contains an aortic valve prosthesis sewn to the aortic annulus and a Dacron tube, which occludes the native coronary ostia in its path to the distal anastomosis with the native ascending aorta

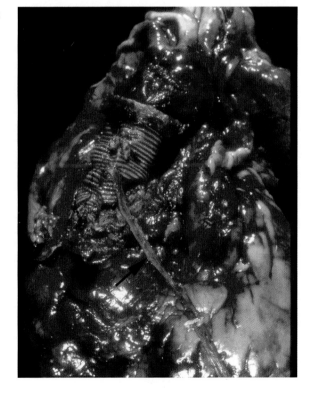

over a biologic prosthesis in a patient younger than 70 because of the better durability of a mechanical valve prosthesis [14]. If, at autopsy, this scenario does not seem to have occurred, consider some contraindication to long-term treatment with Coumadin, i.e., a coagulopathy, an issue of inadequate compliance, or some other issue [15].

Routine Measurements

As one concludes the gross dissection of the operated heart, it is important to document *routine measurements* of the heart. Specific quantification may allow one to optimize clinical-pathologic correlation of morphologic features of the heart and postoperative findings with what is known or can be surmised regarding the hemodynamic pathophysiology of the deceased prior to death. The importance of weighing the heart prior to removing the coronary arteries has been mentioned above. After the heart has been opened, quantification of ventricular wall (myocardial) thickness, measured one centimeter below the tricuspid and mitral annuli, allows the examiner to assess the heart for ventricular hypertrophy. Only then can the pathologist legitimately consider the differential diagnoses of primary hypertrophy versus secondary hypertrophy, eccentric versus concentric hypertrophy, acquired versus congenital hypertrophy, and biventricular hypertrophy versus hypertrophy involving only one of the ventricles [16]. Likewise, measurement of annular circumference of each heart valve will allow one to assess for the presence of remodeling which had resulted in annular dilatation or narrowing, either acquired or congenital. Careful measurement of the diameter of a prosthetic valve at the level of the sewing ring will allow one to calculate valve circumference and avoid removing the prosthesis. However, removing the prosthetic valve by cutting and withdrawing each suture one at a time is an instructive exercise that can simulate the surgeon's task at the time of re-do valve replacement and allow the prosector to visualize the morphologic impact of a seated prosthetic valve on the annular tissue. Beauty here may indeed be in the eye of the beholder.

References

1. Field ML, Al-Alao B, Mediratta N, Sosnowski A. Open and closed chest extrathoracic cannulation for cardiopulmonary bypass and extracorporeal life support: methods, indications, and outcomes. Postgrad Med J 2006;82:323–31.
2. Kamlot A, Bellows SD, Simkhovich BZ, Hale SL, Aoki A, Kloner RA, Kay GL. Is warm retrograde blood cardioplegia better than cold for myocardial protection? Ann Thorac Surg 1997;63:98–104.
3. Nerantzis CE, Lefkidis CA, Smirnoff TB, Agapitos EB, Davaris PS. Variations in the origin and course of the posterior interventricular artery in relation to the crux cordis and the posterior interventricular vein: an anatomical study. Anat Rec 1998;252: 413–7.
4. Michalodimitrakis M, Mavroforou A, Giannoukas AD. Lessons learnt from the autopsies of 445 cases of sudden cardiac death in adults. Coron Artery Dis 2005;16:385–9.

5. Vargas SO, Sampson BA, Schoen FJ. Pathologic detection of early myocardial infarction: a critical review of the evolution and usefulness of modern techniques. Mod Pathol 1999;12:635–45. Review.

6. Nakagawa H, Lazzara R, Khastgir T, Beckman KJ, McClelland JH, Imai S, Pitha JV, Becker AE, Arruda M, Gonzalez MD, Widman LE, Rome M, Neuhauser J, Wang X, Calame JD, Goudeau MD, Jackman WM. Role of the tricuspid annulus and the eustachian valve/ridge on atrial flutter. Relevance to catheter ablation of the septal isthmus and a new technique for rapid identification of ablation success. Circulation 1996;94:407–24.

7. Kirkeby-Garstad I, Tromsdal A, Sellevold OF, Bjorngaard M, Bjella LK, Berg EM, Karevold A, Haaverstad R, Wahba A, Tjomsland O, Astudillo R, Krogstad A, Stenseth R. Guiding surgical cannulation of the inferior vena cava with transesophageal echocardiography. Anesth Analg 2003;96:1288–93.

8. Vander Salm TJ. Coronary sinus cannulation: a technique to overcome an obstructing thebesian valve. Ann Thorac Surg 1993;56:1441–2.

9. Gillinov AM, Bhavani S, Blackstone EH, Rajeswaran J, Svensson LG, Navia JL, Pettersson BG, Sabik JF 3rd, Smedira NG, Mihaljevic T, McCarthy PM, Shewchik J, Natale A. Surgery for permanent atrial fibrillation: impact of patient factors and lesion set. Ann Thorac Surg 2006;82:502–13.

10. Solomon NA, Pranav SK, Naik D, Sukumaran S. Importance of preservation of chordal apparatus in mitral valve replacement. Expert Rev Cardiovasc Ther 2006;4:253–61. Review.

11. Sherrid MV, Chaudhry FA, Swistel DG. Obstructive hypertrophic cardiomyopathy: echocardiography, pathophysiology, and the continuing evolution of surgery for obstruction. Ann Thorac Surg 2003 Feb;75(2):620–32. Review.

12. Tang GH, Rao V, Siu S, Butany J. Thrombosis of mechanical mitral valve prosthesis. J Card Surg 2005;20:481–6.

13. Gao G, Wu Y, Grunkemeier GL, Furnary AP, Starr A. Durability of pericardial versus porcine aortic valves. J Am Coll Cardiol 2004;44:384–8.

14. Zilla P, Human P, Bezuidenhout D. Bioprosthetic heart valves: the need for a quantum leap. Biotechnol Appl Biochem 2004;40:57–66. Review.

15. Lund O, Bland M. Risk-corrected impact of mechanical versus bioprosthetic valves on long-term mortality after aortic valve replacement. J Thorac Cardiovasc Surg 2006;132:20–6.

16. Machackova J, Barta J, Dhalla NS. Myofibrillar remodeling in cardiac hypertrophy, heart failure and cardiomyopathies. Can J Cardiol 2006;22:953–68.

Chapter 5
Putting It All Together

Abstract A series of autopsies done on the deceased at a major tertiary care medical center during the same admission in which cardiac surgery was performed is presented here to illustrate pertinent principles of clinical-pathologic correlation relating to the operated heart. Any relationship between the cause of death and previous heart surgery may remain elusive even after the autopsy is completed. Pertinent variables relating to a given case include the time interval between cardiac surgery and the autopsy, technical issues relating to the cardiac operation(s), subtle complications of underlying heart disease versus surgical complications, comorbidtities at the time of and/or subsequent to cardiac surgery, drug-related complications, and medical-legal issues relating to surgery. This chapter will help the pathologist sort through these parameters in an effort to reach a conclusion based on the autopsy findings and the most likely scenario in a given case.

Keywords Clinicopathologic correlation · Subtle complications · Comorbidtities · Medical-legal issues · Pertinent variables

A careful examination of the operated heart at autopsy based on the guidelines listed above will hopefully allow the pathologist to understand any relationship between the cause of death and previous heart surgery. However, the two events may not be related; or, frustratingly, the relationship may remain elusive even after the autopsy is completed. Multiple scenarios differ according to the pertinent variables relating to a given case:

- Time interval between cardiac surgery and the autopsy
- Technical issues relating to the cardiac operation(s)
- Subtle complications of underlying heart disease versus surgical complications
- Comorbidities at the time of and/or subsequent to cardiac surgery
- Drug-related complications
- Medical-legal issues relating to surgery.

The pathologist must sort through these parameters and formulate his conclusion on the most likely scenario based on the autopsy findings. A series of autopsies

S.L. Houser, *The Operated Heart at Autopsy*, DOI 10.1007/978-1-60327-808-9_5,   53
© Humana Press, a part of Springer Science + Business Media, LLC 2009

done on the deceased at a major tertiary care medical center during the same admission in which cardiac surgery was performed is presented here to illustrate pertinent principles of clinical-pathologic correlation relating to the operated heart. The cases are itemized by operative procedure in the Table of Contents of this manuscript.

Case 1: Nonpulsatile Blood Flow and the Gastrointestinal Tract

History

The patient is a 71-year-old man who presented with increasing exertional symptoms. He was evaluated and showed an aortic stenosis and moderate stenosis of his left anterior descending artery.

Procedure

Aortic valve replacement (23 mm Magna pericardial valve), coronary bypass (left internal mammary to left anterior descending artery).

Hospital Course

On postoperative day 12, the patient was preparing to be discharged home when he had a large bowel movement showing melena. He became hypotensive and required readmission to the Cardiac Surgical ICU. Upper endoscopy revealed multiple bleeding duodenal ulcers. On the 13th day after cardiac surgery, he underwent a truncal vagotomy and an extended pyloroplasty. He developed atrial fibrillation with rapid ventricular response, and he was treated with Amiodarone. Because of recurrent bleeding, he underwent an exploratory laparotomy with oversewing of bleeding ulcers in the third portion of his duodenum, a total gastrectomy with Roux-en-Y esophagojejunostomy and enteroenterostomy. The patient developed increasing respiratory difficulty, and his X-rays began to show evidence of bilateral diffuse infiltrates consistent with ARDS versus Amiodarone toxicity. His Amiodarone was discontinued. His course was further complicated by recurrent gastrointestinal (GI) bleeding, renal failure that required peritoneal dialysis, deep vein thrombosis that was treated with an inferior vena caval filter, and worsening respiratory failure. He died on the 46th day following cardiac surgery.

Autopsy Findings

- Diffuse alveolar damage, organizing phase (combined lung weight = 2805 g).
- Pleural effusion (400 ml) and adhesions, left.

- Cardiomegaly (720 g), with left ventricular hypertrophy and dilatation.
- Fibrinous pericarditis, consistent with prior surgical intervention.
- Coronary artery disease, involving left anterior descending (severe) and right coronary (mild) arteries.
- Patent foramen ovale.
- Atherosclerosis, involving:
   o Aorta (descending and abdominal), moderate.
   o Iliac arteries, moderate.
- Pancreatic abscess (approximately 2 cm), juxtaposed to duodenum.
- Acute renal tubular necrosis, bilateral.
- Hepatomegaly (3450 g), with cholestasis and centrilobular congestion and necrosis.
- Splenic infarct (2.1 cm).
- Chronic acalculous cholecystitis, with focal histiocytic reaction to bile.
- Abdominal adhesions, extensive.
- Nodular prostate, benign hyperplasia.
- Hydrocele, bilateral.
- Scoliosis.

Comment

Autopsy findings show the cause of death to be diffuse alveolar damage, likely secondary to sepsis from a gastrointestinal source. Multiple sections of the pancreas fail to identify a gastrinoma, which is considered a possible cause of multiple bleeding duodenal ulcers (Zollinger-Ellison syndrome). GI complications are uncommon following cardiac surgery, but when they occur, the mortality and morbidity rates are high [1]. Although controversial, the nonpulsatile flow of blood associated with the pump run has been considered important in the cause of postoperative bowel ischemia and ulceration [2]. A recent clinical study [3] found that, although cardiopulmonary bypass did not emerge as a risk factor for GI complications, prolonged bypass (longer than 98 min) was associated with a high incidence of such complications. Furthermore, GI bleeding usually results from stress ulceration and is associated with old age (over 70 years).

Conclusions

- Time interval between cardiac surgery and the autopsy

   - *Important.* Although the autopsy showed a well-seated prosthetic valve and a patent, well-positioned coronary bypass graft, death resulted from postoperative complications.

- Technical issues relating to the cardiac operation(s)

   - *Possibly important.* Length of cross-clamp time and pump run may have been relevant to the patient's outcome.

- Subtle complications of underlying heart disease versus surgical complications

  - *Possibly important.* Postoperative atrial fibrillation may have been related to a decreased compliance of a hypertrophic left ventricle.

- Comorbidities at the time of and/or subsequent to cardiac surgery

  - *Important.* Multi-organ failure resulted from resuscitative efforts to control recurrent GI bleeding and associated hemodynamic instability.

- Drug-related complications

  - *Possibly important.* A questionably adverse effect of treatment with Amiodarone may have been relevant to the patient's outcome.

- Medical-legal issues relating to surgery

  - *None.*

Case 2: Hazard of a Re-Do Sternotomy

History

The patient is a 70-year-old man with a long-standing history of heart disease. In 1976, he had a two-vessel coronary artery bypass. In 1998, he had recurrent angina and had a re-do CABG with LIMA to his LAD and saphenous veins to PDA and the obtuse marginal arteries. He presented recently with syncope. He had a heavily calcified aorta and aortic valve. His vein grafts and his LIMA to his LAD were patent. He presents for aortic valve replacement.

Procedure

Re-do, re-do sternotomy, emergent institution of femorofemoral cardiopulmonary bypass, aortic valve replacement (21 mm pericardial valve), transthoracic intraaortic balloon pump placement.

Hospital Course

During the operation, the sternotomy resulted in injury of a vein graft to the right coronary artery, serious bleeding, and the need to suture-ligate the vein graft. The patient required pressors and multiple transfusions of packed red blood cells for maintenance throughout his operation. After a number of hours of resuscitation, the patient was finally taken up to the cardiac intensive care unit. Despite all efforts to sustain the patient's life, he was pronounced dead the day after surgery.

Autopsy Findings

- Cardiomegaly (1060 g), with biventricular hypertrophy and biatrial dilation.
- Myocardial interstitial fibrosis, patchy.
- Atherosclerotic coronary artery disease:
    70% stenosis of the left main coronary artery.
    >95% stenosis of the left anterior descending coronary artery.
    >95% stenosis of the left circumflex coronary artery.
    >95% stenosis of the right coronary artery.
- Status post coronary artery bypass grafting (1998):
    Left internal mammary artery to LAD, widely patent.
    Saphenous vein graft to obtuse marginal, widely patent.
    Saphenous vein graft to obtuse marginal, with distal obstruction.
    Saphenous vein graft to PDA, with distal obstruction.
    Old saphenous vein graft to LAD, sutured closed
- Status post aortic valve replacement (9/10/2004):
    Bioprosthetic aortic valve intact and in place.
- Atherosclerosis, moderate to severe, involving ascending thoracic and abdominal aorta.
- Bilateral pleural effusions (right = 750 ml, left = 450 ml).
- Hepatic centrilobular congestion.
- Abdominal ascites (1300 ml) and fibrous adhesions.
- Nephrosclerosis, bilateral.
- Renal cortical cyst, simple (8.5 cm)

Comments

Histologically, the myocardium displayed interstitial fibrosis as well as subendo-cardial myocyte vacuolization, which was consistent with ischemia. The mitral valve showed myxomatous degeneration. The cause of death was cardiac failure in the setting of chronic and severe coronary artery disease and recent aortic valve replacement.

There were several pertinent findings at autopsy that related to the patient's past history and current hospital course. Scars on both lower extremities were indicative of previous greater saphenous vein harvest for CABG. A fresh wound closure in the left groin reflected the use of femoral artery and vein to achieve cardiopulmonary bypass, which was done emergently because of injury of a vein graft by the ster-notomy saw. This injury, confirmed at autopsy by the finding of a suture ligature of the vein graft, was a result of adhesion of the heart to the anterior chest wall following previous cardiac surgery... always a hazard in re-do cardiac procedures. An open sternotomy wound covered with a synthetic patch, which was sewn to the skin around the wound, was indicative of the surgeon's inability to close the wound without causing tamponade of a dilated, failing heart. The transthoracic intraaortic balloon pump not only confirmed the serious intraoperative heart failure but also tipped off the pathologist that severe atherosclerosis of the aortoiliac arterial system must have prevented passage of the balloon pump from the routinely used femoral artery access.

Conclusions

- Time interval between cardiac surgery and the autopsy

  - *Important*. Although the autopsy showed a well-seated prosthetic valve, death resulted from a disastrous intraoperative complication.

- Technical issues relating to the cardiac operation(s)

  - *Important*. A heart with a vein graft adherent to the anterior chest wall makes a safe re-do sternotomy a huge technical challenge.

- Subtle complications of underlying heart disease versus surgical complications

  - *Important*. Biventricular hypertrophy increases the vulnerability of myocardium to ischemic injury during the cross-clamp time, increasing the difficulty of myocardial preservation [4]. The blood loss and hemodynamic instability relating to the complication of the sternotomy presumably amplified this difficulty.

- Comorbidities at the time of and/or subsequent to cardiac surgery

  - *Important*. A postoperative coagulopathy was severe and accentuated the patient's hemodynamic instability.

- Drug-related complications

  - *None apparent*.

- Medical-legal issues relating to surgery

  - *None*. The surgical complication in this case is well-recognized and accepted in the surgical community [5].

Case 3: Cardiopulmonary Bypass in a Salvage Mode

History

This 20-year-old female was suffering from end-stage liver disease, diabetes mellitus, and end-stage renal failure. She underwent a liver transplantation 19 years ago for biliary atresia and had developed allograft failure. Now suitable organs (liver, kidney, pancreas) were identified.

Procedure

Exploratory laparotomy, venovenous bypass between femoral vein and axillary vein, hepatectomy of the allograft, sternotomy, cardiopulmonary bypass, attempt of cardiac and pulmonary artery thrombectomy.

Hospital Course

In the operating room, she developed hemodynamic collapse while undergoing re-do orthotopic liver transplantation. She arrested but regained a marginal blood pressure after external CPR. Concomitant with her fall in systolic blood pressure was a dramatic rise in pulmonary artery pressures. Transesophageal echocardiography (TEE) findings were consistent with a clot in the right atrium and pulmonary artery. The Cardiac Surgical Service was consulted for emergent pulmonary embolectomy.

At the time of sternotomy, the patient was asystolic, and internal cardiopulmonary resuscitation was administered. While this was being performed, the patient was systemically heparinized. An arterial perfusor was placed through a double pursestring suture in the ascending aorta. A right angle DLP cannula was placed through a pursestring suture in the superior vena cava. The IVC had been transected in preparation for the new liver, so the second venous line was spliced into the venous femoral line, which was originally part of the centrifugal venovenous bypass circuit. The patient was then placed on a cardiopulmonary bypass and maintained warm. The venous return from the patient was poor and perfusion pressure was just barely adequate. The pulmonary artery was opened longitudinally. There was no clot present within the main pulmonary artery, and attempts to retrieve the clot from the right and left pulmonary arteries were unsuccessful. The right atrium was opened and again no clinically relevant thrombus was found. Visualization of the right ventricle through the tricuspid valve revealed no clot.

During the pump run a number of technical problems occurred, including an electrical power failure, pressurized disconnection of one of the lines, and clotting of the reservoir. These were all dealt with expeditiously. The pulmonary artery and right atrium were closed and the patient's metabolic parameters corrected as much as possible. An attempt to wean the patient from cardiopulmonary bypass with maximal pressors was unsuccessful. Indeed, despite maximal medical therapy, the patient's cardiac function only continued to deteriorate, and eventually she became asystolic. By this time the patient had undergone a prolonged period of extreme hypotension and was anhepatic. The chances of resuscitating her were negligible. Therefore, the patient was declared dead.

Autopsy Findings

- Pulmonary fat emboli, microscopic, few.
- Small left kidney with bile nephrosis (hepatorenal syndrome) and hyaline arteriopathy.

- Pleural effusions, serosanguineous (right: 1059 ml; left: 155 ml).
- Cardiac and pericardial ecchymoses, extensive, resuscitative.
- Hemomediastinum, with dissection of blood into both pulmonary hila and along pulmonary arteries into lungs, resuscitative.
- Cardiac hypertrophy, biventricular.
- Fibrocongestive splenomegaly (882 g).

Note: The liver had been submitted as a surgical specimen and was absent at autopsy. It showed bridging portal fibrosis, patchy loss of bile ducts with marked bile ductular reduplication, and the presence of fibrointimal hyperplasia involving portal venous channels consistent with chronic rejection.

Comments

The cause of the patient's intraoperative cardiovascular collapse was not determined by the morphologic findings. No thromboemboli were present. A fat stain on frozen lung tissue demonstrated multiple small fat emboli, which, in addition to the mediastinal hemorrhage, were considered secondary to resuscitative efforts. An attending surgeon was present during part of the dissection at time of autopsy.

Although transplantation of liver, kidney, and pancreas simultaneously into a patient has been reported [6], it is a scenario which, when combined with emergent establishment of cardiopulmonary bypass and Trendelenburg procedure [7, 8], is clearly uncommon and challenging for the pathologist to assess at autopsy. Interestingly, the use of cardiopulmonary bypass for cardiotomy in conjunction with orthotopic liver transplantation has been done electively for multiple indications[9–14]. Massive intracardiac and pulmonary thromboembolism occurring during orthotopic liver transplantation and the usefulness of TEE in making the diagnosis are well documented in the literature [15]. Whether this complication is due to the use of antifibrinolytic drugs or to an inherited hypercoagulable defect, it can be catastrophic and fatal [16]. On the other hand, the use of cardiopulmonary bypass and surgical embolectomy can be life-saving [17, 18]. However, in the case presented here, the surgical retrieval effort failed to find thromboemboli in the heart or pulmonary arteries despite the TEE findings, and the patient succumbed to persistent cardiovascular collapse.

Without the ability to communicate directly with the surgeon, it would have been difficult for the pathologist to correlate external autopsy findings with specific surgical maneuvers. The left axillary and left femoral skin wounds related to the venovenous bypass used by the transplant team. The cardiac surgical team had achieved cardiopulmonary bypass by cannulating the superior vena cava through a median sternotomy, connecting to the left femoral venous line to complete venous drainage and by cannulating ascending aorta in the usual way to return oxygenated blood to the body. The remaining findings of a pulmonary arteriotomy closure and closed right atriotomy would be self-explanatory to the pathologist after hearing the sequence of operative events. The lack of evidence of intracardiac or pulmonary artery thromboemboli at the time of cardiac surgery, as well as at the time of autopsy, should bring to mind the possibility of a large air embolus as the cause of death [19]. Air embolism has occurred as a complication of liver transplantation [16, 20] and might be impossible to diagnose at the time of autopsy.

Conclusions

- Time interval between cardiac surgery and the autopsy

    – *Important.* As was evident by the lack of any drainage tubes on external examination, death resulted from a catastrophic intraoperative complication.

- Technical issues relating to the cardiac operation(s)

    – *Important.* In addition to the logistical challenge of setting up the machinery for establishing cardiopulmonary bypass in the face of the patient's hemodynamic collapse, a number of other technical complications, as listed in the hospital course above, may have compromised resuscitative efforts.

- Subtle complications of underlying heart disease versus surgical complications

    – *Questionably important.* Biventricular hypertrophy may have increased the vulnerability of the myocardium to ischemic injury following blood loss and hemodynamic instability.

- Comorbidities at the time of and/or subsequent to cardiac surgery

    – *Important.* A postoperative coagulopathy was severe and accentuated the patient's hemodynamic instability.

- Drug-related complications

    – *None apparent.*

- Medical-legal issues relating to surgery

    – *None.* Although the cause of the surgical complication in this case is not well-defined, there is no known reason to address it as anything more than a maloccurrence in a very difficult operation.

Case 4: A Problem of Heart Failure and Hardware

History

The patient is a 58-year-old man with a history of amyloidosis. He had had progressive decline in his cardiac function. Despite inotropic support and the placement of an intraaortic balloon pump, he remained in cardiogenic shock. He was listed for a heart transplant and needed a left ventricular assist device (LVAD) as a bridge to transplantation. Given his body size, he was not a good candidate for a HeartMate XVE. Arrangements were made to place him into the HeartMate II study.

Procedure

LVAD insertion (HeartMate II) and open removal of intraaortic balloon pump.

Hospital Course

His postoperative course thereafter was complicated by some coagulopathy for which the patient returned to the operating room for mediastinal exploration and evacuation of hematoma. He tolerated this procedure well and was extubated at the end of the case. He remained on LVAD support at a fixed rate with flows maintained in the 3.8–4 range. However, his blood pressure remained somewhat difficult to maintain in spite of LVAD support. The patient's condition progressively deteriorated, ending in his demise 58 days following insertion of the LVAD.

Autopsy Findings

- Plasma cell dyscrasia, with systemic lambda light chain amyloidosis, involving heart, lungs, kidneys, tongue, skin, thyroid, colon, small bowel, bladder, and prostate.
- Cardiomegaly (482 g), with biventricular hypertrophy and biatrial dilation.
- Left ventricular assist device (HeartMate II).
- Pulmonary amyloid deposition (1358 g combined weight), interstitial and vascular.
- Pulmonary embolus (0.3 cm), right upper lobe.
- Subpleural hemorrhage, multifocal.
- Hepatic centrilobular congestion.

Comments

The autopsy findings confirm the diagnosis of systemic light chain amyloidosis. The cause of death was progressive heart failure complicated clinically by sepsis. There was no significant coronary artery disease.

   At autopsy, external examination revealed the drive line of the assist device characteristically exiting the abdominal wall of the right upper quadrant. In the mediastinum, the inflow cannula of the device exited the apex of the left ventricle and the outflow graft was sewn end-to-side to the distal ascending aorta. Both of these conduits were attached to the pump, which was lying in a pocket behind the rectus abdominis muscle and anterior to the posterior sheath. Because insertion of the LVAD required establishment of cardiopulmonary bypass, examination at autopsy also revealed the usual suture closure of a right atriotomy in the appendage and a pledgeted suture closure of the aortic cannula site just below the takeoff of the innominate artery.

The HeartMate Vented Electric (XVE), made by Thoratec, is the first generation ventricular assist device and generates pulsatile blood flow. Heartmate II is the second- generation assist device, which has a much smaller pump that generates nonpulsatile blood flow up to 10 l/min. The driveline coming through the skin provides the power by attaching to accessories, including the system controller, batteries, and the power base unit.

Conclusions

- Time interval between cardiac surgery and the autopsy

  - *Not important.* Findings relating to the heart were straightforward and unimpeded by adhesions between the heart and parietal pericardium.

- Technical issues relating to the cardiac operation(s)

  - *Questionably important.* Although the insertion of the LVAD went well, the patient had to be re-explored for bleeding because of a marked coagulopathy.

- Subtle complications of underlying heart disease versus surgical complications

  - *Not important.* Biventricular hypertrophy, which commonly accompanies deposition of amyloid in the myocardium, may have increased the vulnerability of myocardium to ischemic injury, but ischemic injury due to the surgical procedures is unlikely.

- Comorbidities at the time of and/or subsequent to cardiac surgery

  - *Important.* A postoperative coagulopathy resulted in a second surgical procedure. Ongoing heart failure resulted in progressive renal failure. Sepsis due to bacterial and fungal organisms and recurrent pleural effusions further complicated the patient's hospital course.

- Drug-related complications

  - *Important.* One dose of systemic melphalan for his amyloidosis in anticipation of stem cell transplantation was not well-tolerated; he subsequently became profoundly neutropenic with an absolute neutrophil counts below the 200 range.

- Medical-legal issues relating to surgery

  - *None.* The patient's death was not caused by the surgery in this case.

Case 5: Prosthetic Valve Endocarditis

History

This 83-year-old woman had undergone a mitral valve replacement in 1999, utilizing a bioprosthetic valve. She also had been taking steroids for a considerable period of time for autoimmune disease. She presented with progressive congestive heart failure and was found to have prosthetic mitral stenosis with a residual orifice estimated at 0.4 cm.

Subsequently, blood cultures grew out Streptococcus, and evaluation suggested that the mitral stenosis was due to vegetations. Antibiotics were instituted and the patient was transferred for reoperative surgery. Significant pulmonary hypertension and congestive heart failure were present, and there was secondary tricuspid regurgitation.

Procedure

Re-do mitral valve replacement using a 29 mm Medtronic mosaic porcine bioprosthesis; tricuspid valve annuloplasty; ligation of left atrial appendage.

Hospital Course

She weaned from cardiopulmonary bypass with good cardiac output but in a profound state of vasodilation requiring high dose vasopressor drugs. She had received stress steroid coverage. She was taken to the cardiac surgical ICU. Over the course of the first postoperative night and early morning, she developed an evolving picture of severe DIC and the physiology of sepsis. In the morning her pupils were noted to become dilated and fixed, and the question of an intracerebral hemorrhage was raised by the neurologists. She developed progressive acidosis and died the day after her surgery.

Autopsy Findings

- Cardiomegaly (430 g), with:

  - Biventricular hypertrophy, eccentric, severe.
  - Left atrial dilatation, severe.
  - Right atrial dilatation, moderate, with mural thrombi (0.2 cm).
  - Porcine mitral valve prosthesis.
  - Tricuspid annuloplasty ring.

- Atherosclerosis, severe, involving aorta and iliac arteries.

- Hepatic congestion, with cholestasis and centrilobular necrosis.
- Nephrosclerosis.
- Chronic pancreatitis, slight.
- Colonic diverticulosis, sigmoid.
- Petechiae, dura and meninges.
- Microscopic infarct, hippocampus, old.

Comments

Histologic examination of the myocardium showed multiple thrombi in the microvasculature. Myocardial ischemia may therefore have contributed to her low cardiac output state postoperatively. Septic shock is a further consideration.

At autopsy, the heart was relatively free from pericardial adhesions because of the re-do surgery. Otherwise, the pathologist may have had to deal with dense adhesions from the previous surgery in 1999. Sutures in the superior vena cava and inferior aspect of the right atrium represented venous cannulation sites. A pledgeted suture closure in the ascending aorta just below the takeoff of the innominate artery signified the aortic cannulation site, completing the cardiopulmonary bypass circuit. Another pledgeted suture lower on the ascending aorta marked the cannulation site for administration of cardioplegic solution.

A suture line just below and parallel to the interatrial groove marked the left atriotomy site for surgical access to the mitral valve prosthesis, which was replaced. A ligature of the left atrial appendage represented the surgeon's effort to minimize the formation of mural thrombus in the left atrium, which can be a major source of emboli in the setting of chronic atrial fibrillation associated with mitral valve disease. A suture line closure of a right atriotomy is the site for gaining surgical access to the tricuspid valve annulus. In this case, an annuloplasty was done using a suture technique [21] at the commissures adjacent to the posterior leaflet, as well as along the anterior leaflet. Use of a prosthetic ring was avoided because of potential risk of sepsis.

Conclusions

- Time interval between cardiac surgery and the autopsy

  - *Not important*. Findings relating to the heart were straightforward and unimpeded by adhesions between the heart and parietal pericardium.

- Technical issues relating to the cardiac operation(s)

  - *Questionably important*. Re-do cardiac surgery usually is a technical challenge for the surgeon. In this case, however, the procedure apparently went well except for the need for inotropic support off bypass. In the face of ventricular hypertrophy, myocardial preservation during the cross-clamp time is always a concern.

- Subtle complications of underlying heart disease versus surgical complications

  - *Important.* The presence of infectious endocarditis, with vegetations obstructing the old mitral valve prosthesis sets the stage for major complications of infection postoperatively.

- Comorbidities at the time of and/or subsequent to cardiac surgery

  - *Important.* A postoperative clinical picture of disseminated intravascular coagulation (DIC) seems to have been the cause of the patient's course of rapid decline.

- Drug-related complications

  - *Not important.* No toxic drug reaction was apparent.

- Medical-legal issues relating to surgery

  - *None.* The patient's death appears to have been more of a metabolic issue than a technical error.

Case 6: Aortic Root Reconstruction, Old Age, and Comorbidity

History

The patient is a 77-year-old man who presented with shortness of breath. He was found to have a left pleural effusion. There were some malignant cells in it. A pleural biopsy showed some malignant cells of unclear etiology. It was thought that this could be a slow-growing tumor of unclear prognostic significance. At that time, he was found to have a 6 cm aortic root aneurysm. An echocardiogram showed severe aortic insufficiency. After consultation with his thoracic surgeon and thoracic oncologist, it was felt that he should have an aortic root replacement. Cardiac catheterization showed stenosis of his circumflex and left anterior descending artery.

Procedure

Composite porcine aortic root replacement (27 mm free style porcine root replacement and a 26 mm Hemashield ascending aortic graft); double coronary artery bypass (left internal mammary artery to left anterior descending artery and reversed saphenous vein to the obtuse marginal artery).

Hospital Course

Throughout the pump run, the patient was very vasodilated, requiring high flows and alpha agents to maintain the perfusion pressure. He did require norepinephrine to come off the pump. The patient was very coagulopathic both clinically and by laboratory studies and required significant transfusions of red cells, fresh-frozen plasma, and precipitated platelets.

His postoperative course was complicated by significant bleeding for which he was re-explored on postoperative day one. He tolerated this first exploration well and was extubated on postoperative day one. He did well until postoperative day four, when he developed an acute renal insufficiency associated with a change in mental status and decreasing oxygenation. He was reintubated and hemodialysis was initiated. Additionally, the index and middle fingers on his right hand as well as the toes on his feet bilaterally were noted to be ischemic, presumably from microembolic disease. His D-dimer was elevated into the 10,100s. A hematologist was consulted but was unable to identify a clear causal event. The patient remained HIT-negative despite a lower platelet count.

Over the next four days, the patient's oxygenation became progressively worse, and he continued to be in anuric renal failure. He remained ventilator-dependent on increasing FIO2s. He required an increasing dose of Levophed. He died on the 9th postoperative day.

Autopsy Findings

- Disseminated intravascular coagulation, with:

  (a) Cutaneous petechiae.
  (b) Cutaneous bulla.

- Acute bronchopneumonia, bilateral (Klebsiella pneumoniae by culture).
- Diffuse malignant mesothelioma, left pleura and extending into major fissure.
- Pulmonary interstitial fibrosis, regional.
- Pulmonary thromboembolus, recent, small, right.
- Cardiomegaly (543 g), with marked biventricular hypertrophy.
- Coronary bypass grafts (left internal mammary artery to left anterior descending artery and saphenous vein from ascending aorta to obtuse marginal artery), patent as assessed by postmortem angiogram.
- Composite porcine ascending aortic root, with intact reimplanted native coronary ostia.
- Renal cortical and medullary infarcts, hemorrhagic and nonhemorrhagic.
- Pancreatitis, acute.
- Scleral icterus and jaundice, mild.
- Acute tracheitis, diffuse.
- Ascites, serosanguineous, 300 ml.

- Cerebral infarcts, tiny, embolic, age 1–2 weeks.
- Subdural hematomas and subarachnoid blood (coagulopathy by clinical parameters).

Comments

The primary cause of death is disseminated intravascular coagulation (DIC) with dominant cutaneous and renal manifestations. The inciting factor for the patient's DIC is unknown. The patient also had a diffuse malignant mesothelioma that had principally a superficial spreading aspect with little bulk. The tumor cells stained for calretinin, cytokeratin, CK7, Ber-EP4, EMA, and WT-1. The tumor cells did not stain for CK5/6, CK20, or TTF. The patient died with acute pneumonia due to Klebsiella pneumoniae.

The shrunken, pyknotic nuclei within cortical neurons as well as superficial vacuolization is consistent with the patient's terminal hypoxia. The multiple microembolic infarcts are approximately 1–2 weeks in age and likely correspond to an embolic shower at the time of aortic aneurysm repair ten days prior to death. Lastly, the presence of Alzheimer Type II cells in the brain probably reflect a metabolic disturbance associated with multiorgan failure.

Relevant findings at autopsy included a 1–1.5 cm wound on the medial aspect of the distal right thigh. The short length of this vein graft harvest site tells the pathologist that the harvest was done endoscopically using an instrument called Vaso-View. The pledgeted suture closure of the aortic cannulation site was just below the take-off of the innominate artery, well above the more proximal aneurysm. Suture closure of the venous cannulation site was in the right atrial appendage. A suture in the lateral right atrial wall marked the site where the surgeon made a small atriotomy for passage of the cannula used to administer retrograde cardioplegic solution to preserve the myocardium during the cross-clamp time. A suture in the right superior pulmonary vein is evidence that the surgeon used a catheter passed through the vein and into the left ventricle to keep the heart decompressed during the pump run. This drainage of blood from the left ventricle prevents left heart distension, which can result in an adverse effect on contractility after the pump run.

According to protocol, a postmortem coronary injection was done to document patency of the bypass grafts. The technique also focuses the pathologist's attention on the integrity of the proximal anastomosis of each vein graft to the aorta or, in this case, to a Dacron patch used to fill in the gap between the porcine aorta and the patient's aorta anteriorly. Likewise, the reimplantation of the coronary ostia into the porcine aortic root, which otherwise would cover up the ostia, was examined closely. The contrast material used in the injection nicely documented the integrity and patency of the distal anastomoses of the vein graft and internal mammary artery graft.

Conclusions

- Time interval between cardiac surgery and the autopsy
  - *Not important.* Findings relating to the heart were straightforward and unimpeded by adhesions between the heart and parietal pericardium.
- Technical issues relating to the cardiac operation(s)
  - *Important.* The surgery involved a complex operation that required an aortic clamp time that exceeded three hours. Ventricular hypertrophy increases the risk of inadequate myocardial preservation. Furthermore, retrograde cardioplegia alone may sometimes fail to optimally preserve myocardium in this setting [22].
- Subtle complications of underlying heart disease versus surgical complications
  - *Questionably important.* The ventricular hypertrophy may have contributed to the need for norepinephrine coming off bypass. However, the perioperative coagulopathy was the major perioperative complication.
- Comorbidities at the time of and/or subsequent to cardiac surgery
  - *Important.* A postoperative clinical picture of DIC and multiple organ failure led to the patient's demise.
- Drug-related complications
  - *Questionably important.* No toxic drug reaction was documented, but the possibility of a reaction to Vancomycin was entertained.
- Medical-legal issues relating to surgery
  - *None.* From a technical aspect the surgery was carried out in a responsible fashion.

Case 7: Pathology of Off-Pump Coronary Artery Bypass Surgery

History

The patient was a very sick 82-year-old man with symptoms of angina and early heart failure. Cardiac catheterization showed a poor LV ejection fraction of 25% and multivessel coronary disease.

Procedure

Quadruple bypass off pump, with left internal mammary artery to the left anterior descending coronary artery, a saphenous vein from the ascending aorta and then side-to-side to a diagonal coronary artery and end-to-side in sequence to an obtuse marginal coronary artery, and a saphenous vein from the other saphenous vein graft to another diagonal coronary artery.

Hospital Course

His immediate postop course was complicated by a myocardial infarction, with elevated cardiac enzymes. He was pressor- and inotrope-dependent immediately postoperatively on Dopamine and Milrinone infusions. With a borderline cardiac index, he required norepinephrine infusion for blood pressure support and a continuous Lasix infusion to prevent fluid overload and maintain urine output. An IABP was inserted. An antiplatelet antibody assay was positive for heparin-induced thrombocytopenia (HIT), and an early graft failure was suspected. He was started on anticoagulation with Argatroban in order to treat HIT.

At this point he also began to have intermittent episodes of atrial fibrillation, which were poorly tolerated. He was finally able to be weaned off the IABP and at the same time he experienced sustained atrial fibrillation. He was treated with Amiodarone, which converted him to a sinus rhythm. However, on the following day, the patient became tachypneic and was reintubated for respiratory failure. At that time, his sputum was culture-positive for Enterobacter, which was treated with Levoflox.

The patient's cardiac index decreased despite increasing doses of Milrinone. He was taken to the Cath Lab for evaluation of his grafts. A thrombosis of the venous graft to the obtuse marginal branch could not be successfully reopened, despite attempts at thrombectomy.

The patient remained in borderline cardiogenic shock. The decision was made to commence peritoneal dialysis. Amiodarone drip was started for treatment of recurrent atrial fibrillation, and an intraaortic balloon pump was reinserted. The patient had recurrent intermittent runs of ventricular tachycardia, requiring cardioversion. A tracheostomy was performed, and a biventricular pacemaker and automatic implantable cardiac defibrillator (AICD) were implanted. The IABP was removed, but the patient subsequently deteriorated clinically. He died on the 32nd day post-CABG.

Autopsy Findings

- Coronary atherosclerosis, three-vessel, severe.
- Myocardial infarction, anterior and lateral left ventricle, acute, subacute, and old.
- Cardiomegaly, with four-chamber dilatation (810 g).
- Fibrocalcific mitral valve degeneration, mild.
- Thrombosis of the venous Y-graft bypass.
- Organizing blood clot in pericardium.
- Atherosclerosis, generalized, severe in distal aorta.
- Pulmonary edema (combined lung weight 2170 g).

- Pulmonary infarcts, recent, bilateral, with organizing fibrinous pleuritis.
- Organizing pneumonia, subpleural, subacute.
- Hepatic congestion, centrilobular.
- Splenic infarcts, subacute, multiple.
- Acute erosive gastritis.
- Renal infarcts, acute and subacute, bilateral.
- Acute tubular necrosis, bilateral.
- Colonic diverticulosis.
- Hydrocele, right.
- Sacral decubitus ulcer.
- Hydrocephalus, mild.
- Atherosclerosis, cerebral arteries, mild.

Comments

The patient had severe coronary artery disease, which accounted for unstable angina and histologic evidence of old myocardial infarcts. After surgical coronary artery reconstruction, the vein grafts became occluded by thrombus. This thrombosis caused an extensive acute myocardial infarction and cardiac failure. Multiple infarcts in spleen, kidneys, and lungs resulted from showering of atheromatous debris probably related to IABP support [23, 24].

Relevant findings at autopsy included a 1–1.5 cm wound on the medial aspect of the distal right thigh, representing the endoscopic harvest of the greater saphenous vein for use as bypass conduits. Because the CABG procedure was performed off pump, there was no pledgeted suture closure of an aortic cannulation site and no suture closure of a venous cannulation site in the right atrial appendage. Likewise, no access was needed at the operation for administering cardioplegic solution or for placement of a left ventricular sump.

Off-pump coronary bypass surgery (OPCAB) is an alternative to using a cardiopulmonary bypass and cardioplegic solution to arrest the heart while the distal anastomoses are fashioned. OPCAB, which was standardized in the late 1990s when mechanical devices to stabilize the beating heart became available, allows the surgeon to avoid complications which may arise because of adverse physiological effects of cardiopulmonary bypass. These complications include blood loss and transfusion requirements, acute renal failure, myocardial dysfunction, atrial fibrillation, cerebral dysfunction, pulmonary dysfunction, gastrointestinal problems, and systemic inflammation [25]. Recently, OPCAB was shown to be a safe and efficient alternative to conventional on-pump CABG in a long-term follow-up of a group of non-selected patients [26].

In the current case, there was extensive atherosclerosis in the ascending aorta. Cannulating the ascending aorta and using a partially occluding clamp for placement of proximal graft anastomoses would have greatly risked plaque dislodgment and an embolic event [27]. OPCAB avoided this risk. The surgeon noted one soft spot in the ascending aorta and placed a proximal vein graft anastomosis there. To minimize manipulation of the aorta, he used a HEARTSTRING II Proximal Seal System, a mechanical device which maintains hemostasis and facilitates the completion of a proximal anastomosis without application of an aortic clamp [28]. Constructing a Y-graft by sewing the proximal end of one vein to another vein further reduced the need to manipulate a "bad" aorta.

Conclusions

- Time interval between cardiac surgery and the autopsy
  - *Not important.* Findings relating to the heart were straightforward and unimpeded by adhesions between the heart and the parietal pericardium.
- Technical issues relating to the cardiac operation(s)
  - *Questionably important.* Severe atherosclerosis of the ascending aorta influenced the surgeon to perform OPCAB, which is technically more challenging than doing on-pump CABG surgery. However, the patient's poor outcome was apparently a result of the presence of a heparin antibody, causing loss of the vein grafts and a myocardial infarction, a complication that has been documented in the past [29].
- Subtle complications of underlying heart disease versus surgical complications
  - *Important.* The patient's poor left ventricular function going into the operation magnified the impact of any potential perioperative complication.
- Comorbidities at the time of and/or subsequent to cardiac surgery
  - *Important.* A postoperative clinical picture of a low cardiac output state and multiple organ failure led to the patient's demise.
- Drug-related complications
  - *Important.* Anticoagulation with heparin in the presence of an anti-heparin antibody led to a fatal complication.
- Medical-legal issues relating to surgery
  - *None.* From a technical aspect the surgery was carried out in a responsible fashion.

Case 8: Repair of Acute Aortic Dissection—Making Sense of the Findings

History

This is a 57-year-old man with a history of Marfan's syndrome as well as prior bilateral carotid artery dissections, for which he was on chronic Coumadin, and a known history of ascending thoracic aortic aneurysm. He had had chest surgery to repair a pectus excavatum in 1960. He became short of breath with acute chest pain, and ultimately arrived in our emergency room. A CT scan showed a contained rupture of his ascending aorta, which was 5.7 cm in diameter. A type A dissection involved the root of all of the aortic arch vessels and also extended into the descending thoracic and abdominal aorta. The celiac, superior mesenteric, and right renal arteries originated from the true lumen, and the two left renal arteries originated from the false lumen. The dissection stopped in the proximal common iliac artery on the right and the external iliac artery on the left.

Procedure

Emergent repair of a type A aortic dissection, with replacement of aortic root and ascending aorta, coronary artery reimplantation, and vein graft to the LAD.

Hospital Course

The patient tolerated cardiopulmonary bypass and was stable during a period of time in which his extensive aortic dissection was repaired. The findings in the operating room included a contained rupture, involvement of the coronary arteries, and very friable and thin tissues, which lead to significant problems with bleeding from the junction of the valve/conduit and the dilated aortic annulus. In addition, because of an antigen detected in the patient's blood, transfusion of red blood cells from the blood bank was limited.

Despite multiple different maneuvers to control the bleeding, including the creation of a bovine pericardial baffle to channel the bleeding into the right atrium, the attempts were unsuccessful, and the patient subsequently developed intractable hypotension and ultimately asystole. After a period of attempted resuscitation including open cardiac massage, the patient was declared dead in the operating room.

Autopsy Findings

- Marfan syndrome, with a deep pectus excavatum despite previous attempt at surgical repair.
- Aortic dissection, type A, acute, extending along entire length of aorta into both common iliac arteries.
- Cardiomegaly (566 g), with dilatation of all four chambers.
- Hemothorax, bilateral (800 cc right pleura, 200 cc left pleura).
- Hemopericardium (60 cc).
- Emphysema, panacinar, bilateral, severe, with pulmonary hypertensive change and hemosiderin deposition.
- Hepatic congestion, centrilobular.
- Medial necrosis, internal carotid arteries.

- Atherosclerosis, generalized, slight.
- Colonic diverticulosis, extensive.
- Hydrocele, right.

Comments

The autopsy findings confirmed the presence of an acute aortic dissection, type A, by the Stanford classification [30], or type I, by the DeBakey classification [31]. Clot around the tube graft, which reconstructed the ascending aorta, reflected the catastrophic intraoperative bleeding from the anastomotic site between the composite graft and the very friable aortic tissue at the level of the annulus. It was this tissue friability and a marked coagulopathy that caused the patient's death.

At autopsy, a closed wound in the right groin marked the exposure of the femoral vessels prior to the re-do sternotomy. This maneuver served two purposes. It was a precaution that would have allowed emergent establishment of femorofemoral bypass if severe bleeding was encountered because of injury to the aorta or right ventricle by sawing through a sternum that would be dangerously close to mediastinal structures. Secondly, it allowed cannulation of the femoral artery in preparation for a right atrium to femoral artery bypass following a successful sternotomy without injury. It is usually unsafe to try to cannulate the ascending aorta in the conventional manner in the face of a type A dissection.

A resuspension of a prolapsed aortic valve commissure in an acute aortic dissection is usually sufficient to correct the aortic regurgitation. In this case, because of a dilated aortic root, due to the ascending aortic aneurysm being followed clinically, a composite graft was used to replace the aortic valve and reconstruct the ascending aorta. A St. Jude bileaflet mechanical valve prosthesis was sewn inside the proximal end of a Dacron tube graft. After resection of the native valve, the proximal end of the composite graft was then sutured to the aortic annulus. The Teflon pledgets found on the left ventricular outflow tract side of these sutures were used to buttress the sutures, i.e., prevent the sutures from tearing the tissue. Unfortunately, the patient's tissues were so friable that catastrophic bleeding occurred at this anastomosis despite the effort to prevent it.

The Dacron tube of the composite graft excludes the flow of blood from the native coronary ostia. The coronary ostia in this case were therefore reimplanted into the Dacron graft. In addition, a vein bypass was placed between the Dacron graft and the LAD because of decreased left ventricular contractility coming off pump. The surgeon was concerned that rotation of the heart caused by the pectus excavatum might compromise flow through the left main coronary artery. The integrity of all of these suture lines was satisfactory at autopsy.

Finally, a flap of bovine pericardium was found encompassing the area of the aortic root and sewn to the base of the heart and into the right atrium. The surgeon had made an attempt to construct a baffle that would direct the blood from the bleeding aortic root anastomosis into the right atrium, a rather desperate effort to gain control of the bleeding.

Conclusions

- Time interval between cardiac surgery and the autopsy

  - *Important.* An operative death demands close attention to detail at the time of autopsy. The surgeon who loses a patient on the operating table is keen to know if a technical flaw was the cause of the bad outcome. The presence of the surgeon during the dissection of the heart and vascular structures can be an important assistance to the pathologist involved.

- Technical issues relating to the cardiac operation(s)

  - *Important.* This entire scenario is a matter of technical hazards faced by the surgeon at the time of surgery. A re-do sternotomy in a deep pectus excavatum overlying a contained rupture of an aneurysm of an aorta which is acutely dissected can be in itself a surgeon's nightmare. The friable nature of cardiac and vascular tissues in a Marfanoid individual adds an immense challenge to a cardiovascular surgical procedure that is in itself already complex and hazardous.

- Subtle complications of underlying heart disease versus surgical complications

  - *Important.* The patient's heart demonstrated evidence of a dilated cardiomyopathy, which could have compounded an adverse effect of inadequate myocardial preservation during the surgery. Likewise, the bleeding from the suture line at the aortic root could have resulted from one or more poorly placed sutures, extremely friable tissue, or both.

- Comorbidities at the time of and/or subsequent to cardiac surgery

  - *Important.* Bleeding at the time of surgery was attributed to a combination of poor integrity of tissues and a coagulopathy that followed the pump run. Furthermore, the patient's immunologic problem that limited the safe transfusion of blood products was disastrous.

- Drug-related complications

  - *Important.* The patient's chronic use of Coumadin compounded the coagulopathy after the pump run.

- Medical-legal issues relating to surgery

  - *None.* From a technical aspect the surgery was carried out in a responsible fashion. Some problems seem to defy all honest and good effort to solve them.

Case 9: Technical Issues of Coronary Artery Bypass Surgery

History

This 86-year-old female had a history of diabetes, elevated cholesterol, hypertension, and peripheral vascular disease. She also had deep venous thrombosis requiring an IVC filter. She had stable angina for about two years. She recently had an onset of severe angina associated with shortness of breath and was found to have evolved a myocardial infarction. She was transferred here for further evaluation. Cardiac catheterization performed during this hospitalization documented severe three-vessel coronary artery disease with very high-grade lesions in the mid right coronary artery compromising an acute marginal branch and the posterior descending artery. The left anterior descending coronary artery was tightly stenotic in its proximal portion, and the circumflex system also had focally severe disease. Ventricular function was moderately compromised. The patient required not only intravenous therapy but also an intraaortic balloon pump to control her ischemia. Despite the significantly increased risk, the patient desired surgery.

Procedure

Urgent quintuple CABG, with saphenous vein to the obtuse marginal branch of the circumflex, left anterior descending coronary artery, and sequentially side-to-side to the acute marginal branch of the right coronary artery and end-to-side to the posterior descending branch of the right coronary artery; and with the left internal mammary artery to the left anterior descending coronary artery.

Hospital Course

Toward the end of surgery, just before the dressing was applied, the patient developed rather sudden deterioration in her cardiac function, which appeared to result from a loss of atrial capture. Despite the prompt administration of AV sequential pacing and Levophed, the pressure did not respond well and the pulmonary artery pressures began to rise substantially. The chest was then reopened and the heart was found to be very hypocontractile, particularly the right ventricle. All bypass grafts were open, and there was no evidence of any bleeding or tamponade. However, there was a loss of sinus rhythm. The patient's blood pressure was slowly deteriorating despite increasing doses of Levophed. The patient was placed back on bypass and loaded with Milrinone and Amiodarone. Several attempts were made to wean her from cardiopulmonary bypass with different medications. She was finally weaned from bypass after a second total perfusion time of one hour and ten minutes. She was being paced, with the balloon pump on one-to-one, and her systolic blood pressure was 80–90 on substantial doses of Levophed, Milrinone, Dopamine, Prostaglandin E1, and nitroglycerin. Her sternotomy was left open, covered with an Esmarch bandage, and she was transferred to the Intensive Care Unit.

In the Intensive Care Unit, she required increasing doses of Levophed to maintain her pressures. She was tried on several different other pressors (Vasopressin, Neo-Synephrine) without any improvement. The patient was pronounced dead the evening following her surgery. The medical examiner was notified.

Autopsy Findings

- Pulmonary embolus, left upper lobe.
- Cardiomegaly (560 g), with biventricular hypertrophy.
- Myocardial infarction, acute, involving anterior and lateral wall of left ventricle; remote infarct, involving left and right ventricle.
- Atherosclerotic coronary artery disease, severe, triple vessel.
- Quintuple coronary artery bypass grafts:
    - Saphenous vein graft (SVG) to obtuse marginal branch of circumflex coronary artery, which appears obstructed distal to the distal anastomosis of the graft.
    - SVG to right ventricular coronary artery (side-to-side) and right posterior descending coronary artery (end-to-side); probe-patent
    - Left internal mammary artery graft to the left anterior descending artery; patency of distal anastomosis is compromised.
    - SVG to left anterior descending artery is probe-patent.
- Atherosclerosis, thoracic and abdominal aorta, cerebral arteries (circle of Willis), severe.
- Pleural effusion, serosanguineous, bilateral (right: 300 ml, left: 300 ml).
- Thyroid nodule (0.1 cm), benign.
- Hepatic steatosis, mixed micro- and macrovesicular.
- Splenic congestion (weight: 220 g).
- Abdominal adhesions, extensive.
- Renal cortical cyst (1.1 cm), left.
- Nephrosclerosis, bilateral.
- Intracerebral hypoxic/ischemic neuronal injury, acute, diffuse.

Comments

The autopsy revealed a pulmonary embolus in a medium-sized artery of the upper lobe of the left lung, which, combined with an acute myocardial infarction in the anterior and lateral wall of the left ventricle, probably caused the demise of the patient. A postmortem coronary injection showed a lack of filling of the obtuse marginal artery distal to the vein graft. Microscopic examination of the occluded left obtuse marginal artery distal to the distal vein graft anastomosis revealed a fibrin thrombus and atherosclerosis, which occluded the lumen. Focal amyloid deposition (confirmed by a Congo red stain) is identified in the wall of few small myocardial vessels.

External examination of the body at autopsy showed the usual wound closure following endoscopic vein harvest from the right lower extremity. The open sternotomy beneath a synthetic patch sewn to the skin parasternally is indicative of intraoperative heart failure to the extent that closure of the wound would have resulted in tamponade of a distended right ventricle. Three mediastinal drainage tubes exited the skin of the midepigastrium. In addition to the usual temporary pacemaker wires, a small catheter exited the skin on the right subcostal area. The presence of such a catheter in the immediate postoperative period usually means that the surgeon placed a left atrial line, exiting the right superior pulmonary vein, in order to continuously monitor the filling pressure of the left heart to expedite fluid and inotropic therapy.

Examination of the heart and great vessels showed the usual cannulation sites for establishing cardiopulmonary bypass, as well as a suture in the right superior pulmonary vein, which the surgeon had placed to close the insertion site of a left ventricular sump catheter used to keep the left ventricle decompressed during the procedure. However, close inspection showed no evidence that a catheter had been inserted into either the ascending aorta or right atrium for administering cardioplegic solution. Although cardioplegic solution is sometimes delivered into vein grafts after the distal anastomoses are completed, in this case, the distal anastomoses were all done with the heart in ventricular fibrillation and by using intermittent cross-clamping of the aorta [32]. This approach is an alternative to arresting the heart with either warm or cold cardioplegia after a single cross-clamping of the aorta [33].

The vein grafts were all patent and positioned nicely on the heart. The right graft was a sequential, or "snake" graft, which is a prudent technique for the surgeon to use when there is a shortage of vein of adequate quality for the conventional approach of one distal anastomosis per conduit. It also applies well hemodynamically when the side-to-side anastomosis is to a coronary artery that is equal to or smaller than the artery at the more distal end-to-side anastomosis. A clue on initial inspection at autopsy that a sequential graft has been constructed is an "S-shaped" configuration of a conduit. The pathologist should note any kinking of such a graft, which might lead to graft thrombosis.

The fact that a vein graft was placed on the LAD distal to the anastomosis of the left internal mammary artery usually means that the surgeon was for some reason not satisfied with blood flow through the arterial conduit. In fact, the postmortem injection documented a filling defect at that distal anastomosis. Furthermore, by collateral flow, contrast material in the native distal right coronary artery was noted when the vein graft to the LAD was injected but not after injection of the internal mammary graft, a subtle feature which emphasizes the potential value of the contrast study. The valuable information gathered by injecting the graft to the obtuse marginal branch has already been mentioned above.

Finally, a suture line was found in the main pulmonary artery. This finding is uncommon at autopsy following coronary artery bypass surgery. Discussion with the cardiac surgeon or the review of the operative note, always valuable when available, would have indicated to the pathologist that the surgeon had made the arteriotomy to explore the proximal pulmonary arteries with a forceps, looking for a large clot, which could have embolized and caused the rise in pulmonary artery pressure and right heart failure [34] in the operating room. This information should make the pathologist particularly attentive for evidence of emboli when examining the lungs both grossly and microscopically. Such scrutiny actually led to an important finding in this case. From a technical standpoint, the orientation of the incision in the pulmonary artery was transverse to minimize narrowing of the pulmonary artery lumen with closure of the incision. Avoiding longitudinal incisions in blood vessels whenever possible is an important surgical principle.

Conclusions

- Time interval between cardiac surgery and the autopsy

  - *Important*. The death of a patient hours after a surgical procedure, which was complicated by sudden and unexpected heart failure demands close attention to detail at the time of autopsy. The cardiac surgeon is keen to know if a technical flaw was the cause of the bad outcome and if there was any way the fatal complication could have been avoided. The presence of the surgeon during the dissection of the heart and vascular structures can be an important assistance to the pathologist involved.

- Technical issues relating to the cardiac operation(s)

  - *Important*. Two technical issues are relevant in this case. The first is the suboptimal flow in the left internal mammary artery graft, which was astutely appreciated and addressed by the surgeon. Poor flow in an internal mammary artery could be due to an ostial stenosis of the vessel [35], atherosclerotic narrowing of the subclavian artery proximal to the take-off of the internal mammary artery [36], vasospasm [37], or, rarely, to atherosclerosis of the internal mammary artery itself [38]. These occurrences are infrequent but do happen, and any of these problems may be missed in the preoperative evaluation of a patient. Another problem with internal mammary artery flow may relate to a relatively small artery or to injury to the vessel when it is mobilized off the chest wall [39]. The internal mammary artery is routinely taken down with its accompanying veins and surrounding fibromuscular tissue as a pedicle to avoid skeletonizing the vessel, which would increase the risk of injury to it, and because it would deprive the artery of its venous and lymphatic drainage, perhaps adversely affecting its long-term patency [40]. In this case, the surgeon was suspicious of a localized dissection of the vessel and wisely placed a vein graft onto the LAD.

    The second technical issue relates to finding the appropriate site in a coronary artery to make the incision and construct the distal anastomosis of the graft. In this case, significant disease and fibrin deposition obstructed the lumen of the grafted obtuse marginal artery distal to the anastomosis of the vein graft to the artery. The patient had diabetes mellitus, which is commonly associated with diffuse atherosclerotic arterial disease [41]. Coronary angiograms may underestimate the severity of one or more arterial lesions [42]. In addition, successful placement of coronary artery grafts is limited by the size of the distal vessels and, to a lesser extent, the depth of these small vessels in the myocardium [43].

- Subtle complications of underlying heart disease versus surgical complications

  - *Important.* The patient's heart revealed biventricular hypertrophy, which makes the myocardium, especially the subendocardium, increasingly vulnerable to ischemic injury [44]. Left-sided heart failure secondary to ischemia because of distal disease in the obtuse marginal vessel may have been compounded by left ventricular hypertrophy. Furthermore, the patient had a documented acute myocardial infarction preoperatively. Associated myocardial dysfunction may have been compounded by a significant reperfusion injury [45, 46].

- Comorbidities at the time of and/or subsequent to cardiac surgery

  - *Important.* The patient was 86 years old and had a history of diabetes, elevated cholesterol, hypertension, peripheral vascular disease, and rheumatoid arthritis. She had also had deep venous thrombosis, treated with an inferior vena caval filter. Perhaps most important was the acute myocardial infarction and balloon pump-dependent unstable angina. Octogenarians do have higher morbidity and mortality rates following heart surgery than do younger patients [47]. However, octogenarians going from "the floor" to the operating room for open-heart surgery carry a reasonable operative mortality rate and can benefit greatly; whereas, octogenarians going from intensive care unit to the operating room for open-heart surgery carry an operative mortality rate which is significantly higher [48, 49]. Age per se is not a contraindication to open-heart surgery.

- Drug-related complications

  - *Questionably important.* Reversing the effect of systemic heparinization with protamine in diabetic patients is a major concern to the cardiac surgeon [50].

- Medical-legal issues relating to surgery

  - *None.* Multiple issues have been addressed above that could cause one to reflect on concern about medical-legal vulnerability relating to the care of this patient. In the end, despite her age, comorbidities, and the technical complexities involved with her surgical care, an honest and vigorous effort was made to improve the quality of life in an individual who was aware of her high risk for such treatment and chose to take the risk.

Case 10: Aortic Root Abscess and Postoperative Gastrointestinal Complications

History

This is a 43-year-old male who had six weeks of intermittent fever. He was diagnosed with a right lower lobe pneumonia and was treated with outpatient antibiotics. During the current hospital admission, he went into third degree AV block on the day of surgery. He had a cardiac arrest, and a ventricular pacing wire was placed in the cardiac catheterization laboratory. He became profoundly acidotic and had an extremely high pressor requirement. An emergent transesophageal echocardiogram in the medical Intensive Care Unit showed wide-open aortic insufficiency with an aortic to right atrial fistula. He was brought emergently to the operating room in an attempt to salvage his life.

Procedure

Emergent repair of aortic root and aortic valve replacement, using a 21 mm pericardial aortic valve prosthesis; closure of the fistula between the right atrium and left ventricular outflow tract.

Hospital Course

Postoperatively, the patient was managed in the Intensive Care Unit. The patient required a significant amount of pressor support. The patient was seen by multiple consultants, including physicians from sections of Nephrology, Pulmonology, and Infectious Disease.

On the day following surgery, the patient's metabolic acidosis worsened. Therefore, an exploratory laparotomy was performed in the Intensive Care Unit. It was found that the entire small and large bowel were necrotic. At the time, the abdomen was closed and support was withdrawn. The patient was pronounced dead on postoperative day one.

Autopsy Findings

- Subacute endocarditis and aortic root abscess secondary to Streptococcus pneumoniae.
- Pulmonary edema, with early diffuse alveolar damage, (combined lung weight: 2450 g).
- Cardiomegaly (weight: 880 g), with biventricular hypertrophy and dilatation.
- Left ventricular ischemic injury, concentric, acute (<24 hours).
- Gastrointestinal ischemia, involving approximately 75% of the small intestine and focal areas of the large intestine in the regions of the hepatic and splenic flexures.
- Acute tubular necrosis, with acute cortical infarctions, multiple.
- Endophthalmitis, acute.
- Cerebral microinfarcts, acute.

Comments

The pathological changes seen at autopsy are consistent with a cause of death attributed to pneumococcal endocarditis complicated by an aortic root abscess and sepsis. Multiorgan failure was confirmed. The macroscopic and microscopic findings of the left eye confirm the clinical diagnosis of endophthalmitis. Further-more, two areas of fresh cerebral infarcts were identified in the white matter of the left visual cortex and the left frontal lobe, which are likely also related to the endocarditis.

The usual mediastinal and pleural drainage tubes and temporary pacemaker wires exited the skin of the upper epigastrium. An intraaortic balloon pump catheter exited the skin of the right groin. The open sternotomy beneath a green synthetic patch sewn to the skin parasternally is indicative of intraoperative heart failure to the extent that closure of the wound would have resulted in tamponade of a distended right ventricle. In addition, a midline, upper abdominal surgical wound closure is evidence of an intraabdominal complication following heart surgery. In this case, an abdominal exploration was conducted because of the patient's increasing metabolic acidosis. The surgeon found extensive small bowel necrosis and multifocal large bowel necrosis. Nothing further could be done to help the patient.

Examination of the heart and great vessels showed two suture lines in the right atrium reflecting bicaval cannulation by the surgeon and the usual ascending aortic cannulation site for establishing cardiopulmonary bypass. The sutured aortotomy closure in the proximal ascending aorta was circumferential. The typical anterolat-eral aortotomy used to gain access to the aortic valve provided the surgeon sub-optimal exposure of the aortic root, so the surgeon transected the aorta to improve his exposure.

A bovine pericardial valve prosthesis appeared to be well-seated at the aortic annulus. A pericardial patch was sutured over the fistula between the subaortic left ventricular outflow tract and right atrium. A roughened endocardial surface reflected the surgical debridement of the devitalized tissue in the aortic root.

Conclusions

- Time interval between cardiac surgery and the autopsy

  - *Questionably important.* The death of this patient hours after a surgical pro-cedure, although a sad outcome, was not surprising. The patient had been in marked heart failure and septic preoperatively. His infectious endocarditis was complicated by an aortic root abscess, intracardiac fistula, and heart block, any one of which carries a high mortality rate [51, 52].

- Technical issues relating to the cardiac operation(s)

  - *Important.* The aortic root abscess had left nonviable tissue, which the surgeon had to debride aggressively. In addition, the infection had eroded the subaortic septum, creating a fistula between the left ventricular outflow tract and right atrium. As a result, the aortic root had to be reconstructed with a pericardial patch, part of which closed the fistula and part of which served as a reconsti-tuted aortic annulus, to which the valve prosthesis was sewn. These technical problems can be quite challenging [53].

- Subtle complications of underlying heart disease versus surgical complications

  - *Important*. The patient's heart revealed biventricular hypertrophy, which makes the myocardium, especially the subendocardium, increasingly vulnerable to ischemic injury [44]. Left-sided heart failure secondary to severe aortic insufficiency resulting from infectious endocarditis and destruction of the aortic valve may have been compounded by perioperative myocardial ischemic injury due to left ventricular hypertrophy, particularly during a cross-clamp time at surgery.

- Comorbidities at the time of and/or subsequent to cardiac surgery

  - *Important*. Intestinal necrosis resulting from a prolonged low cardiac output state proved to be a fatal complication of surgery in this case. Gastrointestinal complications of heart surgery are uncommon, but when they occur, they carry a high mortality rate [54].

- Drug-related complications

  - *Questionably important*. High doses of alpha blockers to achieve an adequate blood pressure probably contributed to vasoconstriction and ischemic injury of the bowel [55].

- Medical-legal issues relating to surgery

  - *None*. The autopsy showed no findings that were suggestive of inappropriate care of the patient.

Case 11: Mitral Valve Plus Coronary Bypass Surgery on an Obese Diabetic

History

The patient is a 79-year-old man with a history of diabetes, hypertension, and morbid obesity. Following a myocardial infarction about 12 years ago, he underwent a pericardiectomy for treatment of restrictive pericarditis. Since then he has had chronic angina that has gotten worse, including angina at rest. He had a cardiac catheterization that showed severe three-vessel coronary artery disease as well as severe mitral regurgitation. He presents for revascularization.

Procedure

Re-do sternotomy, quadruple coronary artery bypass grafts to the left anterior descending artery, posterior descending artery, first and second obtuse marginal arteries in sequence; mitral valve replacement (31 mm mosaic).

Hospital Course

At the end of the operation, after the patient was separated from bypass, he was hypotensive. He was put back on bypass and started on milrinone with an improvement in his ventricular function. He had a serious coagulopathy. Because he was hypotensive with his chest closed, his chest was reopened and left open and covered with an Esmarch patch. The patient was then transferred to the Cardiac Surgical Intensive Care Unit for postoperative care.

On the second postoperative day, the patient was taken back to the operating room for mediastinal exploration for bleeding. He continued to require significant numbers of blood products to remain normotensive, and his chest was again left open. Throughout his postoperative course, he was maintained on maximum ventilatory support with only marginal oxygenation. His chest radiograph was consistent with ARDS, and he could not be weaned from the ventilator.

Over the next few days, he continued to be anuric as a result of acute renal failure. He was started on hemodialysis. His pressor requirement continued to rise, and he needed escalating levels of bicarbonate to control his worsening metabolic acidosis. The patient died on the 10th postoperative day.

Autopsy Findings

- Hemorrhagic diffuse alveolar damage.
- Cardiomegaly (1000 g), with biventricular hypertrophy.
- Coronary artery disease, severe, with near occlusion of the left anterior descending and circumflex arteries, and >90% stenosis of the right coronary artery; patent vein bypass grafts to the left anterior descending artery, posterior descending branch of the right coronary artery, and 1st and 2nd obtuse marginal arteries (in sequence).
- Organizing pericarditis.
- Pulmonary arteriopathy, grade 2–3/4.
- Atherosclerosis, severe, involving the aorta and carotid arteries.
- Hepatic congestion, with steatosis and mild steatohepatitis.
- Splenic congestion and multiple infarcts.
- Pancreatitis, acute and chronic, with calcification.
- Testicular hemorrhage, bilateral.
- Prostatic hypertrophy.
- Lipoma, cerebellar vermis.
- Procedures:
- Coronary artery bypass graft × 4, mitral valve replacement; re-do sternotomy for bleeding.

Comments

The cause of death was diffuse alveolar damage, associated with a marked coagulopathy. The autopsy findings confirm multiple-organ failure, which resulted from a low cardiac output state following heart surgery. The lipoma of the cerebellar vermis is an incidental finding and, given the underlying focal cerebellar malformation, is most likely congenital.

The usual mediastinal and pleural drainage tubes and temporary pacemaker wires exited the skin of the upper epigastrium. The open sternotomy beneath a green synthetic patch sewn to the skin parasternally is indicative of intraoperative heart failure to the extent that closure of the wound would have resulted in tamponade of a distended right ventricle. A double-lumen left subclavian venous catheter had been used for hemodialysis.

Examination of the heart and great vessels showed two suture lines in the right atrium reflecting bicaval cannulation by the surgeon and the usual ascending aortic cannulation site for establishing cardiopulmonary bypass. A sutured closure of a left atriotomy, parallel and just posterior to the interatrial groove on the right, marked the site of surgical access to the mitral valve for its replacement. In this case, a porcine Mosaic bioprosthesis, a new generation stented porcine valve [56], had been used. Compared to previous generations of porcine bioprostheses, the Mosaic valve leaflets undergo a more physiologic fixation with glutaraldehyde. They are then treated with α-aminooleic acid to reduce the potential for calcification and mounted on an appropriately sized Hancock II flexible stent made of acetyl copolymer covered with Dacron fabric [57]. A close inspection of the mitral annulus would have revealed that the anterior leaflet had been resected, but the posterior leaflet remained attached to its chordal attachments. Leaving at least part of the underlying suspension apparatus of the mitral valve intact when the valve is replaced helps to preserve left ventricular function over the years following mitral valve replacement, an important surgical principle [58].

Examination of the surface of the heart showed three venous conduits, all of which were flat throughout, indicating their patency. A thrombus distends vein grafts and makes them firm to the touch. Three proximal anastomoses were present on the ascending aorta. However, as each graft was mobilized off the epicardial surface, the vein to the circumflex artery was attached side-to-side to the first obtuse marginal branch and end-to-side to the second obtuse marginal branch in sequence. Finally, examination of the chest plate at the beginning of the autopsy revealed that the left internal mammary artery had been mobilized off the chest wall by the surgeon. However, no internal mammary artery graft was observed on the heart at autopsy. In fact, the graft to the left anterior descending artery, the usual site for a left internal mammary artery graft, was a vein graft. This scenario usually means the internal mammary artery was inadequate for use as a bypass graft. In this case, the surgeon had found that flow in the artery was inadequate.

Conclusions

- Time interval between cardiac surgery and the autopsy

    – *Important*. The death of this patient, although not precipitous following surgery, occurred because of a perioperative coagulopathy requiring many physiologically stressful transfusions [59] and low cardiac output state, which could not be reversed.

- Technical issues relating to the cardiac operation(s)

  – *Important*. An important factor which added to the routine complexity of valve replacement plus coronary artery reconstruction was the patient's morbid obesity [60]. Exposure of the mitral valve and, indeed, of the heart itself is complicated by a thick layer of adipose tissue on the anterior chest wall. This reality becomes readily apparent to the pathologist at autopsy as he or she peers into the open sternotomy wound. The fact that this patient had undergone a previous pericardiectomy forced the surgeon to deal with the risk of injury to the heart as a re-do sternotomy is performed and as mobilization of the heart from surrounding adhesions is done in preparation for a complex second procedure. Furthermore, a coronary artery reconstruction in the face of chronic fibrotic epicarditis presents a challenging test of a surgeon's endurance.

- Subtle complications of underlying heart disease versus surgical complications

  – *Questionably important*. The patient's heart revealed biventricular hypertrophy, which makes the myocardium, especially the subendocardium, increasingly vulnerable to ischemic injury [44], particularly in the face of triple-vessel coronary artery disease while the aortic cross-clamp is on. Left-sided heart failure secondary to diffuse coronary artery disease and an old infarct may have been compounded by perioperative myocardial ischemic injury due to left ventricular hypertrophy, particularly during a cross-clamp time at surgery.

- Comorbidities at the time of and/or subsequent to cardiac surgery

  – *Important*. Extremely obese patients undergoing cardiac surgery are at a higher risk of developing renal failure and respiratory failure postoperatively than nonobese patients [60]. The patient was a diabetic, with diffuse coronary artery disease, which can complicate any attempt by the surgeon to bypass all significant disease and increase the likelihood of postoperative heart failure [61]. The coagulopathy, resulting tamponade, and the need for multiple transfusions of blood products, combined with respiratory failure, precluded a successful outcome in this case.

- Drug-related complications

  – *Questionably important*. Although no specific drug reaction was observed, large doses of inotropic agents may have contributed to ischemia in peripheral vascular beds and to metabolic acidosis [55].

- Medical-legal issues relating to surgery

  – *None*. The autopsy showed no findings that were suggestive of inappropriate care of the patient.

Case 12: An Extraanatomic Approach to Treatment of Aortic Stenosis

History

This 67-year-old man underwent previous revascularization surgery. He initially did well, but presented with evidence of aortic stenosis. On longitudinal follow-up, his aortic stenosis worsened and is now critical. Preoperative investigation demonstrated that he had calcification in his ascending aorta, and a previous patent right-sided bypass graft appeared adherent to the back of the sternum. For these reasons, it was elected to manage his critical aortic stenosis by left ventricular apex-to-aortic conduit placement.

Procedure

Left ventricular apex-to-aortic valve conduit implantation; open insertion of intraaortic balloon pump into left femoral artery.

Hospital Course

The surgical procedure was complicated by bleeding from the LV apex-to-conduit connection and low systemic vascular resistance (SVR). Although LV appeared to be good initially, it deteriorated when the blood pressure (BP) decreased. Bleeding around the appliance in the LV apex caused tamponade that was relieved by resecting a "window" of pericardium. The bleeding was controlled by additional sutures around the appliance. Although he initially weaned from bypass and was stable on several occasions, as SVR and BP declined, LV function was adversely affected, requiring escalating doses of vasoconstrictor drugs. An intraaortic balloon pump was inserted but provided inadequate hemodynamic support. The patient expired on the operating table.

Autopsy Findings

- Cardiomegaly (600 g), with left ventricular hypertrophy.
- Triple-vessel coronary artery atherosclerosis, severe, with a patent left internal mammary artery bypass to the left anterior descending artery and patent saphenous vein grafts to the right posterior descending artery, diagonal branch, and obtuse marginal artery.
- Myocardial infarction, acute, involving left ventricular free wall.
- Aortic valve stenosis, severe.
- Mitral valve calcification, severe.

Comments

The autopsy findings support acute myocardial ischemia as the cause of death. A tetrazolium stain shows evidence of diffuse acute infarction of the left ventricular subendocardium. Local contraction band necrosis is identified in the left ventricular anterior and lateral walls histologically. Patchy myocardial fibrosis reflects evidence of remodeling, probably due to ischemia in the presence of progressive myocyte hypertrophy.

At autopsy, there was a healed vertical midline scar over the sternum and a suture closure of a fresh surgical wound over the left chest. These findings should alert the pathologist that a re-do sternotomy was avoided and that surgical access to the heart had been gained through an anterolateral thoracotomy. Preoperative evaluation had revealed a calcific ascending aorta and patent bypass grafts, with the right vein graft perhaps adherent to the anterior chest wall. Hence, care should be taken in the removal of the chest plate at autopsy in order to avoid tearing adherent myocardium and/or bypass graft tissue.

Because of the surgeon's approach through a thoracotomy, the left femoral artery and femoral vein were used for the pump run. A sutured wound in the left groin served not only for establishing femorofemoral cardiopulmonary bypass but also for placement of an intraaortic balloon pump, which was exiting the skin of the wound at autopsy. No drainage tubes or temporary pacemaker wires were present on external examination, since the patient had died prior to closure of the thoracotomy.

Examination of the heart and great vessels showed an elbow-like device situated within a core-like opening in the left ventricular apex, fixed to the surrounding epimyocardium by multiple sutures buttressed by Teflon pledgets. The device was contiguous with a Dacron tube graft, which was sewn end-to-side to the distal descending thoracic aorta. Close to this anastomosis, within the tube graft, a tilting disc metallic valve prosthesis was situated, a Medtronic Hall valve prosthesis, which is similar in appearance and function to that of a Bjork-Shiley valve.

Examination of the surface of the heart required careful removal of a partially adherent parietal pericardium by sharp dissection. Four venous conduits were noted, all of which were flat throughout, indicating their patency. Patency of the grafts had been documented by coronary angiogram preoperatively, which argues against the need for a postmortem coronary injection. However, if an embolic event to the coronaries is a consideration, the injection might still be helpful.

The left ventricular wall was markedly thickened. The aortic valve was found to be tightly stenotic and calcified. In addition, the mitral valve was also calcific. The association of aortic plus mitral valve disease as demonstrated by this case is consistent with a postinflammatory valvular heart disease, viz., rheumatic valvular heart disease in most incidences [62].

Conclusions

- Time interval between cardiac surgery and the autopsy

  - *Important.* Death in the operating room simply means that the patient did not tolerate the operation. Three scenarios need to be entertained. First, with or without comorbidities, the heart was "too sick" going in. Second, a technical error precluded a satisfactory surgical outcome. Third, some physical or physiologic maloccurrence prevented recovery of cardiac function.

- Technical issues relating to the cardiac operation(s)

  - *Important.* It was clearly because of cumbersome technical issues that the surgeon abandoned the usual approach to aortic valve replacement and chose an uncommon alternative to treating a severe aortic stenosis [63]. He thereby avoided almost certain injury to the right coronary artery bypass graft by doing a re-do sternotomy with the oscillating saw. Even if the sternotomy had been completed without injury to the underlying heart, he would have been unable to safely cross-clamp or incise the atheromatous and calcific ascending aorta in order to gain access to the aortic valve. Such manipulation of an aorta with this degree of disease would have carried a major risk of injury to the aorta and/or a dangerous embolic event. However, an approach through a left thoracotomy limits the surgeon's options regarding techniques of myocardial preservation by precluding any attempt to administer an antegrade or retrograde cardioplegic solution.

- Subtle complications of underlying heart disease versus surgical complications

  - *Important.* The patient's marked left ventricular hypertrophy makes the myocardium of the LV, especially the subendocardium, increasingly vulnerable to ischemic injury [44] in a relatively low-flow state. Left-sided heart failure secondary to peripheral vasodilation resulting from the stress of the pump run [64] may have been compounded by intraoperative myocardial ischemic injury due to left ventricular hypertrophy.

- Comorbidities at the time of and/or subsequent to cardiac surgery

  - *Questionably important.* Even though the patient's coronary bypass grafts were patent, his severe coronary artery disease could have contributed to the myocardial ischemic injury found at autopsy.

- Drug-related complications

  - *Questionably important.* Although no specific drug reaction was observed, large doses of intraoperative inotropic agents may have contributed to ischemia in peripheral vascular beds [55].

- Medical-legal issues relating to surgery

  - *None*. The autopsy showed no findings that were suggestive of inappropriate care of the patient.

Case 13: An Acute Aortic Dissection Involving the Left Main Coronary Artery

History

The patient is a 52-year-old male who presented with 45 min of chest pain and was noted on EKG to have ST segment elevation in the inferior and lateral leads.

Procedure

Emergent coronary artery bypass grafting x2 and replacement of ascending aorta.

Hospital Course

The patient was brought to the catheterization lab, at which time he was found to have left main coronary artery occlusion. This artery was successfully stented, although the patient became unstable. He required Levophed and dopamine for maintenance of his blood pressure. He developed ventricular tachycardia and was defibrillated twice for a return of his rhythm. The cardiac surgery team was notified, and he was taken emergently to the operating room. In the operating room, a transesophageal echocardiogram revealed an ascending aortic dissection, which involved the left main coronary artery. Following an ascending aortic reconstruction and CABG to the left anterior descending artery and right coronary artery, multiple attempts were required to come off cardiopulmonary bypass. An intraaortic balloon pump, which had been inserted in the cardiac catheterization lab, was left in place. Because of a coagulopathy, multiple transfusions of blood products were required before the patient could be transported from the operating room.

Upon arrival in the cardiac intensive care unit, the patient had a blood pressure of 40/20 and had no inherent electrical rhythm in his ECG. The patient's family decided that further measures should not be pursued to maintain the patient's life. The infusing medications and intraaortic balloon pump were stopped and the patient was pronounced dead a few hours following surgery.

Autopsy Findings

- Aortic dissection (type A), acute, involving left main coronary artery, the brachio-cephalic trunk, left common carotid artery, left subclavian artery, and descending thoracic aorta.

- Cardiomegaly (936 g), with left ventricular hypertrophy.
- Myocardial infarction, acute (<24 hours old), transmural, involving anterior and lateral left ventricle and anterior right ventricle.
- Atherosclerotic coronary artery disease, with focal 40% stenosis of the proximal left circumflex artery and <20% stenoses of the left main, left anterior descending, and right coronary arteries.
- Intravascular stents (2), in left main coronary artery.
- Saphenous vein bypass grafts, patent, to left anterior descending and posterior descending arteries.
- Cardiac hemangioma (0.4 cm), anterior right ventricular wall, incidental.
- Pulmonary edema (right lung = 840 g, left lung = 900 g).
- Hepatic steatosis, marked, with centrilobular congestion.
- Renal arteriosclerosis and glomerulosclerosis, mild.

Comments

The autopsy findings showed that the cause of death of this patient was an acute aortic dissection, involving the left anterior descending artery, causing a massive acute myocardial infarction. There was no evidence of a dissection arising from the left main coronary artery itself. Histologically, the aortic wall showed only mild medial degeneration with minimal atherosclerosis and no evidence of active aortitis. The etiology of the acute dissection is most likely related to the patient's history of hypertension.

At autopsy, there was a suture closure of a fresh median sternotomy wound, below which the usual mediastinal and pleural drainage tubes and temporary pacemaker wires exited the skin. One 40 cm freshly closed surgical wound on the medial right thigh marked the site of open harvest of the greater saphenous vein used for bypass grafts. An open technique is faster than an endoscopic technique and therefore certainly appropriate in this surgical emergency. An intraaortic balloon pump exiting the skin of the left groin reflected the patient's need for support of failing left ventricular dysfunction.

A suture line in the right atrial appendage marked the site of cannulation for venous return to the pump. In acutely dissected aortas, a femoral artery is usually used to complete the cardiopulmonary bypass circuit. However, the pathologist found no wound in the right groin and concluded that the surgeon was able to cannulate the aorta. The tube graft used to reconstruct the ascending aorta had a small sidearm of Dacron, which was oversewn with suture. This sidearm had been used by the surgeon to cannulate after the distal anastomosis between the tube graft and proximal aortic arch had been completed. This anastomosis was done with the patient cooled and in complete cardiac arrest to avoid a clamp injury to the always friable dissected tissue. Once the distal anastomosis is completed, the surgeon can safely clamp the tube graft and restore perfusion of the body through the sidearm graft.

The proximal anastomosis of the tube graft was made just above the aortic valve, effectively excluding the intimal tear and flow of blood into the false lumen, which is the surgical goal in treatment of a type A dissection. This anastomosis also resuspended the aortic valve, restoring its competence that was compromised by the dissection. Had this valve resuspension been inadequate to restore competence, a composite graft would have had to be used, in which case, reimplanting the coronary ostia into the tube graft would probably not have been done in face of the acute dissection.

The two vein grafts were patent, with proximal anastomoses to the aortic tube graft. During the period of circulatory arrest, while the distal anastomosis was being fashioned, and during the time that the tube graft was clamped to allow the surgeon to complete the aortic reconstruction, myocardial preservation could have been achieved by administering cardioplegic solution either antegrade through the vein grafts or retrograde through the coronary sinus. In this case, the distal anastomoses of the vein grafts were completed once cardiopulmonary bypass was established, and the former technique was used.

The left ventricular wall was markedly thickened, not surprising given the high incidence of hypertension in patients with aortic dissections [65, 66]. A massive area of dark mottling in the myocardial distribution of the left main coronary artery marked the acute infarction that resulted from the occlusion of the left main at the time of aortic dissection. An extensive reperfusion injury undoubtedly occurred when perfusion was restored by the placement of stents and/or by perfusion of the CABG [67].

Conclusions

- Time interval between cardiac surgery and the autopsy

  - *Important.* The death of this patient only a few hours after a surgical procedure, although a sad outcome, was not surprising. The patient had been in marked heart failure secondary to a massive acute infarct going into the operation. Surgical treatment of the acute dissection was needed to prevent rupture of the aorta and pericardial tamponade. However, the large loss of left ventricular function, as documented at autopsy, was irreversible. Review of the of the hospital record indicated that the patient's family had stipulated that use of a left ventricular assist device and heart transplantation were not to be done.

- Technical issues relating to the cardiac operation(s)

  - *Important.* The surgical challenges in this case were multiple. Reconstruction of an acutely dissected aorta is complicated by marked tissue friability, complicating suture techniques that can easily tear the tissue. Circulatory arrest, although a standardized surgical technique, requires great attention to detail in order to preserve function of the central nervous system as well as of the myocardium [68, 69].

- Subtle complications of underlying heart disease versus surgical complications

  - *Questionably important.* The patient's marked left ventricular hypertrophy, makes the myocardium of the LV, especially the subendocardium, increasingly vulnerable to ischemic injury [44] in a relatively low-flow state, as during the time of circulatory arrest and clamping of the tube graft. However, given the massive infarction of the LV going into the operation, the stress of the pump run [64] may not have significantly compounded left ventricular dysfunction.

- Comorbidities at the time of and/or subsequent to cardiac surgery

  - *Questionably important.* The adverse effects of the patient's coagulopathy and bleeding after the pump run were hemodynamically detrimental, but probably not determinate in the patient's outcome.

- Drug-related complications

  - *Questionably important.* Although no specific drug reaction was observed, large doses of intraoperative inotropic agents may have contributed to ischemia in peripheral vascular beds [55].

- Medical-legal issues relating to surgery

  - *None.* The autopsy showed no findings that were suggestive of inappropriate care of the patient. The autopsy findings support the contention that, without the use of a left ventricular assist device, which the patient's family refused, the patient's life could not be salvaged.

Case 14: ECMO Following Treatment of Congenital Heart Disease

History

This is a 4-month-old male with a very complicated history that dates back to his birth. He was born with intrauterine growth retardation and was found to have a tetralogy of Fallot, an omphalocele, renal anomalies, and a deletion of chromosome 6q. He underwent repair of his kidneys, repair of his omphalocele, and two subsequent operations for bowel obstruction, after which he was ventilator-dependent with a Pseudomonas and Enterobacter pneumonia. His VSD continued to be a problem, and ultimately it was determined that the next thing that needed to be done was to repair his VSD even though he still had colonization of his airways and copious sputum production. After maximization of his medical care, he was scheduled for operative repair of his heart. A new Broviac line was placed.

Procedure

Closure of VSD with pericardial patch and closure of RVOT incision with pericardial patch.

Hospital Course

An echocardiogram showed right ventricular dilation with diffuse hypokinesis. There was dilation of the main and branch pulmonary arteries, with moderate tricuspid regurgitation. There was valvular pulmonic stenosis, with a peak gradient of 25, and a large VSD, with overriding aorta and bidirectional shunt. An ASD or PFO showed a left to right shunt. The patient remained hemodynamically stable prior to his VSD repair.

On postoperative day 3, the patient had respiratory decompensation, with difficulty in movement of the chest with bag-to-endotracheal tube ventilation. Suctioning did not improve ventilation and a chest X-ray did not reveal a pneumothorax. The endotracheal tube was replaced multiple times using various sized tubes, cuffed and uncuffed. During this time, the patient manifested poor perfusion, and the chest was opened by the cardiac surgeons. Open cardiac massage was performed. The patient was emergently placed on extracorporeal membrane oxygenation, or ECMO [70, 71].

Over the ensuing 24 hours, the patient developed anuria, severe metabolic acidosis, and liver failure, and the pupils became fixed and dilated. After a family meeting, the parents decided that due to the poor prognosis, withdrawal of care was best. ECMO was discontinued, and the patient was pronounced dead on postoperative day 4.

Autopsy Findings

- 4-month-old male infant (3800 g; <10th percentile for age) with 46XY6q-.
- Congenital cardiac abnormalities, multiple, including:

  - Ventricular septal defect, large, status post patch repair
  - Patent foramen ovale.
  - Dilated pulmonary artery root.
  - Myocardial infarcts, acute, involving right and left ventricular walls and interventricular septum.

- Pulmonary atelectasis, bilateral, with marked mucous and hemorrhagic plugging of the tracheobronchial tree.
- Bronchopneumonia, organizing, multifocal.
- Pulmonary hemorrhage and hemosiderosis.
- Congenital absence of the pericardium and thymus.
- Dysmorphic facies, including:

  - Low set and deformed ears with flattened pinnae.
  - Flattened nasal bridge.

- – Prominent epicanthal folds.
- – Thin upper lip.
- – Enlarged intercanthal distance.

- Skeletal abnormalities, including crossed third and fourth fingers.
- Fibrous adhesions, small and large intestines, marked.
- Acute tubular necrosis.
- Renal cortical cysts.
- Splenic infarcts.
- Hepatic necrosis, centrilobular.
- Brain (470 g), with:

- – Incomplete inferior vermis.
- – Delayed myelination pattern for gestational and marked volume reduction.
- – Ischemic/hypoxic neuronal injury, acute.

Comments

Microscopic sections of the heart showed multiple subendocardial and focally transmural infarctions involving the right ventricle, interventricular septum, and left ventricle. These infarctions involved approximately one-third of the total heart tissue, and showed abundant hemorrhage with scattered inflammatory cells, suggesting they occurred at the time of the ventricular septal defect repair, three days prior to death. In addition, the pulmonary hemorrhage/congestion, centrilobular hepatic necrosis, and acute tubular necrosis are likely secondary to the extensive myocyte necrosis, resulting in cardiac dysfunction.

Gross and microscopic examination reveals a delayed myelination pattern for gestational age that involves the centrum semiovale, corpus callosum, anterior commissure, and the anterior limb of the internal capsule. Since the cerebral cortex is well developed and there is no decreased number of axons in the white matter, the marked reduction of the white matter is most likely due to reduced myelination. In addition to the other congenital abnormalities, there is an incomplete vermis.

The multiple congenital malformations in this infant are consistent with the documented chromosomal deletion of 6q- [72–74]. Although no definite syndrome has been described with this deletion, several papers have documented congenital heart defects, craniofacial and hand anomalies, all seen in this case.

At autopsy, the parietal pericardium was congenitally absent. Absence of the pericardium is a feature of the pentalogy of Cantrell [75, 76], which is ectopia cordis, a midline supraumbilical wall defect, a defect of the lower sternum, absent pericardium, and an anterior diaphragmatic defect. To this author's knowledge, it has not been associated with tetralogy of Fallot in the literature. The presence of a VSD has also been associated with of the pentalogy of Cantrell [77]. The lack of documentation at autopsy in the current case of right ventricular hypertrophy, overriding aorta, and subpulmonic and/or pulmonic valve stenosis suggests, particularly in view of the patient's past history of an omphalocele, that the infant had some variant of the pentalogy of Cantrell rather than a tetralogy of Fallot.

Sutures in the inferior and superior venae cavae marked the cannulation sites for the cardiopulmonary bypass. A suture in the ascending aorta marked the aortic cannulation site, completing the circuit. A right atriotomy closure and patched right ventriculotomy indicated the two exposures of the VSD, which the surgeon had used to close the defect with a bovine pericardial patch. A patent foramen ovale was noted.

ECMO has been shown in prospective randomized trials to improve survival of neonates with severe respiratory failure [70]. Venoarterial ECMO, which is similar to standard cardiopulmonary bypass used in cardiac surgery, allows support for both the heart and lungs as blood is drained into a gas exchanger where oxygen is added and CO_2 is removed and then pumped back into the arterial system. Indeed, the infant in this case was recannulated in the right atrium and ascending aorta, since the sternum was already open when the decision to use ECMO was made. ECMO has also been established using the internal jugular vein or femoral vein, and the carotid or femoral artery. In patients with isolated pulmonary failure, venovenous ECMO returns blood to a large central vein rather than to an artery.

Conclusions

- Time interval between cardiac surgery and the autopsy

  - *Important.* Histologically, there was evidence that at least some of the myocardial infarct dated back to the day of surgery, suggesting that, during the aortic clamp time, myocardial preservation with cardioplegic solution had been suboptimal. However, the large hemorrhagic component of the infarct is consistent with ongoing myocyte damage correlating with the patient's severe respiratory insufficiency postoperatively.

- Technical issues relating to the cardiac operation(s)

  - *Questionably important.* Repair of the VSD appeared to be straightforward. Adequate myocardial preservation may have been problematic. The heart was reported to have been contracting well at the end of the procedure. However, inotropic support was being administered after the pump run.

- Subtle complications of underlying heart disease versus surgical complications

  - *Questionably important.* The right ventricle was noted at autopsy to be dilated, probably a result of overload caused by the left-to-right shunt through the VSD [77]. An accompanying decrease in right ventricular function could have compounded the degree of heart failure postoperatively.

- Comorbidities at the time of and/or subsequent to cardiac surgery

  - *Important.* The patient had been treated for pneumonia preoperatively. Postoperatively, respiratory failure was a profound complication in the patient's course.

- Drug-related complications

  - *Questionably important*. No specific drug reaction was observed, although multiple drugs were administered to support the patient.

- Medical-legal issues relating to surgery

  - *None*. The autopsy showed no findings that were suggestive of inappropriate care of the patient.

Case 15: Assessing Placement of a Biventricular Assist Device

History

This is a 56-year-old man who presented with idiopathic dilated cardiomyopathy a number of years ago. He has been treated medically since that time, including dual chamber pacing. Recently, he developed increasing dyspnea and shortness of breath. He was admitted to the hospital and eventually required maximal doses of pressors and afterload reducing agents. Despite this treatment and the addition of an intraaortic balloon pump, the patient was spiraling into cardiogenic shock, with rising creatinine, worsening respiratory status, and mental confusion. Therefore, it was suggested that the patient undergo urgent placement of a biventricular assist device. The patient consented.

Procedure

Placement of thoracic biventricular assist device and surgical removal of an intraaortic balloon pump.

Hospital Course

The procedure was complicated by some postoperative bleeding for which the patient was taken back to the operating room and reexplored; the bleeding was surgically controlled. The patient did not have a problem with his bilateral ventricular assist device throughout his hospitalization; indeed, his flows remained adequate throughout his stay, his right being approximately 4.5 and his left 5.2 l/min. However, within 2–3 weeks following insertion of his assist device, his clinical course began to trend downwards. He developed multiorgan failure and also became septic. He began to develop a Levophed requirement despite adequate flows in to his BIVAD.

His postoperative pulmonary course was marked by difficulty weaning from his ventilator. Extubation was attempted approximately two weeks postoperatively; however, he required reintubation because of inadequate oxygenation and ventilation. In addition, he also grew Klebsiella out of his sputum, for which he was placed on a combination of Vancomycin and Meropenem.

The patient had profound liver failure that worsened postoperatively. His total bilirubin peaked at 53 and he had persistent elevation of his liver enzymes. It was thought that this elevation was secondary to a combination of hemolysis and to his underlying liver disease, likely secondary to his history of alcoholism.

The patient had a baseline chronic renal insufficiency. Postoperatively, when he developed a combination of liver failure and a possible sepsis, his renal function began to deteriorate. He became anuric and required hemodialysis.

As time passed, it became quite clear that a meaningful recovery was unlikely given his multiple organ dysfunction. His family ultimately requested that supportive measures be discontinued. He died 32 days following placement of the biventricular assist device.

Autopsy Findings

- Hemorrhagic and organizing pneumonia, bilateral.
- Pleural adhesions, left lung.
- Pleural effusions, serosanguineous, (left: 100 ml, right: 50 ml).
- Cardiomegaly (683 g), with

  - Four-chamber cardiac dilatation and biventricular hypertrophy.
  - Patchy fibrosis consistent with old myocardial infarction, left ventricle.
  - Vegetation, small, tricuspid valve.

- Chronic pericarditis, mild.
- Pancreatitis with fat necrosis.
- Ascites (3000 ml, serosanguineous).
- Renal tubular necrosis, acute, bilateral.
- Simple renal cortical cysts, bilateral.
- Hemorrhagic gastroenteritis.
- Hepatomegaly (2342 g), with incomplete cirrhosis
- Splenomegaly (641 g) with multiple infarctions (up to $4.0 \times 3.0 \times 3.0$ cm).
- Atherosclerosis, abdominal aorta, mild
- Diverticula, sigmoid colon.

Comments

The autopsy findings indicated that the patient's demise was likely secondary to a combination of pneumonia and multiorgan failure, which was ultimately related to his extensive underlying dilated cardiomyopathy. Microscopic sections of the lung showed numerous intraalveolar lymphocytes, histiocytes, and giant cells admixed with hemorrhage and fibrosis. These findings are consistent with a hemorrhagic organizing pneumonia complicated by aspiration. Sections of the liver showed fibrosis of the perilobular and centrilobular zones, with bridging fibrosis that formed an incomplete pattern of cirrhosis. These findings are consistent with poor cardiac function.

At autopsy, the median sternotomy wound showed evidence of early healing. A hemodialysis catheter exited the skin over the left femoral vein. As the chest and abdomen were opened, the biventricular assist device was observed. Two pumping units were buried in the soft tissue of the upper abdominal wall, one on each side of the midline. Each unit had an inflow tube and an outflow tube. On the left, the inflow tube originated from a cannula exiting the apex of the left ventricle, and the outflow tube was tunneled deep into the soft tissue of the left chest wall and sewn end-to-side to the ascending aorta. On the right, the inflow tube originated from a cannula in the right atrium, and the outflow tube was sewn end-to-side to the main pulmonary artery. The drive line of each component of the device exited the skin laterally.

Multiple soft, fibrous adhesions surrounded the heart and tubes of the assist device, since a month had elapsed between the surgery and the autopsy. The inflow tube of the right ventricular component entered the right atrium through the appendage, which was also the site of cannulation for establishing cardiopulmonary bypass. A pledgeted suture in the aortic arch marked the arterial cannulation site to complete the circuit. A pledgeted suture in the ascending aorta below the left outflow tube graft marked the site of catheter insertion for administration of antegrade cardioplegic solution, indicating that resecting the core of the left ventricular apex and securing the cannula in the apical opening had been done with the heart in cardioplegic arrest.

Each component of the biventricular assist device was a HeartMate Vented Electric (XVE), made by Thoratec, which is a first generation ventricular assist device and generates pulsatile blood flow. The drive line coming through the skin provides the power by attaching to accessories, including the system controller, batteries, and the power base unit. Another similar ventricular assist device is the Novacor, made by Baxter Healthcare. A comparison study [78] has shown that both devices offer significant improvement in quality of life for patients with end-stage heart failure and similar rates of survival to transplantation. However, with long-term use, further study is needed to compare mechanical failure, mortality rates, and the incidence of complications such as thromboembolism, infection, and bleeding associated with the two devices.

Conclusions

- Time interval between cardiac surgery and the autopsy

  - *Important.* The fact that the patient survived for a month after placement of the assist device indicates that his death was not due to some catastrophic event at the time of surgery. The need for anticoagulation to prevent thrombus formation in the device did complicate the management of the patient, who was apparently bleeding in his gastrointestinal tract, requiring multiple blood transfusions.

- Technical issues relating to the cardiac operation(s)

    - *Questionably important.* Although the surgical procedure was technically rather straightforward, any major operation on a heart that is already in end-stage failure carries a technical challenge.

- Subtle complications of underlying heart disease versus surgical complications

    - *Questionably important.* Dilated cardiomyopathy is commonly associated with mural thrombus formation within trabecular grooves in the ventricles [79]. Dislodgment of such thrombi, causing an embolic event, could be confused with thrombus formation within the ventricular assist device.

- Comorbidities at the time of and/or subsequent to cardiac surgery

    - *Important.* Postoperatively, the patient could not be extubated because of respiratory insufficiency. He developed pneumonia, sepsis, and deterioration of renal and hepatic function, which had already been compromised preoperatively. He died because of a cascade of severe comorbidities.

- Drug-related complications

    - *Questionably important.* No specific drug reaction was observed, although multiple drugs were administered to support the patient, in addition to many transfusions of blood products.

- Medical-legal issues relating to surgery

    - *None.* The autopsy showed no findings that were suggestive of inappropriate care of the patient.

Case 16: Cardiac Surgery Through the Right Chest

History

This 76-year-old male underwent previous coronary revascularization. He has required subsequent angioplasty of the proximal left anterior descending artery to resolve recurrent ischemia. He subsequently underwent pacemaker implantation because of bradycardia in the setting of atrial fibrillation, and has required lead revision. He subsequently developed progressive tricuspid regurgitation and now has substantial systemic venous congestion, including a pulsatile liver and a considerable peripheral edema. Right ventricular function is depressed. His most recent cardiac catheterization revealed 50% stenosis of the left main coronary artery, 70% stenosis of the left anterior descending artery, 80% stenosis of the circumflex coronary artery, 70% stenosis of the posterior descending artery, stenosis of the posterior left ventricular artery, occluded left internal mammary artery graft to the left anterior descending artery, patent saphenous vein grafts to the obtuse marginal branch and posterior descending artery, and severe tricuspid regurgitation. He is admitted now for a tricuspid valve reconstruction.

Procedure

Tricuspid valve reconstruction by ring annuloplasty, utilizing a right thoracotomy approach.

Hospital Course

Surgery was done on a beating heart with minimal cooling. Following the annuloplasty, he had excellent tricuspid valve function with a considerable decrease in his central venous pressure. However, he had a very difficult postoperative course. Initially, he had low systemic vascular resistance and required pressor agents to maintain his blood pressure despite adequate cardiac output. High-grade ventricular ectopy was noted, antiarrhythmic medications were given, and an intraaortic balloon pump was inserted to provide additional hemodynamic stability.

A picture of acute respiratory distress syndrome (ARDS) developed. In addition, there was evidence of hepatic failure with jaundice and encephalopathy. Renal failure was noted, consistent with a hepatorenal syndrome, and hemodialysis was started. Despite antiarrhythmic medications, intermittent ventricular tachycardia occurred. His condition continued to deteriorate, even with aggressive supportive measures. He expired on the seventh postoperative day.

Autopsy Findings

- Diffuse alveolar damage (combined lung weight: 3200 g), with hemorrhage and pneumonia, bilateral.
- Emphysema, marked, bilateral.
- Cardiomegaly (784 g), with biventricular hypertrophy and four-chamber dilatation, and tricuspid valve ring annuloplasty.
- Coronary artery disease (left main: 50%, left anterior descending: 90%, circumflex: 70%, posterior descending: 70%, with patent vein grafts to right and circumflex coronary arteries).
- Myocardial infarction, acute, circumferential, involving the left and right ventricular walls.
- Mediastinal hematoma, 50 ml, right.
- Hepatomegaly (1370 g), with centrilobular congestion, necrosis, fibrosis, cholestasis, and mild steatosis.
- Pancreatic hemorrhage, focal.
- Acute tubular necrosis, severe.
- Splenomegaly (242 g), with infarction.

Comments

This patient, with a long history of coronary artery disease, cardiomegaly, and tricuspid regurgitation, developed an acute myocardial infarction involving both ventricles. A concomitant diffuse alveolar damage with bilateral pneumonia and multiple organ failure led to the patient's demise.

At autopsy, a median sternotomy wound from the past CABG surgery was well healed. A fresh anterior right thoracotomy wound closure indicated a relatively uncommon approach to open-heart surgery. In this case, the previous bypass surgery would have made a re-do sternotomy hazardous because of possible injury to the patent vein bypass graft to the posterior descending branch of the right coronary artery. Furthermore, the goal of the operation was just to repair the tricuspid valve, which can be exposed very nicely through the right chest. Mitral valve surgery is also quite amenable to this approach [80].

When a right thoracotomy approach to the heart is used, the right femoral artery is frequently used for establishing cardiopulmonary bypass. However, a pledgeted suture in the ascending aorta indicated the site that the surgeon in this case chose. Sutures also marked the sites of bicaval cannulation for the pump run. A right atrial suture line marked the site of surgical access to the tricuspid valve. Two pacemaker leads entered the right atrium from the superior vena cava, traversed the tricuspid valve, and were seated in the apex of the right ventricle. Fibrous encapsulation of the tips of the pacemaker leads is a common occurrence over time, necessitating lead replacement because of a decrease in electrical threshold as a result of the reactive endocardial scarring process. In the process of replacing a malfunctioning lead, if the lead cannot be safely withdrawn from the heart because of the firm fibrous encapsulation, a new lead is simply implanted, leaving the old lead in place. Other indications for lead replacement have been reported [81]. Review of this patient's record indicates that the second lead was placed a year after the initial lead insertion.

The tricuspid valve leaflets were normal, and an annuloplasty ring was well seated on the tricuspid annulus, indicating that the surgeon had concluded that the patient's tricuspid insufficiency had been due to annular dilatation brought about by myocardial remodeling, which was reflected by biventricular hypertrophy and dilatation [82]. Placement of an appropriately sized annuloplasty ring effectively reduces the circumference of the annulus to allow better coaptation of the valve leaflets, improving the competency of the valve.

Interestingly, even though the CABG surgery had been performed more than ten years previously, no pericardial adhesions were found at autopsy. This absence of adhesions allowed the pathologist easy access to the surface of the heart. Two patent vein grafts and an occluded left internal mammary artery were noted, corresponding to the preoperative coronary angiogram. Minimal evidence of atherosclerotic disease was found in the vein grafts, which is also surprising, since the superiority of patency in internal mammary artery grafts over that of vein grafts has been well established [83, 84]. Over time, vein grafts develop atherosclerosis and occlude because of progressive thickening of intimal plaque. Internal mammary artery grafts are much less susceptible to atherosclerosis than are vein grafts [85]. Occlusion of these arterial grafts tends to occur at the anastomotic site because of technical problems, or may occur elsewhere in the arterial conduit because of graft shrinkage, a so-called "string sign," due to chronic competitive flow through a coronary artery with moderate disease [86].

Conclusions

- Time interval between cardiac surgery and the autopsy
  - *Important.* The patient was in a low cardiac output state early on after his surgery, which was associated with ventricular ectopy. He quickly developed ARDS and renal failure. In summary, the postoperative course was one of rapid deterioration.

- Technical issues relating to the cardiac operation(s)
  - *Questionably important.* A right thoracotomy is not the usual approach to tricuspid valve surgery, but it is a standardized approach and yields straightforward access to the right atrium. A re-do cardiac procedure adds challenge to heart surgery. Any manipulation of old vein grafts for whatever reason can result in distal embolization of atheromatous debris, which can result in myocardial infarction [87].

- Subtle complications of underlying heart disease versus surgical complications
  - *Important.* The patient went into the operation with moderately impaired left ventricular function and diffuse right ventricular hypokinesis. He had severe triple-vessel coronary artery disease with two patent >10-year-old vein grafts. The lesion in the proximal left anterior descending artery was more stenotic than the coronary angiogram had indicated preoperatively, not an unusual occurrence [42]. As mentioned above, myocardial infarcts can result from surgical manipulation of old vein grafts if an aortic cross-clamp is not in place at the time of manipulation. Finally, dilated cardiomyopathy is commonly associated with mural thrombus formation within trabecular grooves in the ventricles [79]. Dislodgment of such thrombi, causing an embolic event, could also result in myocyte damage. Consideration of all of these realities makes it difficult to distinguish between adverse effects of underlying disease and technical complications of surgery.

- Comorbidities at the time of and/or subsequent to cardiac surgery
  - *Important.* Postoperatively, the patient had acute myocardial injury compounding baseline cardiac dysfunction, resulting in a low cardiac output state and a cascade of multiorgan failure.

- Drug-related complications
  - *Questionably important.* No specific drug reaction was observed, although multiple drugs were administered to support the patient.

- Medical-legal issues relating to surgery

  - *None*. One might wonder in retrospect if an attempt at repeat angioplasty of
    the proximal left anterior descending artery might have been helpful. Given
    the whole clinical picture in this case, the answer to the question raised is a
    "tough call."

Case 17: ECMO One Day After Cardiac Surgery Through the Left Chest

History

The patient was a fifty-three-year-old male who was less than 24 hours status post
left thoracotomy for re-do coronary artery bypass grafting. The patient had had previous coronary artery bypass grafting and multiple catheter-based procedures for
severe coronary atherosclerosis. At the end of his operation, the patient seemed to
have good blood flow in the graft. However, the left lung, as it was being reinflated,
developed a large physiologic shunt and signs of pulmonary edema with poor pulmonary function. The patient was developing severe hypoxemia despite significantly
high ventilator pressures. In addition, he had ongoing issues with cardiac failure and
required high-dose vasopressors for support.

Procedure

Cannulation for extracorporeal membrane oxygenation (ECMO).

Hospital Course

Extracorporeal membrane oxygenation was instituted for venous arterial bypass,
using the left femoral vein and artery. Good flows of 3–4 l/min were initially
achieved, with rapid hemodynamic improvement of the patient. There was no bleeding. The left leg initially appeared to have reasonable capillary refill, though the
patient still had very cool extremities throughout related to his high-dose Levophed
and ongoing epinephrine therapy.

By the second hospital day, the patient had worsening metabolic acidosis and
hyperkalemia and needed to be placed on hemodialysis for acute renal failure. This
acute renal failure was secondary to his prolonged hypoperfusion from cardiogenic
shock. The patient was found to have a markedly swollen, tense, and cold left lower
extremity, the side on which the ECMO catheter was placed in the femoral artery.
It appeared that the patient had a compartment syndrome, with a tense leg and elevated creatine kinases. The patient had an additional arterial perfusor placed to the
left superficial femoral artery for this left lower extremity ischemia and left lower
extremity fasciotomies to relieve the compartment syndrome.

Despite hemodialysis, it was very difficult to correct the patient's severe metabolic acidosis and hyperkalemia. The patient's status continued to decline, and in accordance with the family's request, support was withdrawn. The patient was declared dead on the third day following re-do CABG.

Autopsy Findings

- Cardiomegaly (800 g), with biventricular hypertrophy.
- Myocardial infarct, posterolateral, old, with subacute and acute posterolateral extension, involving posterior papillary muscle.
- Coronary artery disease, three-vessel disease, severe.
  - Patent left internal mammary artery bypass graft to the left anterior descending artery
  - Stent occlusion, obtuse marginal branch of circumflex
  - Distally occluded saphenous vein bypass graft to ramus medialis (thrombus at distal anastomosis).
- Pulmonary hemorrhagic infarction mostly peripheral, severe, bilateral (left greater than right).
- Splenomegaly (267 g).
- Hepatomegaly (1900 g), with marked steatosis and incomplete septal cirrhosis.

Comments

The patient died from acute respiratory distress, acute bilateral peripheral pulmonary hemorrhagic infarction, and an acute myocardial infarction associated with thrombosis at the anastomosis to the saphenous vein bypass graft. The pattern of the pulmonary infarctions is unusual. The infarctions are peripheral and may represent an unusual form of reexpansion injury [88, 89].

At autopsy, two cannulae in the left groin represented the ECMO lines. A median sternotomy wound and multiple scars on the lower extremities from the past CABG surgery were all well healed. A fresh anterolateral left thoracotomy wound closure indicated the relatively uncommon approach to CABG surgery. In this case, the previous bypass surgery would have made a re-do sternotomy hazardous because of possible injury to the patent left internal mammary bypass graft to the left anterior descending coronary artery. Furthermore, the goal of the operation was just to construct one vein bypass graft to the ramus medialis, which can be exposed adequately through the left chest [90]. This operation had been done off pump. Alternatively, it could have been accomplished using cardiopulmonary bypass, usually by a femoral venous and arterial circuit or left atrial to femoral arterial bypass. At autopsy, no inguinal incision or suture ligature of the left atrial appendage was noted.

Conclusions

- Time interval between cardiac surgery and the autopsy

  - *Important*. The patient was in a low cardiac output state early on after his surgery, which was associated with an acute lung injury due to surgical manipulation. He quickly developed ARDS and renal failure. In summary, the postoperative course was one of rapid deterioration.

- Technical issues relating to the cardiac operation(s)

  - *Important*. A left thoracotomy is not the usual approach to CABG surgery, but it can be useful in re-do procedures [90]. A re-do cardiac procedure adds challenge to heart surgery. Any manipulation of old vein grafts for whatever reason can result in distal embolization of atheromatous debris, which can lead to myocardial infarction [87]. Injury of a patent left internal mammary artery graft by a re-do sternotomy might lead to catastrophic difficulty [5]. A caveat to this approach, however, is to avoid technical difficulties that may be problematic in a less commonly used approach. The recently constructed vein graft between the descending thoracic aorta and ramus medialis was found to be thrombosed at the distal anastomosis, suggesting obstruction due to a possible tension on or angulation of the suture line.

- Subtle complications of underlying heart disease versus surgical complications

  - *Important*. A myocardial ischemic injury secondary to underlying severe coronary artery disease and ventricular hypertrophy would be compounded by acute thrombosis of a coronary artery bypass graft and a postoperative ARDS.

- Comorbidities at the time of and/or subsequent to cardiac surgery

  - *Important*. Postoperatively, the patient had acute myocardial injury compounding baseline cardiac dysfunction, resulting in a low cardiac output state and a cascade of multiorgan failure.

- Drug-related complications

  - *Questionably important*. No specific drug reaction was observed, although multiple drugs were administered to support the patient.

- Medical-legal issues relating to surgery

  - *None*. The use of a left thoracotomy, in retrospect, did not in the end prove beneficial for the patient at the time of his most recent CABG surgery. However, the reasoning behind the use of this approach seems valid.

Case 18: Aortic Valve Replacement and Failure Coming Off Pump

History

The patient is a 79-year-old woman who has exertional dyspnea, fatigue, angina, and recent presyncopal episodes. Her echocardiogram showed critical aortic stenosis with a peak gradient of 67, mean gradient 38, and valve area of $0.7\,cm^2$. The left ventricular function was normal. Angiography showed no significant coronary artery disease. The valve was crossed at catheterization and the valve area was calculated at $0.6\,cm^2$. Pulmonary artery pressure was normal.

Procedure

Aortic valve replacement, 2-vessel coronary artery bypass, insertion of intraaortic balloon pump.

Hospital Course

Cardiac catheterization showed that the left main coronary artery was normal. Her proximal LAD had a mild 30% stenosis on its proximal one-third. There was a 25% stenosis after her major diagonal branch take-off. Her left circumflex coronary artery was normal. Her right coronary artery was normal.

The patient was taken to the operating room, where she underwent replacement of her aortic valve with a bovine pericardial valve. The patient was very difficult to wean off the pump. Several attempts were made, and one was associated with ventricular tachycardia and ischemic ECG changes. At this time, because of her failure to wean off the pump, there was concern that she might have left coronary artery obstruction, so two vessel coronary artery bypass grafts were performed. An intraaortic balloon pump was placed, and at this time she was on several vasopressors to maintain a blood pressure. She was in critical condition and was transferred up to the Cardiac Surgery Intensive Care Unit.

On arrival in the Intensive Care Unit, her blood pressure was 56/31. She was atrial-paced at a heart rate of 101. Her pulmonary artery pressure was 40/11, her CVP was 17 on a very high vasopressor requirement. Since it did not look as if she would survive, the patient's family requested withdrawal of support. She expired on the day following surgery.

Autopsy Findings

- Myocardial infarction, acute, involving left ventricular free wall, diffuse.
- Coronary artery atherosclerosis, with >60% stenosis of proximal left anterior descending and >70% stenosis of proximal circumflex coronary arteries.

- Left ventricular hypertrophy (1.6 cm).
- Aortic atherosclerosis, mild.
- Pulmonary edema, mild (left: 590 g; right: 630 g).
- Pleural effusion, bilateral, serous (left: 300 ml, right: 400 ml).

Comments

The autopsy findings reveal the cause of death as a perioperative acute myocardial infarction, causing left ventricular failure. She had a normal ejection fraction preoperatively and poor function coming off bypass. At autopsy, the pathologist needs to consider the following possible scenarios leading to an acute myocardial infarction after aortic valve replacement:

1. Inadequate myocardial preservation during the operation, particularly during the aortic clamp time.
2. Compromise of coronary ostial blood flow by the aortic valve prosthesis.
3. An embolic event leading to compromise of coronary arterial blood flow.
4. Atherosclerotic coronary artery disease, causing deficient coronary flow.

During the cross-clamp time, the surgeon had administered cold cardioplegic solution first into the aortic root and then intermittently directly into the coronary ostia. While the distal vein graft anastomoses were being constructed, both antegrade and retrograde cardioplegic solution was administered. In the presence of ventricular hypertrophy, it is sometimes difficult to achieve optimal cooling of the myocardium with antegrade cardioplegia [91]. Significant coronary artery disease might compound this problem [92, 93].

A small aortic root challenges the surgeon to replace the valve with a prosthesis that is large enough to allow an adequate hemodynamic result, i.e., by not leaving the patient with a significant pressure gradient across the valve prosthesis, while at the same time avoiding obstruction of blood flow into the coronary ostia. Sometimes it is necessary for the surgeon to enlarge the aortic root to accomplish proper seating of an adequately sized valve prosthesis. Techniques of dealing with a small aortic root vary, and they can add to the complexity of valve replacement [94–97].

Coronary artery emboli comprise a rare cause of myocardial infarction [98]. They can originate from mural thrombi in the left ventricle or atrium [99], atheromatous debris from vein graft manipulation at the time of re-do heart surgery [87], and fragmentation of vegetations on an infected valve or valve prosthesis [100]. A postmortem coronary injection could be particularly helpful in localizing one or more coronary emboli [101].

Significant coronary artery disease that is not defined on a preoperative coronary angiogram can jeopardize the myocardium during the course of valve replacement, because the surgeon lacks the known indication for combining valve replacement with CABG. Rupture of a mild to moderate coronary plaque can result in sudden coronary artery thrombosis and acute myocardial infarction in the perioperative period, which defies clinical predictability [102].

At autopsy, pertinent findings included left ventricular hypertrophy, as anticipated in an individual with long-standing aortic stenosis. The aortic valve prosthesis, a bovine pericardial valve, was well seated and not obstructing the coronary ostia. The vein grafts were patent. There was no evidence of embolic debris in the careful breadloafing examination of the epicardial coronary arteries or histological study of myocardial vessels. Significant atherosclerotic stenoses were found in the proximal LAD and circumflex arteries.

Conclusions

- Time interval between cardiac surgery and the autopsy

  - *Important*. The patient demonstrated left ventricular failure as cardiopulmonary bypass was discontinued, which defined an adverse intraoperative event as the cause of heart failure.

- Technical issues relating to the cardiac operation(s)

  - *Questionably important*. The valve replacement had been straightforward. However, in the face of left ventricular hypertrophy and unrecognized coronary artery disease, the level of myocardial preservation during the cross-clamp time remains questionable.

- Subtle complications of underlying heart disease versus surgical complications

  - *Important*. A myocardial ischemic injury secondary to underlying significant coronary artery disease and ventricular hypertrophy would compound an adverse effect relating to the administration of cardioplegic solution.

- Comorbidities at the time of and/or subsequent to cardiac surgery

  - *Not important*. Postoperatively, the patient's precipitous demise was caused by refractory left ventricular failure secondary to an acute myocardial injury.

- Drug-related complications

  - *Questionably important*. No specific drug reaction was observed, although multiple drugs were administered to support the patient.

- Medical-legal issues relating to surgery

  - *None*. Given the underestimation of the patient's coronary artery disease on the preoperative coronary angiogram, second guessing relating to the care of this patient is speculative.

Case 19: Postoperative Complex Congenital Heart Disease at Autopsy

History

The patient is a 5-month-old, 5-kg girl who was born with an unbalanced AV canal. Echocardiogram and cardiac catheterization showed an unbalanced AV canal with a common atrium, a parachute morphology of the left-sided component of the AV valve, and a small left ventricle, which we considered would not be adequate to support the systemic circulation. She also had a tunnel-type subaortic stenosis and a small aortic valve. She had pulmonary hypertension, which was considered to be reactive. We therefore thought that she would need a single ventricular repair and a systemic to pulmonary artery shunt. She had had a colon pull-through operation for Hirschsprung's disease.

Procedure

Damus-Kaye-Stansel Procedure.

Central pulmonary artery reconstruction with autologous pericardial patch, right modified Blalock-Taussig shunt (4 mm Gortex).

Ligation and division of patent ductus arteriosus.

Hospital Course

The intraoperative course was complicated by cardiac arrest and open-chest CPR and stat return to cardiopulmonary bypass and revision of the Blalock-Taussig (BT) shunt. The early postoperative course was remarkable for progressive hypoxia and hypotension, which required CPR, epinephrine, and emergent opening of the patient's chest soon after her arrival in the pediatric intensive care unit. She was placed on ECMO, which was continued for 16 days. She had multiple episodes of bradycardia, requiring pacing. She required escalating vasopressor and inotropic support, which included dopamine, dobutamine, little to no epinephrine.

While ECMO was continued, she was anticoagulated with heparin. She required multiple transfusions of packed cells, platelets, fresh frozen plasma, and various factors to maintain her coagulation parameters in the normal range. Because of continuing postoperative bleeding, she was treated with aprotinin and Amicar and had numerous revisions of the Esmarch to relieve tamponade.

Cardiac catheterization on postoperative day 6 demonstrated the DKS anastomosis, a widely patent 4-mm BT shunt with no distortion or stenosis, widely patent pulmonary arteries, and normal pulmonary venous return. There was no stenosis of the pulmonary veins. Systemic arterial saturation was 89, venous saturation was 61, pulmonary venous saturation was 98.

Soon after placement on the ECMO she developed acute renal failure with hypernatremia, which responded well to diuretics with normalization of diuretics and fluid management. However, she later developed signs of infection, including urinary tract infection and ventilator assisted pneumonia, treated with multiple antibiotics.

The patient was never able to tolerate ECMO flows less than 300 without desaturation and hypotension. At her family's request, she was allowed to expire on the 16th postoperative day.

Autopsy Findings

- Complete atrioventricular canal defect (right ventricular dominant), with:
    - Right ventricular hypertrophy.
    - Hypoplastic left heart syndrome.
    - Left superior vena cava.
    - Double outlet right ventricle.
- Pulmonary congestion (combined weight: 135 g).
- Pulmonary arteriopathy, consistent with pulmonary hypertension.
- Polydactyly, involving feet and left hand.

Comments

The autopsy findings are consistent with pulmonary hypertension. There was pulmonary arteriopathy and arterial intimal thickening, as well as diffuse myocardial hypertrophy of the right ventricle. The cause of death was increased hypoxia secondary to progressive pulmonary hypertension and compromised blood flow to the lungs.

The cardiac findings include: a common atrium with a left superior vena cava, which drains into the common atrium; an innominate vein connecting both superior venae cavae was absent; the pulmonary artery is about twice the size of the aorta; a single atrioventricular valve emptying mainly into the right ventricle and partially into the hypoplastic left ventricle; a membranous ventricular septal defect; and a hypertrophic, double outlet right ventricle. There was inflammation of the epicardium, with a notable presence of eosinophils. A Brown-Hopps stain showed no definite organisms.

Externally, two ECMO cannulae were found in the neck, one in the left common carotid artery and the other in the left internal jugular vein. Examination of the heart and vessels found sutures in the right atrial appendage and aortic arch, marking the sites of cannulation to achieve cardiopulmonary bypass. Another suture in the ascending aorta marked the site of catheter placement for administration of cardioplegic solution. A double ligature was found occluding the ductus arteriosus.

The Damus-Kaye-Stansel (DKS) procedure has proved to be a useful approach to complex congenital cardiac anomalies [103]. It has been used successfully in cases resembling that of this patient, viz., a functional single ventricle with features of hypoplastic left heart syndrome and double outlet right ventricle [104]. The physiological problem here was an inadequate left ventricle, with a small outflow tract and small aortic valve, and excessive flow to the lungs. A DKS procedure channels pulmonary arterial flow into the ascending aorta by transecting the pulmonary artery proximal to its bifurcation and sewing the proximal transected end to the side of the aorta. In this case, a piece of autologous pericardium was used to reconstruct the proximal pulmonary artery, which was then sewn to a long slit in the ascending aorta and arch to funnel blood into the systemic circulation. This technique comprised a modification of the original DKS operation.

The distal end of the transected pulmonary artery was found oversewn. In order to establish blood flow to the lungs, a shunt had been created surgically. At autopsy, a Gortex graft (polytetrafluoroethylene, or PTFE) was found between the right subclavian artery and right pulmonary artery, a modification of the original Blalock-Taussig shunt, in which the distal right subclavian artery was transected and brought down end-to-side to the right pulmonary artery [105]. Historically, systemic-to-pulmonary artery communications have been constructed to achieve the same result. These shunts, or fistulae, include the Glenn shunt, anastomosis between the superior vena cava and right pulmonary artery; the Waterston shunt, ascending aorta to right pulmonary artery; and the Potts shunt, descending thoracic aorta to left pulmonary artery [106].

Conclusions

- Time interval between cardiac surgery and the autopsy

  - *Questionably important.* The patient would not have survived without surgical treatment, and 16 days seems a reasonable "trial" of reconstructive surgery of a difficult complex of congenital heart defects.

- Technical issues relating to the cardiac operation(s)

  - *Important.* The primary repair of a complete AV canal, or endocardial cushion, defect in children less than 2 years old has been well established as a successful surgical procedure [107]. However, when an AV canal defect is associated with other complex anomalies, as in this case, technical issues become confounding. When a large pulmonary artery is transected and a systemic to pulmonary arterial shunt is created, striking a balance between too much pulmonary blood flow and not enough flow can be a difficult judgment call at the time of surgery [108]. Furthermore, although progress has been made over the past two decades with the Norwood and Fontan procedures [109–111], a hypoplastic left heart presents the surgeon a technical challenge that is often impossible to overcome [112].

- Subtle complications of underlying heart disease versus surgical complications

  - *Important.* Distinguishing between the effect of a technical mishap surgically and an adverse effect of an already established cardiopulmonary disability is difficult in this case.

- Comorbidities at the time of and/or subsequent to cardiac surgery

  – *Questionably important*. The development of pneumonia and urinary tract infection probably expedited the realization of the patient's physicians that successful weaning from ECMO support would not be achievable [113] and that heart transplantation, a reasonable choice of treatment of some pediatric patients with severe congenital heart disease [114], was contraindicated.

- Drug-related complications

  – *Questionably important*. No specific drug reaction was observed, although multiple drugs were administered to support the patient.

- Medical-legal issues relating to surgery

  – *None*. The autopsy showed no findings that were suggestive of inappropriate care of the patient.

Case 20: Right Ventricular Failure Following Transplantation

History

The patient is a 67-year-old female who has had prolonged hospitalization with multiple medical problems and has recently been discharged from the hospital on home Dobutamine. She has a restrictive cardiomyopathy, for which she is currently listed as status 1b on the transplant list. Although she appears to be stable, she has limited exercise tolerance on her Dobutamine. She has marked fatigue, has not had paroxysmal nocturnal dyspnea, orthopnea, presyncope, or syncope. Her AICD has not discharged.

Procedure

1. Orthotopic cardiac transplantation.
2. Femoral intraaortic balloon pump insertion.
3. Left ventricular assist device insertion.
4. Right ventricular assist device insertion.

Hospital Course

Following transplantation of the heart, the graft developed fulminant right heart failure. Being unable to wean the patient from the pump, the surgeon inserted an IABP, followed by implantation of biventricular assist devices. Unfortunately, the patient remained extremely hypotensive, with a very low cardiac index. She was also bleeding profusely from all chest tube sites. She arrived in the intensive care unit having received multiple blood products and still bleeding profusely. She was hypotensive and had no measurable CI. She expired the night of her surgery.

Autopsy Findings

- Diffuse, patchy myocardial infarction, histologically consistent with ~12–24 hour duration.
- Coronary artery disease, triple vessel, mild to moderate.
- Pericardial effusion, sanguineous (100 cc).
- Pulmonary hemosiderosis, bilateral, with pulmonary arterial and venous hypertensive changes consistent with chronic left atrial hypertension.
- Pleural effusion, sanguineous (right = 350 cc, left = 450 cc).
- Renal tubular necrosis, acute.
- Nephrosclerosis.
- Renal cortical angiomyolipoma (0.4 cm), right.

Comments

The autopsy findings support the diagnosis of biventricular failure of the allograft heart following transplantation as the cause of death. The initial right ventricular failure may have been secondary to pulmonary hypertension given the histological findings of pulmonary arteriopathy and venous sclerosis and diffuse hemosiderosis. These vascular changes were probably reactive to the documented restrictive cardiomyopathy of the patient's native heart [115, 116]. Compounding the poor function of the allograft were widespread focal areas of myocardial ischemic injury, which may be attributed to a reperfusion injury relating to the period of ischemia from the time of graft harvest to the time of reperfusion of the graft in the recipient [117, 118]. In addition, epicardial coronary artery disease was evident histologically as notable intimal hyperplasia, involving the left main and right coronary arteries, and moderately severe atherosclerotic plaque in the left anterior descending and circumflex arteries [119, 120]. A rare case of an embolus of myocardial tissue occluding the right coronary artery and causing an infarct and graft failure has been reported [121]. Another consideration in this rapid failure of the allograft is acute antibody mediated rejection [122]. Although she had been highly sensitized preoperatively, she was treated for her positive serum antibody panel, and she was identified as a suitable immunologic match for the donor. Furthermore, the allograft myocardium was negative for C4d immunostaining, evidence against a diagnosis of acute humoral rejection [123, 124].

At autopsy, the body presented to the untrained eye a somewhat daunting spectacle of a torso, much of which was covered with a tan-brown plastic-like material, from which a complex array of drains exited the skin. Beneath the plastic material (Vi-Drape), an open sternotomy wound was covered with a blue-green rubbery material (Esmarch), which, when removed, allowed exposure of a sternal retractor maintaining the open mediastinum to prevent cardiac tamponade. There were five plastic tubes exiting the skin of the mid-epigastrium to drain the mediastinum and pleural spaces. There were six blue pacemaker wires exiting the wound connected to a collection of electrodes. Two ventricular assist devices labeled "ABIOMED BVS 5000" were buried in the wall of the upper abdomen, one on each side of the midline. The inflow tube of the LVAD exited the right superior pulmonary vein, draining the left atrium. The outflow tube of the LVAD was sewn end-to-side to the ascending aorta. The inflow tube of the RVAD exited the right atrium, and the outflow tube was sewn end-to-side to the main pulmonary artery. Two small white plastic lines exiting the skin bilaterally were the drive lines to the devices.

There was a 6.0 × 5.5 cm elevated area on the upper left chest wall where a dual chamber AICD battery lay in a subcutaneous pocket. A Power PICC (Peripherally Inserted Central Catheter) was inserted in the right upper arm for giving intravenous fluids and therapeutic drugs. An intraaortic balloon pump exited the skin of a freshly closed surgical would in the right groin. This line had two lumens, one of which was labeled "arrow 30 cc" and the other of which was labeled "one way valve" and "He."

Suture closure of cannulation sites in the recipient's inferior and superior venae cavae and ascending aorta above the outflow tube of the LVAD defined the cardiopulmonary bypass circuit used during implantation of the allograft heart. Five suture lines demonstrated the technique used by the surgeon to implant the graft. One connected the donor and recipient left atria. The other four anastomoses joined donor and recipient ascending aortas, main pulmonary arteries, and inferior and superior venae cavae end-to-end. Until recently, the standard surgical technique of using two atrial-cuff anastomoses had been used in the majority of transplant centers. The recently introduced technique of bicaval anastomoses has been associated with a lower incidence of tricuspid regurgitation during the late postoperative period and is now considered to be the preferred technique of cardiac implantation in some institutions [125].

Conclusions

- Time interval between cardiac surgery and the autopsy

  - *Important.* The patient clearly died as a result of a problem that occurred in the operating room during the procedure of transplantation. The problem seemed to have originated with right ventricular failure. Meticulous collaboration between the surgeon and pathologist is necessary to optimally clarify the etiology of the intraoperative heart failure.

- Technical issues relating to the cardiac operation(s)

  - *Questionably important.* The surgical procedure appeared to be straightforward and uncomplicated until cardiopulmonary bypass was tapered. A surgeon in this situation nevertheless "relives" every step of the operation until he is satisfied that all "bases" were or were not covered appropriately.

- Subtle complications of underlying heart disease versus surgical complications

  - *Important.* The impact of the patient's pulmonary vasculopathy and of the graft coronary artery disease are difficult to distinguish from periimplantation ischemic injury resulting from the period of nonperfusion of the graft from harvest to reperfusion in the recipient.

- Comorbidities at the time of and/or subsequent to cardiac surgery

  - *Questionably important.* Pulmonary hypertension, if it indeed was the cause of the initial right ventricular failure coming off bypass, was perhaps a crucial comorbidity in this case.

- Drug-related complications

  - *Questionably important.* No specific drug reaction was observed, although multiple drugs were administered to support the patient.

- Medical-legal issues relating to surgery

  - *None.* The autopsy showed no findings that were suggestive of inappropriate care of the patient. Donor heart selection in the complicated medical scenario of this recipient bears careful reexamination, however.

References

1. Yoshida K, Matsumoto M, Sugita T, Nishizawa J, Matsuyama K, Tokuda Y, Matsuo T. Gastrointestinal complications in patients undergoing coronary artery bypass grafting. Ann Thorac Cardiovasc Surg 2005;11:25–8.
2. Andersson B, Nilsson J, Brandt J, Hoglund P, Andersson R. Gastrointestinal complications after cardiac surgery. Br J Surg 2005;92:326–33.
3. Sanisoglu I, Guden M, Bayramoglu Z, Sagbas E, Dibekoglu C, Sanisoglu SY, Akpinar B. Does off-pump CABG reduce gastrointestinal complications? Ann Thorac Surg 2004;77:619–25.
4. Takeuchi K, Buenaventura P, Cao-Danh H, Glynn P, Simplaceanu E, McGowan FX, del Nido PJ. Improved protection of the hypertrophied left ventricle by histidine-containing cardioplegia. Circulation 1995 Nov 1;92(9 Suppl):II395–9.
5. Byrne JG, Karavas AN, Adams DH, Aklog L, Aranki SF, Filsoufi F, Cohn LH. The preferred approach for mitral valve surgery after CABG: right thoracotomy, hypothermia and avoidance of LIMA-LAD graft. J Heart Valve Dis 2001;10:584–90.
6. Starzl TE, Todo S, Fung J, Demetris AJ, Venkataramman R, Jain A. FK 506 for liver, kidney, and pancreas transplantation. Lancet 1989;2:1000–4.
7. Mazzoni G, Koep L, Starzl T. Air embolus in liver transplantation. Transplant Proc 1979;11:267–8.
8. Meyer JA. Friedrich Trendelenburg and the surgical approach to massive pulmonary embolism. Arch Surg 1990;125:1202–5.

9. Te HS, Jeevanandam V, Millis JM, Cronin DC, Baker AL. Open cardiotomy for removal of migrating transjugular intrahepatic portosystemic shunt stent combined with liver transplantation. Transplantation 2001;71:1000–3.

10. Befeler AS, Schiano TD, Lissoos TW, Conjeevaram HS, Anderson AS, Millis JM, Albertucci M, Baker AL. Successful combined liver-heart transplantation in adults: report of three patients and review of the literature. Transplantation 1999;68:1423–7. Review.

11. Zimmerman AA, Howard TK, Huddleston CB. Combined lung and liver transplantation in a girl with cystic fibrosis. Can J Anaesth 1999;46:571–5.

12. Massad MG, Benedetti E, Pollak R, Chami YG, Allen BS, DeCastro MA, Wiley T, Layden TJ. Combined coronary bypass and liver transplantation: technical considerations. Ann Thorac Surg 1998;65:1130–2. Review.

13. Mitruka SN, Griffith BP, Kormos RL, Hattler BG, Pigula FA, Shapiro R, Fung JJ, Pham SM. Cardiac operations in solid-organ transplant recipients. Ann Thorac Surg 1997;64:1270–8.

14. Wallwork J, Williams R, Calne RY. Transplantation of liver, heart, and lungs for primary biliary cirrhosis and primary pulmonary hypertension. Lancet 1987;2:182–5.

15. Pivalizza EG, Ekpenyong UU, Sheinbaum R, Warters RD, Estrera AL, Saggi BH, Mieles LA. Very early intraoperative cardiac thromboembolism during liver transplantation. J Cardiothorac Vasc Anesth 2006;20:232–5.

16. Ramsay MA, Randall HB, Burton EC. Intravascular thrombosis and thromboembolism during liver transplantation: antifibrinolytic therapy implicated. Liver Transpl 2004;10:310–4.

17. De Weese JA. The role of pulmonary embolectomy in venous thromboembolism. J Cardiovasc Surg (Torino) 1976;17:348–53.

18. Manji M, Isaac JL, Bion J. Survival from massive intraoperative pulmonary thromboembolism during orthotopic liver transplantation. Br J Anaesth 1998;80:685–7.

19. Vignaux O, Borrego P, Macron L, Cariou A, Claessens YE. Cardiac gas embolism after central venous catheter removal. Undersea Hyperb Med 2005;32:325–6.

20. Thiery G, Le Corre F, Kirstetter P, Sauvanet A, Belghiti J, Marty J. Paradoxical air embolism during orthoptic liver transplantation: diagnosis by transoesophageal echocardiography. Eur J Anaesthesiol 1999;16:342–5.

21. Goksin I, Yilmaz A, Baltalarli A, Goktogan T, Karahan N, Turk UA, Kara H, Sagban M. Modified semicircular constricting annuloplasty (Sagban's annuloplasty) in severe functional tricuspid regurgitation: alternative surgical technique and its mid-term results. J Card Surg 2006;21:172–5.

22. Hirata N, Sakai K, Ohtani M, Sakaki S, Ohnishi K. Assessment of myocardial distribution of retrograde and antegrade cardioplegic solution in the same patients. Eur J Cardiothorac Surg 1997;12:242–7.

23. Boffa DJ, Tak V, Jansson SL, Ko W, Krishnasastry KV. Atheroemboli to superior mesenteric artery following cardiopulmonary bypass. Ann Vasc Surg 2002;16:228–30.

24. Kumbasar SD, Semiz E, Sancaktar O, Yalcinkaya S, Deger N. Mechanical complications of intra-aortic balloon counterpulsation. Int J Cardiol 1999;70:69–73.

25. Raja SG. Pump or no pump for coronary artery bypass: current best available evidence. Tex Heart Inst J 2005;32:489–501. Review.

26. El-Hamamsy I, Cartier R, Demers P, Bouchard D, Pellerin M. Long-term results after systematic off-pump coronary artery bypass graft surgery in 1000 consecutive patients. Circulation 2006;114(1 Suppl):I486–91.

27. Demirsoy E, Unal M, Arbatli H, Yagan N, Tukenmez F, Sonmez B. Extra-anatomic coronary artery bypass graftings in patients with porcelain aorta. J Cardiovasc Surg (Torino) 2004;45:111–5.

28. Vicol C, Oberhoffer M, Nollert G, Eifert S, Boekstegers P, Wintersperger B, Reichart B. First clinical experience with the HEARTSTRING, a device for proximal anastomoses in coronary surgery. Ann Thorac Surg 2005;79(5):1732–7.

29. Burke AP, Mezzetti T, Farb A, Zech ER, Virmani R. Multiple coronary artery graft occlusion in a fatal case of heparin-induced thrombocytopenia. Chest 1998;114:1492–5.

30. Gallo A, Davies RR, Coe MP, Elefteriades JA, Coady MA. Indications, timing, and progno-
    sis of operative repair of aortic dissections. Semin Thorac Cardiovasc Surg 2005;17:224–35.
31. Zeebregts CJ, Schepens MA, Vermeulen FE. Spontaneous resolution late after aortic dissec-
    tion. Eur J Cardiothorac Surg 1997;12:513–5.
32. Casula RP, Velissaris TJ, Dar M, Athanasiou T. Is early hospital discharge feasible following
    normothermic coronary artery surgery on the fibrillating heart? J Cardiovasc Surg (Torino)
    2003;44:583–9.
33. Minatoya K, Okabayashi H, Shimada I, Tanabe A, Nishina T, Nandate K, Kunihiro M. Inter-
    mittent antegrade warm blood cardioplegia for CABG: extended interval of cardioplegia.
    Ann Thorac Surg 2000;69:74–6.
34. Watts JA, Zagorski J, Gellar MA, Stevinson BG, Kline JA. Cardiac inflammation con-
    tributes to right ventricular dysfunction following experimental pulmonary embolism in rats.
    J Mol Cell Cardiol 2006;41:296–307.
35. Yoshitatsu M, Nomura F, Izutani H, Toda K, Katayama A, Tamura K, Katayama K, Ihara K.
    Impact of ostial stenosis on the Doppler flow profiles in internal thoracic artery graft. Circ J
    2005;69:253–6.
36. Fortier S, Demaria RG, Perrault LP. Subclavian artery stenosis impairs flow in left internal
    mammary artery grafts. Ann Thorac Surg 2002;74:1293–4.
37. Tabel Y, Hepaguslar H, Erdal C, Catalyurek H, Acikel U, Elar Z, Aslan O. Diltiazem pro-
    vides higher internal mammary artery flow than nitroglycerin during coronary artery bypass
    grafting surgery. Eur J Cardiothorac Surg 2004;25:553–9.
38. Castano M, Silva J, Fortuny R, Lopez J, Vallejo JL. Internal thoracic artery atherosclerosis
    after coarctation repair in an adult. Ann Thorac Surg 1998;66:1424–6.
39. Charitou A, Panesar SS, DeL Stanbridge R, Athanasiou T. Novel use of a magnetic coupling
    device to repair damage of the internal thoracic artery. J Card Surg 2006;21:89–91.
40. Del Campo C. Pedicled or skeletonized? A review of the internal thoracic artery graft. Tex
    Heart Inst J 2003;30(3):170–5. Review.
41. L'allier PL, Lesperance J. Role of angiography for the assessment of coronary artery disease
    in patients with diabetes mellitus. Can J Cardiol 2006;22 Suppl A:34–7.
42. Escolar E, Weigold G, Fuisz A, Weissman NJ. New imaging techniques for diagnosing coro-
    nary artery disease. CMAJ 2006;174:487–95. Review.
43. Oz MC, Cooper MM, Hickey TJ, Rose EA. Exposure of the intramyocardial left anterior
    descending artery. Ann Thorac Surg 1994;58:1194–5.
44. Rajappan K, Rimoldi OE, Dutka DP, Ariff B, Pennell DJ, Sheridan DJ, Cam-
    ici PG. Mechanisms of coronary microcirculatory dysfunction in patients with aor-
    tic stenosis and angiographically normal coronary arteries. Circulation 2002;105(4):
    470–6.
45. Chehal MK, Granville DJ. Cytochrome p450 2C (CYP2C) in ischemic heart injury and
    vascular dysfunction. Can J Physiol Pharmacol 2006;84:15–20.
46. Cannon RO 3rd. Mechanisms, management and future directions for reperfusion
    injury after acute myocardial infarction. Nat Clin Pract Cardiovasc Med 2005;2:88–94.
    Review.
47. Johnson WM, Smith JM, Woods SE, Hendy MP, Hiratzka LF. Cardiac surgery in octogenar-
    ians: does age alone influence outcomes? Arch Surg 2005;140:1089–93.
48. Houser SL, Hashmi FH, Lehmann TJ, Chawla SK. Cardiac surgery in octogenarians: are the
    risks too high? Conn Med 1988;52:579–81.
49. Chiappini B, Camurri N, Loforte A, Di Marco L, Di Bartolomeo R, Marinelli G. Outcome
    after aortic valve replacement in octogenarians. Ann Thorac Surg 2004;78:85–9. Review.
50. Takenoshita M, Sugiyama M, Okuno Y, Inagaki Y, Yoshiya I, Shimazaki Y. Anaphylactoid
    reaction to protamine confirmed by plasma tryptase in a diabetic patient during open heart
    surgery. Anesthesiology 1996;84:233–5.
51. Bozbuga N, Erentug V, Erdogan HB, Kirali K, Ardal H, Tas S, Akinci E, Yakut C. Surgical
    treatment of aortic abscess and fistula. Tex Heart Inst J 2004;31:382–6.

52. Graupner C, Vilacosta I, SanRoman J, Ronderos R, Sarria C, Fernandez C, Mujica R, Sanz O, Sanmartin JV, Pinto AG. Periannular extension of infective endocarditis. J Am Coll Cardiol 2002;39:1204–11.

53. Yankah AC, Pasic M, Klose H, Siniawski H, Weng Y, Hetzer R. Homograft reconstruction of the aortic root for endocarditis with periannular abscess: a 17-year study. Eur J Cardiothorac Surg 2005;28:69–75.

54. Bolcal C, Iyem H, Sargin M, Mataraci I, Sahin MA, Temizkan V, Yildirim V, Demirkilic U, Tatar H. Gastrointestinal complications after cardiopulmonary bypass: sixteen years of experience. Can J Gastroenterol 2005;19:613–7.

55. Muniz AE, Evans T. Acute gastrointestinal manifestations associated with use of crack. Am J Emerg Med 2001;19:61–3.

56. Fradet G, Bleese N, Busse E, Jamieson E, Raudkivi P, Goldstein J, Metras J. The mosaic valve clinical performance at seven years: results from a multicenter prospective clinical trial. J Heart Valve Dis 2004;13:239–46.

57. Wong SP, Legget ME, Greaves SC, Barratt-Boyes BG, Milsom FP, Raudkivi PJ. Early experience with the mosaic bioprosthesis: a new generation porcine valve. Ann Thorac Surg 2000;69:1846–50.

58. Kouris N, Ikonomidis I, Kontogianni D, Smith P, Nihoyannopoulos P. Mitral valve repair versus replacement for isolated non-ischemic mitral regurgitation in patients with preoperative left ventricular dysfunction. A long-term follow-up echocardiography study. Eur J Echocardiogr 2005;6:435–42.

59. Madjdpour C, Heindl V, Spahn DR. Risks, benefits, alternatives and indications of allogenic blood transfusions. Minerva Anestesiol 2006;72:283–98.

60. Wigfield CH, Lindsey JD, Munoz A, Chopra PS, Edwards NM, Love RB. Is extreme obesity a risk factor for cardiac surgery? An analysis of patients with a BMI > or = 40. Eur J Cardiothorac Surg 2006;29:434–40. Review.

61. Scognamiglio R, Negut C, Ramondo A, Tiengo A, Avogaro A. Detection of coronary artery disease in asymptomatic patients with type 2 diabetes mellitus. J Am Coll Cardiol 2006;47:65–71.

62. Choudhary SK, Talwar S, Juneja R, Kumar AS. Fate of mild aortic valve disease after mitral valve intervention. J Thorac Cardiovasc Surg 2001;122:583–6.

63. Gammie JS, Brown JW, Brown JM, Poston RS, Peirson RN 34e, Odonkor PN, White CS, Gottdiener JS, Griffith BP. Aortic valve bypass for the high-risk patient with aortic stenosis. Ann Thorac Surg 2006;81:1605–10.

64. Westerberg M, Gabel J, Bengtsson A, Sellgren J, Eidem O, Jeppsson A. Hemodynamic effects of cardiotomy suction blood. J Thorac Cardiovasc Surg 2006;131:1352–7.

65. Mehta RH, Manfredini R, Hassan F, Sechtem U, Bossone E, Oh JK, Cooper JV, Smith DE, Portaluppi F, Penn M, Hutchison S, Nienaber CA, Isselbacher EM, Eagle KA; International Registry of Acute Aortic Dissection (IRAD) investigators. Chronobiological patterns of acute aortic dissection. Circulation 2002;106:1110–5.

66. Roberts WC. Frequency of systemic hypertension in various cardiovascular diseases. Am J Cardiol 1987;60:1E–8E. Review.

67. Okuda M. A multidisciplinary overview of cardiogenic shock. Shock 2006;25:557–70. Review.

68. Buckberg GD. Stroke and extra-cardiac perfusion: new vantage points in brain protection. Eur J Cardiothorac Surg 2004;26 Suppl 1:S62–5; discussion S65–7. Review.

69. Immer FF, Lippeck C, Barmettler H, Berdat PA, Eckstein FS, Kipfer B, Saner H, Schmidli J, Carrel TP. Improvement of quality of life after surgery on the thoracic aorta: effect of antegrade cerebral perfusion and short duration of deep hypothermic circulatory arrest. Circulation 2004;110(11 Suppl 1):II250–5. Review.

70. Zwischenberger BA, Clemson LA, Zwischenberger JB. Artificial lung: progress and prototypes. Expert Rev Med Devices 2006;3:485–97.

71. Huang SC, Wu ET, Chen YS, Chang CI, Chiu IS, Chi NH, Wu MH, Wang SS, Lin FY, Ko WJ. Experience with extracorporeal life support in pediatric patients after cardiac surgery. ASAIO J 2005;51:517–21.

72. Pandya A, Braverman N, Pyeritx RE et al. Interstitial deletion of the long arm of chromosome 6 associated with unusual limb anomalies: report of two new patients and review of the literature. Am J Med Genet 1995;59:38–43.

73. Sulaumar S, Wang S, Hoang K et al. Subtle overlapping deletions in the terminal region of chromosome 6q242–q26: three cases studied using FISH. Am J Med Genet 1999;87: 17–22.

74. Wakahama Y, Nakayama M, Rujimura A. Autopsy findings in interstitial deletion 6q. Pediatric Pathol 1991;11(1):97–103.

75. Kohli V, Nooreyazdan S, Das BN, Kaul S, Singh J, Parmar V. Surgical reconstruction for absence of sternum and pericardium in a newborn. Indian J Pediatr 2006;73:367–8.

76. Correa-Rivas MS, Matos-Llovet I, Garcia-Fragoso L. Pentalogy of cantrell: a case report with pathologic findings. Pediatr Dev Pathol 2004;7:649–52.

77. Mann D, Qu JZ, Mehta V. Congenital heart diseases with left-to-right shunts. Int Anesthesiol Clin 2004;42:45–58. Review.

78. Kalya AV, Tector AJ, Crouch JD, Downey FX, McDonald ML, Anderson AJ, Bartoszewski CJ, Hosenpud JD. Comparison of Novacor and HeartMate vented electric left ventricular assist devices in a single institution. J Heart Lung Transplant 2005;24:1973–5.

79. Mazzone M, La Sala M, Portale G, Ursella S, Forte P, Carbone L, Testa A, Pignataro G, Covino M, Gentiloni Silveri N. Review of dilated cardiomyopathies. Dilated cardiomyopathies and altered prothrombotic state: a point of view of the literature. Panminerva Med 2005;47:157–67. Review.

80. Pratt JW, Williams TE, Michler RE, Brown DA. Current indications for left thoracotomy in coronary revascularization and valvular procedures. Ann Thorac Surg 2000;70:1366–70.

81. Fleck T, Khazen C, Wolner E, Grabenwoger M. The incidence of reoperations in pacemaker recipients. Heart Surg Forum 2006;9:E779–82.

82. Filsoufi F, Salzberg SP, Coutu M, Adams DH. A three-dimensional ring annuloplasty for the treatment of tricuspid regurgitation. Ann Thorac Surg 2006;81:2273–7.

83. Calafiore AM, Di Mauro M. Bilateral internal mammary artery grafting. Expert Rev Cardiovasc Ther 2006;4:395–403.

84. Goldman S, Zadina K, Moritz T, Ovitt T, Sethi G, Copeland JG, Thottapurathu L, Krasnicka B, Ellis N, Anderson RJ, Henderson W; VA Cooperative Study Group #207/297/364. Long-term patency of saphenous vein and left internal mammary artery grafts after coronary artery bypass surgery: results from a Department of Veterans Affairs cooperative study. J Am Coll Cardiol 2004;44:2149–56.

85. Gaudino M, Cellini C, Pragliola C, Trani C, Burzotta F, Schiavoni G, Nasso G, Possati G. Arterial versus venous bypass grafts in patients with in-stent restenosis. Circulation 2005;112(9 Suppl):I265–9.

86. Berger A, MacCarthy PA, Vanermen H, De Bruyne B. Occlusion of internal mammary grafts: a review of the potential causative factors. Acta Chir Belg 2004;104:630–4. Review.

87. Grondin CM, Pomar JL, Hebert Y, Bosch X, Santos JM, Enjalbert M, Campeau L. Reoperation in patients with patent atherosclerotic coronary vein grafts. A different approach to a different disease. J Thorac Cardiovasc Surg 1984;87:379–85.

88. Garantziotis S, Bhalla KS, Long GD, Vredenburgh JJ, Folz RJ. Fatal re-expansion pulmonary edema associated with increased lung IL-8 levels following high-dose chemotherapy and autologous stem cell transplant. Respiration 2002;69:351–4.

89. Jackson RM, Veal CF. Re-expansion, re-oxygenation, and rethinking.Am J Med Sci 1989;298:44–50. Review.

90. Shapira OM, Natarajan V, Kaushik S, DeAndrade KM, Shemin RJ. Off-pump versus on-pump reoperative CABG via a left thoracotomy for circumflex coronary artery revascularization. J Card Surg 2004;19:113–8.

91. Natsuaki M, Itoh T, Okazaki Y, Rikitake K, Ohtubo S, Furukawa K. Risk factors associated with perioperative myocardial damage in patients with severe aortic stenosis. J Cardiovasc Surg (Torino) 2004;45:271–7.

92. Onorati F, Renzulli A, De Feo M, Santarpino G, Gregorio R, Biondi A, Cerasuolo F, Cotrufo M. Does antegrade blood cardioplegia alone provide adequate myocardial protection in patients with left main stem disease? J Thorac Cardiovasc Surg 2003;126:1345–51.

93. Noyez L, van Son JA, van der Werf T, Knape JT, Gimbrere J, van Asten WN, Lacquet LK, Flameng W. Retrograde versus antegrade delivery of cardioplegic solution in myocardial revascularization. A clinical trial in patients with three-vessel coronary artery disease who underwent myocardial revascularization with extensive use of the internal mammary artery. J Thorac Cardiovasc Surg 1993;105:854–63.

94. Hashimoto K. Patient-prosthesis mismatch: the Japanese experience. Ann Thorac Cardiovasc Surg 2006;12:159–65.

95. Castro LJ, Arcidi JM Jr, Fisher AL, Gaudiani VA. Routine enlargement of the small aortic root: a preventive strategy to minimize mismatch. Ann Thorac Surg 2002;74:31–6; discussion 36.

96. Petracek MR. Assessing options for the small aortic root. J Heart Valve Dis 2002;11 Suppl 1:S50–5. Review.

97. Santini F, Pentiricci S, Messina A, Mazzucco A. Coronary ostial enlargement to prevent stenosis after prosthetic aortic valve replacement. Ann Thorac Surg 2004;77:1854–6.

98. Iwama T, Asami K, Kubo I, Kitazume H. Hypertrophic cardiomyopathy complicated with acute myocardial infarction due to coronary embolism. Intern Med 1997;36:613–7.

99. Bodor E, Janosi A, Szilard D, Balogh O. Surgically treated intraoperative coronary embolism. Thorac Cardiovasc Surg 2006;54:142–4.

100. Bracco D, Noiseux N, Duong P, Prieto I, Basile F. Aortic vegetation and acute coronary embolism. Can J Cardiol 2006;22:113.

101. Gurtu R, Grocott-Mason R, Mason M, Ilsley C, William Dubrey S. Paradoxical coronary emboli following a long-haul airline flight. Eur J Echocardiogr 2007;8(5):390–2.

102. Shin J, Edelberg JE, Hong MK. Vulnerable atherosclerotic plaque: clinical implications. Curr Vasc Pharmacol 2003;1:183–204. Review.

103. Carter TL, Mainwaring RD, Lamberti JJ. Damus-Kaye-Stansel procedure: midterm follow-up and technical considerations. Ann Thorac Surg 1994;58:1603–8.

104. Lim HG, Kim WA, Lee YT, Han JJ, Kim SC, Lim C, Na CY. Staged biventricular repair of Taussig-Bing anomaly with subaortic stenosis and coarctation of aorta. Ann Thorac Surg 2003;76:1283–6.

105. Moulton AL, Brenner JI, Ringel R, Nordenberg A, Berman MA, Ali S, Burns J. Classic versus modified Blalock-Taussig shunts in neonates and infants. Circulation 1985;72: II35–44.

106. Schoen FJ, Edwards WD. Pathology of cardiovascular interventions, including endovascular therapies, revascularization, vascular replacement, cardiac assist/replacement, arrhythmia control, and repaired congenital heart disease. In: Silver MD, Gotlieb AI, Shoen FJ (eds.) Cardiovascular Pathology, 3rd edn., Churchill Livingstone, New York, 2001, p. 711.

107. Berger TJ, Kirklin JW, Blackstone EH, Pacifico AD, Kouchoukos NT. Primary repair of complete atrioventricular canal in patients less than 2 years old. Am J Cardiol 1978; 41:906–13.

108. Photiadis J, Hubler M, Sinzobahamvya N, Ovroutski S, Stiller B, Hetzer R, Urban AE, Asfour B. Does size matter? Larger Blalock-Taussig shunt in the modified Norwood operation correlates with better hemodynamics. Eur J Cardiothorac Surg 2005;28:56–60.

109. Stasik CN, Goldberg CS, Bove EL, Devaney EJ, Ohye RG. Current outcomes and risk factors for the Norwood procedure. J Thorac Cardiovasc Surg 2006;131:412–7.

110. Pizarro C, Malec E, Maher KO, Januszewska K, Gidding SS, Murdison KA, Baffa JM, Norwood WI. Right ventricle to pulmonary artery conduit improves outcome after stage I Norwood for hypoplastic left heart syndrome. Circulation 2003;108 Suppl 1:II155–60.

111. Walker SG, Stuth EA. Single-ventricle physiology: perioperative implications. Semin Pediatr Surg 2004;13:188–202. Review.
112. Singh TP, Vasquez JC, Delius R, Walters HL 3rd. Neonatal heart transplantation to a physiologic single lung. J Heart Lung Transplant 2006;25:362–4.
113. Hoskote A, Bohn D, Gruenwald C, Edgell D, Cai S, Adatia I, Van Arsdell G. Extracorporeal life support after staged palliation of a functional single ventricle: subsequent morbidity and survival. J Thorac Cardiovasc Surg 2006;131:1114–21.
114. Shaffer KM, Denfield SW, Schowengerdt KO, Towbin JA, Radovancevic B, Frazier OH, Price JK, Gajarski RJ. Cardiac transplantation for pediatric patients. With inoperable congenital heart disease. Tex Heart Inst J 1998;25:57–63.
115. Braun S, Schrotter H, Schmeisser A, Strasser RH. Evaluation of pulmonary vascular response to inhaled iloprost in heart transplant candidates with pulmonary venous hypertension. Int J Cardiol 2007;115:67–72.
116. Delgado JF, Conde E, Sanchez V, Lopez-Rios F, Gomez-Sanchez MA, Escribano P, Sotelo T, Gomez de la Camara A, Cortina J, de la Calzada CS. Pulmonary vascular remodeling in pulmonary hypertension due to chronic heart failure. Eur J Heart Fail 2005;7:1011–6.
117. Kjellman UW, Shariari A, Svensson G, Wiklund L, Bengtsson A, Ekroth R. Predictors of allograft ischemic injury in clinical heart transplantation. Scand Cardiovasc J 2002;36:313–8.
118. Tanaka M, Gunawan F, Terry RD, Inagaki K, Caffarelli AD, Hoyt G, Tsao PS, Mochly-Rosen D, Robbins RC. Inhibition of heart transplant injury and graft coronary artery disease after prolonged organ ischemia by selective protein kinase C regulators. J Thorac Cardiovasc Surg 2005;129:1160–7.
119. Gaudin PB, Rayburn BK, Hutchins GM, Kasper EK, Baughman KL, Goodman SN, Lecks LE, Baumgartner WA, Hruban RH. Peritransplant injury to the myocardium associated with the development of accelerated arteriosclerosis in heart transplant recipients. Am J Surg Pathol 1994;18:338–46.
120. Grauhan O, Patzurek J, Hummel M, Lehmkuhl H, Dandel M, Pasic M, Weng Y, Hetzer R. Donor-transmitted coronary atherosclerosis. J Heart Lung Transplant 2003;22:568–73.
121. Miralles A, Serrano T, Calbet JM, Castells E. Early graft failure after heart transplantation due to coronary artery embolization with myocardial tissue. Eur J Cardiothorac Surg 1996;10:916–8.
122. Reinsmoen NL, Nelson K, Zeevi A. Anti-HLA antibody analysis and crossmatching in heart and lung transplantation. Transpl Immunol 2004;13:63–71. Review.
123. Rodriguez ER, Skojec DV, Tan CD, Zachary AA, Kasper EK, Conte JV, Baldwin WM 3rd. Antibody-mediated rejection in human cardiac allografts: evaluation of immunoglobulins and complement activation products C4d and C3d as markers. Am J Transplant 2005;5:2778–85.
124. Moll S, Pascual M. Humoral rejection of organ allografts. Am J Transplant 2005;5:2611–8. Review.
125. Park KY, Park CH, Chun YB, Shin MS, Lee KC. Bicaval anastomosis reduces tricuspid regurgitation after heart transplantation. Asian Cardiovasc Thorac Ann 2005;13:251–4.

Chapter 6
Congenital Heart Disease and Surgical Footprints

Abstract The purpose of this chapter is to illustrate and discuss a series of cases of congenital heart disease that will provide for some pathologists in practice, and particularly for those in training, a point of reference by which skills can be developed in this area of complex morphologic changes of the heart and what they mean at autopsy. Images of a collection of formalin-fixed hearts with congenital defects of variable complexity will be presented. Surgical approaches will be discussed in an attempt to reinforce the need for the pathologist to identify those "footprints" described earlier in this manuscript. The final case in this chapter, although not an example of congenital heart disease, will signal caution to the observer to maintain an overall perspective when examining the heart.

Keywords Congenital heart disease · Pathophysiology · Combined anomalies · Hemodynamic insults

A report four years ago [1] indicated that congenital heart disease (CHD) has a prevalence of 1 in 100 live births and accounts for most of prenatal deaths. It went on to say that 3 per 1000 live births will need an intervention, either catheter-based or surgical, to correct congenital heart defects in the first year of life. The Congenital Cardiac Defects Committee of the American Heart Association recently reported that the population of adults with CHD is growing by about 5% per year and, accordingly, that adults living with CHD have for the first time exceeded the number of children with the disease [2]. Although these authors focus in their reports on the scientific progress that has already been made and yet needs to be made regarding our understanding of the etiology of CHD, their data are relevant to this manuscript by revealing an ongoing need on the part of the pathologist at autopsy to be on the lookout for complex congenital heart defects either with or without surgical treatment and to be able to interpret the anatomic and physiologic impact of these findings.

The purpose of this chapter then is to illustrate and discuss a series of cases of CHD that will provide for some pathologists in practice, and particularly for those in training, a point of reference by which skills can be developed in this area of complex morphologic changes of the heart and what they mean at autopsy.

S.L. Houser, *The Operated Heart at Autopsy*, DOI 10.1007/978-1-60327-808-9_6,
© Humana Press, a part of Springer Science+Business Media, LLC 2009

An exhaustive review of the pathology of congenital heart disease is beyond the scope of this chapter and is not the intent of this author. However, a few guidelines to consider when thinking about CHD include the following:

1. Was the resulting pathophysiology one of cyanotic or noncyanotic heart disease?
2. Can an etiology be determined, i.e., related to drugs, chemicals, or infections?
3. Is the congenital defect isolated or in association with other cardiac and/or non-cardiac defects?
4. Can a known syndrome be associated with the cardiac findings?
5. How amenable is the CHD to medical and/or surgical treatment?

Images of a collection of formalin-fixed hearts with congenital defects will be presented. The anomalies will vary in a range of complexity from straightforward, simple defects to multiple, combined anomalies. Some defects have been untreated, and surgical approaches will be discussed. Other specimens will demonstrate important "footprints" of surgical treatment that have been a focus of this manuscript. After reviewing this series of hearts, the reader will hopefully have a better understanding of how to approach findings of CHD at autopsy.

Epstein's Anomaly

Here (Fig. 6.1), we are looking into the right ventricle of an explanted heart. Because of the need to preserve native atrial tissue for incorporating the allograft expediently, the surgeon has mobilized the explant at the plane of the skeletal axis of the heart. The patient underwent a cardiac transplantation because of a congeni-

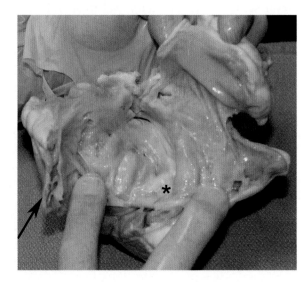

Fig. 6.1 The right ventricular myocardium of an explanted heart binds an extension of redundant tricuspid valve leaflet tissue all the way to the apex (*asterisk*), giving the impression of expansion of the right atrium, or right atrialization of the right ventricle

tal anomaly that compromised right ventricular outflow. Notice the extension of redundant tricuspid valve leaflet tissue all the way to the apex of the right ventricle (asterisk). The leaflet tissue is bound to the underlying myocardium of the right ventricle, in effect, giving the impression of expansion of the right atrium, or right atrialization, of the right ventricle, which is the essence of Epstein's anomaly. The inflow portion of the right ventricular wall can be paper thin (arrow) in this anomaly. Forceps (Fig. 6.2, arrow) from the right ventricular outflow tract demonstrate the hemodynamically significant comprise of flow of blood from the right ventricle by redundant tricuspid valve leaflet tissue. Figure 6.3 clearly shows the degree to which blood flow through the right ventricular outflow tract (arrow) was compromised.

Fig. 6.2 Forceps (*arrow*) from the right ventricular outflow tract demonstrate the hemodynamically significant compromise of flow of blood from the right ventricle by redundant tricuspid valve leaflet tissue

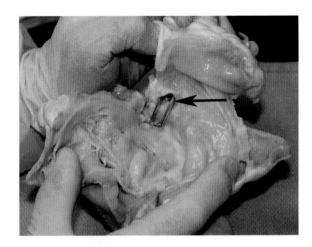

The heart in Fig. 6.4 illustrates an Epstein's anomaly treated by replacement of the tricuspid valve with a tilting disk (Bjork-Shiley) prosthesis, correcting a hemodynamically significant tricuspid valve insufficiency. Similar to the case above, redundant tricuspid valve leaflet tissue extends all the way to the apex of a dilated right ventricle, with extensive attachment to underlying myocardium. However, flow through the right ventricular outflow tract (arrow) in this heart is not compromised. Figure 6.5 shows a markedly dilated right atrium, a result of long-standing tricuspid valve regurgitation. Note the pericardial patch (asterisk) over the secundum atrial septal defect, which is commonly present in this anomaly. The extent of the right atrial dilatation is somewhat difficult to appreciate. Interestingly, a eustacian valve (arrowhead) adds to the complexity of this anomalous heart and may have frustrated the surgeon at the time of passage of the right atrial cannula into the inferior vena cava (double asterisk). Finally, a permanent epicardial pacemaker wire (arrow) is implanted in the right atrial wall, a surgical maneuver commonly done when a long-term need for a pacemaker is necessary. Not shown is a similar wire placed on the right ventricular wall.

Epstein first described this cardiac anomaly in 1866, and it now represents less than 1% of all congenital heart defects [3]. Illustrated by these two hearts are the

Fig. 6.3 Flow from the right
ventricle into the pulmonary
artery is compromised to a
marked degree (*arrow*)

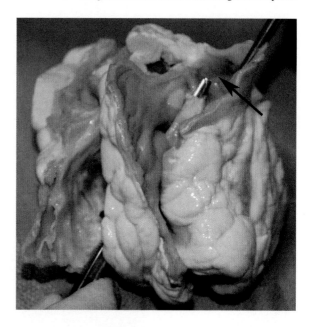

Fig. 6.4 Epstein's anomaly
treated by replacement of the
tricuspid valve with a tilting
disk (Bjork-Shiley)
prosthesis, correcting a
hemodynamically significant
tricuspid valve insufficiency.
Flow through the right
ventricular outflow tract
(*arrow*) is not compromised
by redundant valve leaflet
tissue

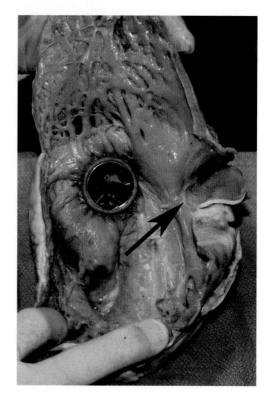

Fig. 6.5 A dilated right atrium reveals a pericardial patch (*asterisk*) over a secundum atrial septal defect. A eustacian valve (*arrowhead*) overlies the inferior vena cava (*double asterisk*). A permanent epicardial pacemaker wire (*arrow*) is implanted in the right atrial wall

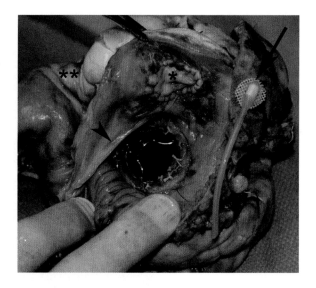

characteristic features of this anomaly, including adherence of the tricuspid valve leaflet tissue to the underlying ventricular myocardium, apical displacement of a functional tricuspid annulus, a dilated (atrialized) inflow portion of the right ventricle with variable thinning of the ventricular wall, a redundant anterior tricuspid leaflet, and a dilated true tricuspid annulus. As Carpentier et al. [4] pointed out, the clinical course of patients with this anomaly is determined by the adequacy of the right ventricular volume, the degree of restriction of the anterior tricuspid leaflet, and the degree of obstruction of the RVOT. An associated ASD, which we note above, can result in a significant right-to-left shunt and cyanosis and requires closure if the heart is salvageable.

Single Ventricle

Figure 6.6 shows cross-sections of an adult heart with an anomalous single ventricle. In the upper panel, note the absence of an interventricular septum. A probe and forceps pass through the tricuspid and mitral valves, respectively, into a common chamber, the wall of which is concentrically thickened. In Fig. 6.7, a dome-shaped, tightly stenotic pulmonary valve (arrow) is visualized through a dilated main pulmonary artery. Because of this pulmonary valve stenosis, the lungs had escaped volume overload and the commonly fatal pulmonary edema associated with anomalous single ventricles. Approximately one-third of these patients will have a so-called balanced circulation as a result of pulmonary valve stenosis and may survive 10 years or more [5].

In contrast, the heart in Fig. 6.8 is that of an infant with a single ventricle (asterisk) and no pulmonary valve stenosis to prevent pulmonary edema and

Fig. 6.6 These cross-sections
of an adult heart with an
anomalous single ventricle
lack an interventricular
septum. A probe and forceps
pass through the tricuspid and
mitral valves, respectively,
into a common chamber, the
wall of which is
concentrically thickened

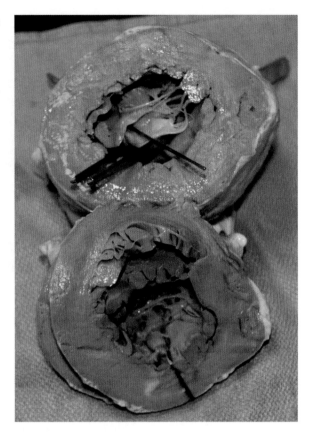

provide the balance in circulation necessary for these individuals to survive very
long. In addition, a large right atrium (asterisk), seen in Fig. 6.9, is explained
by the next image (Fig. 6.10), showing right-to-left passage of a probe through a
PFO, which, because of a tricuspid atresia (not well illustrated below the probe),
reflects the only means of right atrial decompression during the short life of the
patient. An early surgical option of banding the PA [6] was probably passed over
in view of the complicating tricuspid valve atresia. However, surgical intervention
to establish cavopulmonary circulation can be considered in some cases of tricuspid
atresia [7].

In univentricular hearts, the ventricular structure may have the morphology of
a normal right ventricle, normal left ventricle, or neither. There are usually two
atria, either with both AV valves opening into the single ventricle or one atretic
AV valve, both occurrences illustrated by the cases above. With mixing of systemic venous return and pulmonary venous return in the ventricle, cyanosis can
result. The clinical course, as described above, will be determined by how much
blood flows into the lungs from the single ventricle. Definitive surgical repair entails
construction of an artificial septum, so-called septation. Although the criteria for

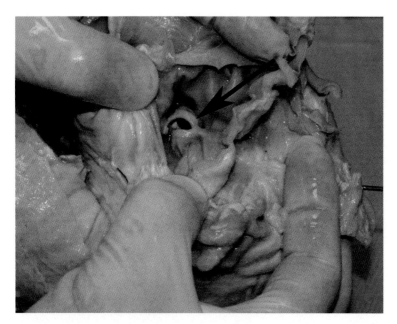

Fig. 6.7 A dome-shaped, tightly stenotic pulmonary valve (*arrow*) is visualized through a dilated main pulmonary artery

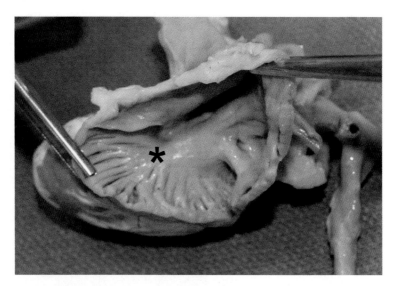

Fig. 6.8 An infant heart with a single ventricle (*asterisk*) lacks a protective pulmonary valve stenosis to prevent pulmonary edema and provide the balance in circulation necessary for long-term survival

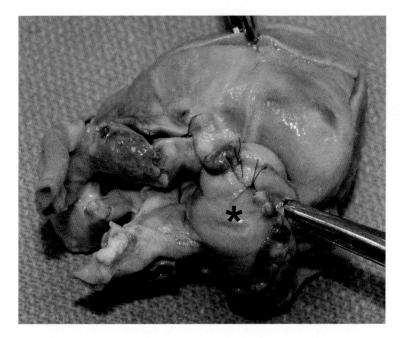

Fig. 6.9 The right atrium (*asterisk*) is dilated

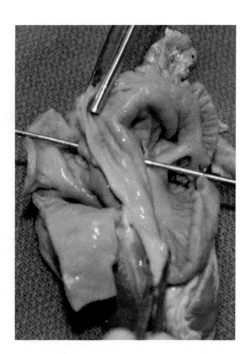

Fig. 6.10 A right-to-left passage of a probe through a PFO is illustrated

proceeding with this operation are strict, and the mortality rate has been relatively high, a report by Margossian et al. [8] suggests the procedure may be a
reasonable alternative to the Fontan operation in some patients with univentricular
hearts.

Double Outlet Right Ventricle

This adult heart (Fig. 6.11) demonstrates a very uncommon [9] congenital anomaly.
One notes that both the aorta (arrow head) and pulmonary artery (arrow) drain a
very hypertrophic and dilated right ventricle, hence, a so-called double-outlet right
ventricle (DORV). Common in this anomaly is a ventricular septal defect, through
which forceps pass from left to right. The tricuspid valve, seen just below the tip
of the forceps, and mitral valve are commonly continuous through the VSD. The
orientation of the VSD is relevant to classifying the type of DORV [10]. The VSD
can commit to the pulmonary valve, aortic valve, both the aortic and pulmonary
valves (doubly committed), or to neither valve (noncommitted). When the pulmonary trunk mildly overrides the VSD, a so-called Taussig-Bing anomaly exists.
In patients with this anomaly, an arterial switch operation has been favored by some
surgeons [11].

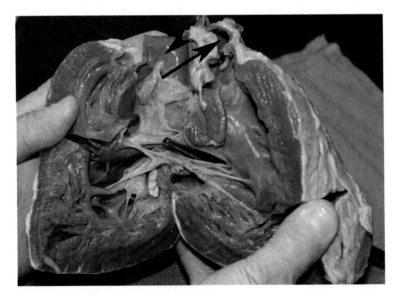

Fig. 6.11 In a double-outlet right ventricle (DORV), the aorta (*arrow head*) and pulmonary artery
(*arrow*) drain a very hypertrophic and dilated right ventricle. There is a ventricular septal defect,
through which forceps pass from left to right. The tricuspid valve, seen just below the tip of the
forceps, and mitral valve are commonly continuous through the VSD

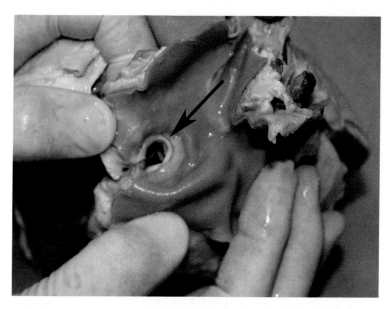

Fig. 6.12 A pulmonary valve stenosis is visualized through a dilated main pulmonary artery

In the case illustrated, the VSD appears to be committed essentially to the aorta, and the pulmonary trunk emerges completely from the right ventricle. Another interesting finding in this heart is a significant pulmonary valve stenosis (Fig. 6.12), which is seen here through a dilated main pulmonary artery. Similar to the case of a single ventricle described above, pulmonary stenosis in the patient with DORV prevents excessive perfusion of the lungs and early, clinically intolerable pulmonary edema. The complexities of surgical treatment in a spectrum of patients with DORV are discussed in a review by Bradley and colleagues [12].

AV Canal Defect

An atrioventricular canal defect, also known as endocardial cushion disease (Fig. 6.13) is a complex congenital anomaly. A VSD (arrow) subtends a combined anterior leaflet of an anomalous atrioventricular canal that needs to be fixed. Note the attachment of the clefted anterior leaflet of the common AV valve (arrowhead) to the anterior papillary muscle of the right ventricle, consistent with a type II Rastelli AV canal disorder [13, 14]. In addition to the primum ASD (below the band of tissue bound by a string), there is a secundum ASD above the band of septal tissue, which would require an additional patch of parietal pericardium for closure. As a result of the hemodynamic stress on the right ventricle due to the

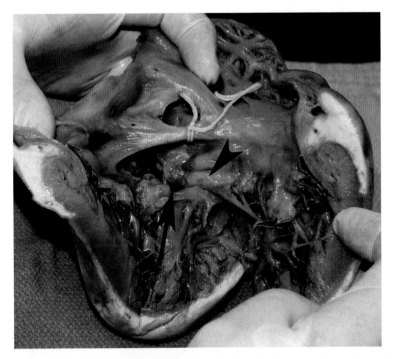

Fig. 6.13 A VSD (*arrow*) subtends a combined anterior leaflet of an anomalous atrioventricular canal. The clefted anterior leaflet of the common AV valve (*arrowhead*) has chordal attachment to the anterior papillary muscle of the right ventricle

complex shunting of blood in the heart, a notable right ventricular hypertrophy has developed.

Another heart (Fig. 6.14) nicely demonstrates a repair of a complete AV canal. A view into the right side of the heart reveals the endothelialized patch closure of the VSD (arrow) and septum primum ASD (arrowhead), which are bounded above by the fossa ovalis (asterisk), on the left by the posterior leaflet of the tricuspid valve (double asterisk), and on the right by the anterior leaflet of the tricuspid valve (triple asterisk). One can even see blue "dots" of suture material surrounding the patches, a definitive "footprint" of a surgeon who has spent time and effort inside this heart in the past.

A patch repair of an A-V canal defect in this heart (Fig. 6.15) closes both a VSD and septum primum ASD. Note the Dacron pledgets (arrows) used by the surgeon to buttress the sutures used to sew in the patch to the muscular wall around the defects. The fossa ovalis (asterisk) is seen above the patch. Valvular tissue eludes identification in this image. The importance of making an accurate assessment of surgical anatomy and preservation of valve tissue in patients undergoing repair of AV canal defects has long been known [15].

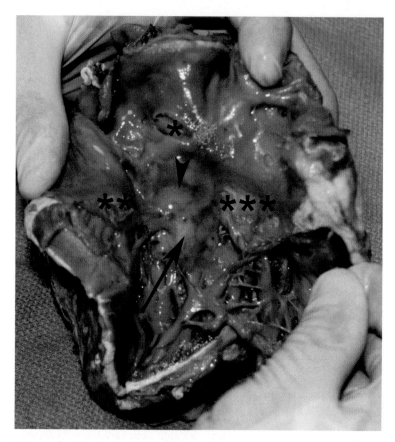

Fig. 6.14 A repair of a complete AV canal consists of an endothelialized patch closure of the VSD (*arrow*) and septum primum ASD (*arrowhead*), which are bounded above by the fossa ovalis (*asterisk*), on the left by the posterior leaflet of the tricuspid valve (*double asterisk*), and on the right by the anterior leaflet of the tricuspid valve (*triple asterisk*). Blue "dots" of suture material are seen on the periphery of the patches

Fig. 6.15 A patch repair of an AV canal defect in this heart closes both a VSD and septum primum ASD. Dacron pledgets (*arrows*) were used by the surgeon to buttress the sutures used to sew in the patch to the muscular wall tissue eludes identification in this image around the defects. The fossa ovalis (*asterisk*) is seen above the patch

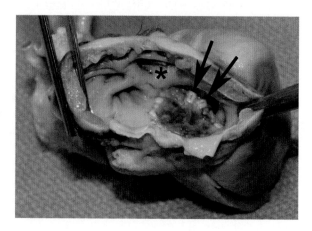

AQ

Ventricular Septal Defect

The most prevalent congenital anomaly of the heart is a VSD, and the commonest site of a VSD is behind the septal leaflet of the tricuspid valve, a so-called membranous, or perimembranous, VSD [16]. In Fig. 6.16, a probe is passing from the left ventricle into the right ventricle through such a defect. The defect is adjacent to the posterior leaflet of the tricuspid valve (arrow), which relates to the coronary sinus above (asterisk) and opposite the anterior leaflet of the tricuspid valve (arrowhead) subtended by the anterior papillary muscle (double asterisk). The thumb-width hypertrophy of the right ventricular free wall conveys the stress of the physiologic volume overload that the left-to-right shunt produced over time. This finding alone at autopsy would trigger in the mind of an astute pathologist a particular interest in examination of the lungs for evidence of pulmonary hypertension.

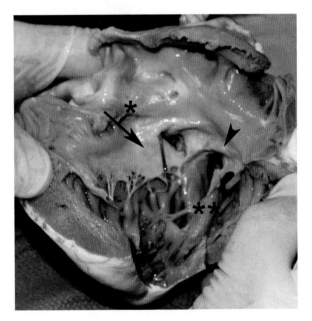

Fig. 6.16 A probe is passing from the left ventricle into the right ventricle through a VSD. The defect is adjacent to the posterior leaflet of the tricuspid valve (*arrow*), which relates to the coronary sinus above (*asterisk*) and opposite the anterior leaflet of the tricuspid valve (*arrowhead*) subtended by the anterior papillary muscle (*double asterisk*)

Beyond hemodynamic stress on the right side of the heart, a VSD left unprepared carries a risk of significant consequences. Figure 6.17 shows a probe passed from the left ventricle through a VSD into the right ventricle. Vegetations on the posterior and septal leaflets of the tricuspid valve (arrows) illustrate a frequently unrecognized complication of an unrepaired VSD, viz., valvular endocarditis. In Fig. 6.18, above the probe in the VSD, vegetations are found on the pulmonic valve as well (arrows). Here the valvular disease is in addition to marked RVH (arrowhead) and

Fig. 6.17 A probe passes from the left ventricle through a VSD into the right ventricle. Vegetations on the posterior and septal leaflets of the tricuspid valve (*arrows*) illustrate the presence of valvular endocarditis

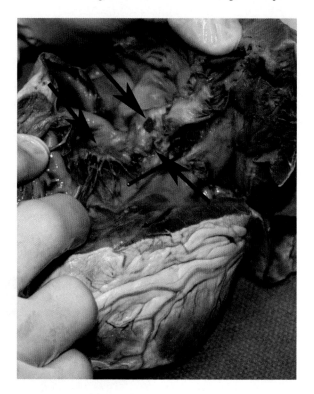

atherosclerotic plaque (asterisk) in the main pulmonary artery, clear evidence of pulmonary hypertension as a result of a long-standing left-to-right shunt through a large VSD.

VSDs can be supracristal, i.e., high in the RVOT above the crista supraventricularis, and they can occur in the muscular portion of the interventricular septum below the crista. The hemodynamic significance of the defect relates to its size, the left and right ventricular pressures, and the degree of pulmonary vascular resistance. Open surgical closure of the defect with a patch of prosthetic material, usually Dacron, is indicated before development of pulmonary hypertension, which can result in reversal of the left-to-right shunt (Eisenmenger syndrome). Closure is usually accomplished through a right atriotomy if the VSD is isolated to the membranous portion of the septum. Otherwise, or if associated with other anomalies, a right ventriculotomy may be used for access to repair the defect [17].

Tetralogy of Fallot

A piece of cloth in Fig. 6.19, Dacron in this case (asterisk), sewn into the anterior wall of the right ventricle (arrows pointing to sutures) over the right ventricular outflow tract (PA = pulmonary artery) is a major clue at autopsy that the

Fig. 6.18 Above the probe in the VSD, vegetations are found on the pulmonic valve (*arrows*). The marked RVH (*arrowhead*) and atherosclerotic plaque (*asterisk*) in the main pulmonary artery are clear evidence of pulmonary hypertension as well

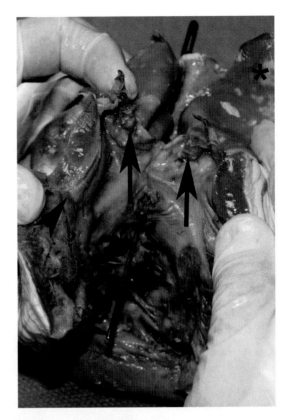

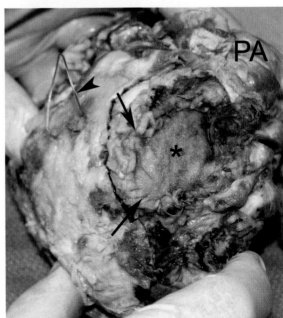

Fig. 6.19 A Dacron patch (*asterisk*) is sewn into the anterior wall of the right ventricle (arrows pointing to sutures) over the right ventricular outflow tract (PA = pulmonary artery). Adjacent to the patch is a temporary pacemaker wire (*arrowhead*)

deceased had undergone an operation to relieve a narrowing of the outflow tract and/or a pulmonary valve stenosis, commonly found in a tetralogy of Fallot (TOF). The infundibular obstruction in this anomaly is due to anterior displacement of a markedly thickened interventricular septum. Adjacent to the patch is a temporary pacemaker wire (arrowhead), which the surgeon placed onto the surface of the right ventricle as a matter of routine.

Figure 6.20 shows where interventricular septal muscle had been resected (arrow) to "open up" the RVOT obstruction in this heart. Above the surgical, muscular channel is a Dacron patch (arrowhead) used to close a VSD. Note also the marked hypertrophy of the right ventricular wall adjacent to the individual's thumb, depicting in this image the third of four characteristic features of TOF. Not seen here is the overriding aorta, which completes the tetralogy. However, if one looks at the ascending aorta (Fig. 6.21) from above (arrowhead) and passes a probe through the aortic valve (not done here), one gathers a sense of the aorta's overriding the right ventricle by observing the angle of direction taken by the probe. Note also in this heart the marked pulmonary valve stenosis, which may occur in place of or in association with an underlying infundibular stenosis, causing RVOT obstruction in a TOF.

Fig. 6.20 Interventricular septal muscle has been resected (*arrow*) to "open up" the RVOT obstruction in this heart. Above the surgical, muscular channel is a Dacron patch (*arrowhead*) used to close a VSD

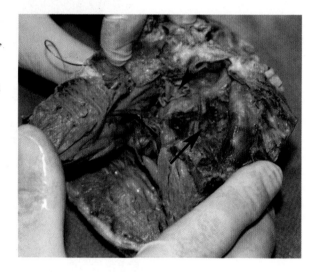

In the small heart of a younger patient, treatment of the associated stenotic pulmonary valve in TOF may not be amenable to valve replacement or mere valvulotomy. In Fig. 6.22, a Dacron graft (arrowhead) was sewn to the RVOT proximally and main pulmonary artery distally to improve blood flow to the lungs. In Fig. 6.23, the distal anastomosis (arrow) illustrates the technical challenge of connecting a tube graft to a relatively much smaller vessel. Looking at the RVOT from inside the right ventricle (Fig. 6.24), one sees the three leaflets of the bioprosthetic valve (arrows) which the tube graft had to accommodate in order to prevent unacceptable

Fig. 6.21 The ascending aorta (*arrowhead*) overrides the right ventricle. In addition, there is a marked pulmonary valve stenosis (*arrow*)

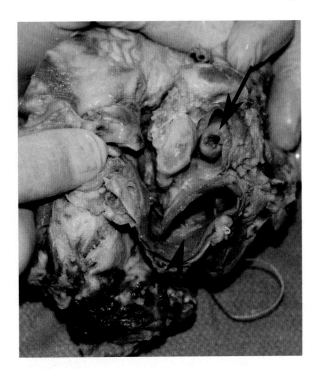

regurgitation of blood. Adjacent to the RVOT (asterisk) is a Dacron patch (arrowhead) closure of the VSD in this anomalous heart.

The heart in Fig. 6.25 is that of a 40-year-old male who died after one of a series of operations for another complex TOF. The epicardial blood is consistent with the patient's perioperative death. Note the old suture line closure of a previous right ventriculotomy over the outflow tract (arrow). In Fig. 6.26, note the remarkable biventricular hypertrophy (arrow points to the left anterior descending coronary artery). Opening the right side of this heart (Fig. 6.27), shows multiple important findings. Sequential pacemaker wires, a J-wire in the atrium and an endocardial ventricular lead below it, are evidence of a heart block, the etiology of which is of interest given the surgical repairs that are evident. The right atrium is markedly dilated and contains one side of a partially endothelialized Cardioseal, or clam shell, device (asterisk) reflecting a previous endovascular closure of a secundum ASD. The presence of a Carpentier-Edwards tricuspid valve annuloplasty ring (arrow) reflects prior valvular incompetence, which is common in association with annular dilatation due to significant remodeling associated with severe right ventricular hypertrophy [18]. Barely seen (arrowhead), is the patch closure of a VSD behind the septal leaflet of the tricuspid valve. Figure 6.28 shows a view of the right ventricular outflow tract above the apical pacemaker wire. Note the fibrosis (asterisk) marking the site of resection of muscle which had narrowed the infundibulum. In addition, an associated pulmonary valve stenosis had been corrected by replacement with a St. Jude

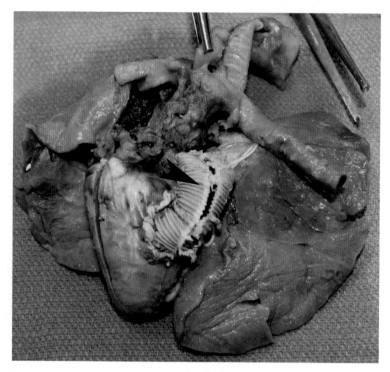

Fig. 6.22 A Dacron graft (*arrowhead*) is sewn to the RVOT proximally and the main pulmonary artery

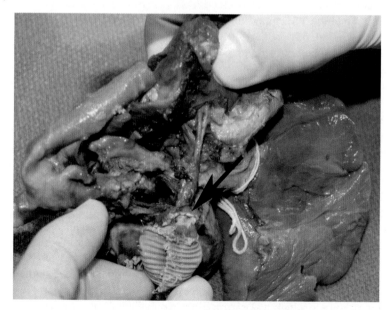

Fig. 6.23 The anastomosis of a tube graft to the main pulmonary artery (*arrow*) illustrates the technical challenge of connecting such a graft to a relatively much smaller vessel

Fig. 6.24 A view of the
RVOT from inside the right
ventricle shows the three
leaflets of the bioprosthetic
valve (*arrows*) which the tube
graft had to accommodate in
order to prevent unacceptable
regurgitation of blood.
Adjacent to the RVOT
(*asterisk*) is a Dacron patch
(*arrowhead*) closure of the
VSD in this anomalous heart

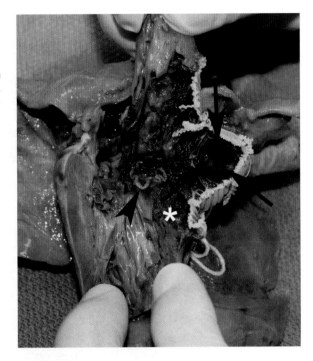

prosthesis (arrow). A second St. Jude prosthesis (Fig. 6.29, arrow) was also used to replace the native aortic valve, which had been made incompetent due to prolapse of the right coronary leaflet, presumably "pulled down" by the left-to-right shunt through a high VSD [19]. Note the suture line closure (arrowhead) of the ascending aortotomy used by the surgeon to gain access to the incompetent native aortic valve and replace it.

This saga of surgical efforts to address multiple hemodynamic insults in a heart with a complex congenital anomaly ended, unfortunately, with an operative problem. As a result of multiple previous operations, adhesions between the heart and great vessels, a reality which the informed pathologist understands at the time of autopsy, were "as usual" challenging. During the mobilizing of planes in order to gain access to the source of paravalvular aortic insufficiency, the left main coronary artery was inadvertently severed, which resulted in the death of the patient. This case illustrates the need for a pathologist at autopsy of a heart previously operated in a scenario of a complex congenital heart disease in order to understand, not only the disease, which the pathologist does with exceptional skill, but the "footprints of a surgeon" to a degree that the findings at autopsy simply fall into place rather than "defy understanding" on analysis. Verheugt et al. [20] have investigated the availability of data on long-term survival and morbidity in adults with common congenital heart defects and found that these data are sparse in adults over 40.

Fig. 6.25 The epicardial
blood is consistent with the
patient's perioperative death.
Note the old suture line
closure of a previous right
ventriculotomy over the
outflow tract (*arrow*)

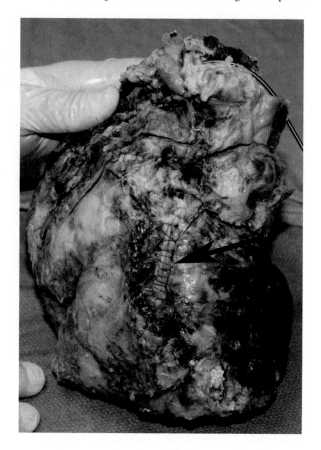

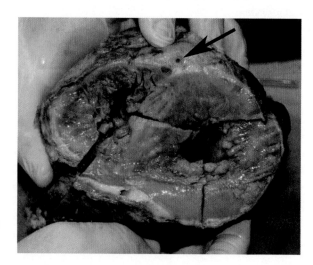

Fig. 6.26 Biventricular
hypertrophy is remarkable in
this heart (*arrow* points to the
left anterior descending
coronary artery)

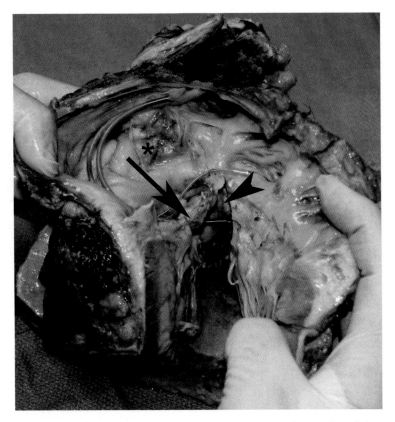

Fig. 6.27 Sequential pacemaker wires, a J-wire in the atrium and an endocardial ventricular lead below it, are well placed. The right atrium is markedly dilated and contains one side of a partially endothelialized Cardioseal, or clam shell, device (*asterisk*), reflecting a previous endovascular closure of a secundum ASD. A Carpentier-Edwards tricuspid valve annuloplasty ring (*arrow*) reflects prior valvular incompetence associated with severe right ventricular hypertrophy. Barely seen (*arrowhead*), is the patch closure of a VSD behind the septal leaflet of the tricuspid valve

Patent Foramen Ovale

Open repair of a patent foramen ovale (PFO), unlike that of most clinically significant secundum atrial septal defects, does not necessitate use of a patch, which usually comprises a piece of autologous parietal pericardium sewn over the defect with a running suture technique. Figure 6.30 shows two Dacron pledgets (arrows) used to buttress the simple suture closure of the relatively small entrance into the somewhat tunnel-like gap between the septum secundum and septum primum of a PFO, which allows an abnormal communication between the right and left atria, resulting in a risk of a paradoxical embolus [21]. For orientation, the posterior leaflet of the

Fig. 6.28 The right ventricular outflow tract above the apical pacemaker wire is fibrotic (*asterisk*), marking the site of resection of muscle which had narrowed the infundibulum. An associated pulmonary valve stenosis had been corrected by replacement with a St. Jude prosthesis (*arrow*)

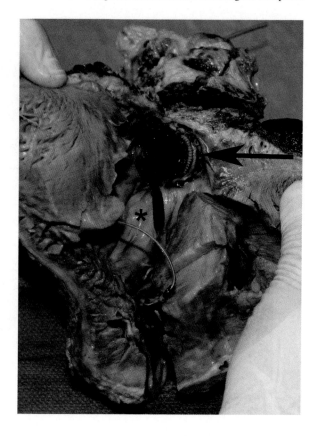

tricuspid valve and the overlying coronary sinus (arrowhead) can be seen below the fossa ovalis, which has been distorted somewhat by surgical manipulation. Endovascular closure of PFOs, as illustrated above, has its own distinct characterization at autopsy, and the pathologist needs to recognize it, in contrast to that of surgical closure. Wechsler [22] has made an important effort in current assessment of the need for PFO closure to prevent stroke, data of interest to pathologists as well as to clinicians.

Coronary Artery Anomaly

In addition to a thickened and calcified aortic valve, this autopsy specimen (Fig. 6.31) reveals a coronary artery anomaly which is a variant of the left-sided arteries originating from the right side, either from the right coronary sinus or from the proximal right coronary artery. Here the circumflex coronary artery (arrowhead) arises from the right coronary artery just beyond the right coronary sinus. Note the

Fig. 6.29 A St. Jude
prosthesis (*arrow*) was used
to replace the native aortic
valve. The suture line closure
(*arrowhead*) of the ascending
aortotomy marks the access
used by the surgeon to
replace the valve

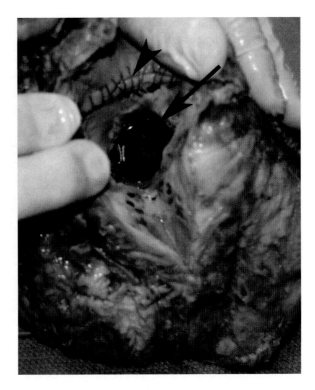

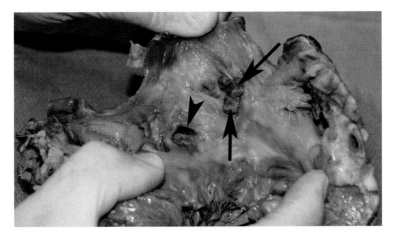

Fig. 6.30 Two Dacron pledgets (*arrows*) were used to buttress the simple suture closure of a
PFO. For orientation, the posterior leaflet of the tricuspid valve and overlying coronary sinus
(*arrowhead*) can be seen below the fossa ovalis, which has been distorted somewhat by surgical
manipulation

Fig. 6.31 The circumflex
coronary artery (*arrowhead*)
arises from the right coronary
artery just beyond the right
coronary sinus. A "pinhole"
opening (*arrow*) of the
circumflex vessel must have
compromised flow to the
lateral wall of the left
ventricle (*asterisk*). The left
anterior descending artery
(*double arrow*) had originated
normally from the left
coronary sinus, which here
has been removed

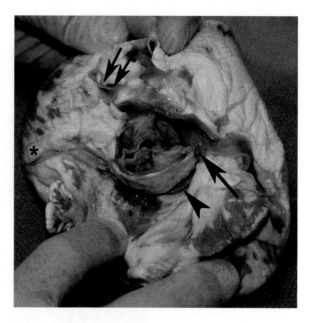

"pinhole" opening (arrow) of the circumflex vessel, which must have compromised flow to the lateral wall of the left ventricle (asterisk). Interestingly, the left anterior descending artery (double arrow) had originated normally from the left coronary sinus, which here has been removed.

When the left main coronary artery arises from the right side, the LAD can take one of four pathways to the anterior wall of the left ventricle [23–25]. It can pass dorsal, or posterior, to the aorta, as the circumflex did in this case. Alternatively, passing anterior to the aorta, the LAD can follow a course between the ascending aorta and main pulmonary artery, a situation which can lead to compression of the LAD between the two great vessels during vigorous exercise and sudden cardiac death due to myocardial ischemia. A second anomalous anterior course of the LAD is across the right ventricular outflow tract, which is known to occur in patients with TOF and at risk of injury at the time of right ventriculotomy for corrective surgery. Finally, the LAD from the right side can take an intramyocardial course through the parietal band at the base of the right ventricle. When the circumflex coronary artery arises from the proximal RCA, it takes one of two paths. One is between the pulmonary artery and aorta, and the other, as we see in this case, dorsal to the ascending aorta [26].

Coronary artery anomalies have been reported to appear in 0.64–5.5% of patients having coronary angiograms [27]. They have been classified according to their origination and course, intrinsic coronary arterial anatomy, coronary termination, and presence of anastomotic vessels that are anomalous [28]. In a significant number of cases, no intervention is necessary. However, when myocardial ischemia results from anomalous coronary anatomy, patients are at risk for sudden cardiac death without appropriate intervention [29]. In the case illustrated here, the pinhole-sized take-off of the anomalous circumflex could have resulted in fatal ischemia of the free wall of left ventricle, which was already thickened, and hence increasingly vulnerable to ischemia, as a result of aortic stenosis. The presence of this particular anomaly has been reported once before by Turkoglu and Ozdemir [24].

Bicuspid vs. Unicuspid Aortic Valve

Figure 6.32 shows an adult heart with bicuspid aortic valve, a congenital defect that affects about 1–2% of the population and brings patients to surgical aortic valve replacement a mean of 10 years sooner than patients with the much more common degenerative valve disease, which causes the so-called senile calcific aortic stenosis [30]. Note the raphe in place of the normal third commissure, which never formed in this valve. The thickened, calcific leaflets result in compromise of flow from the left ventricle and contribute to a long-term turbulence, the significance of which will be discussed shortly. For now, the reader might consider the impact of aortic stenosis requiring aortic valve replacement in a relatively young patient and, based on previous discussion in this manuscript, what type of valve prosthesis the patient and surgeon might choose in this setting.

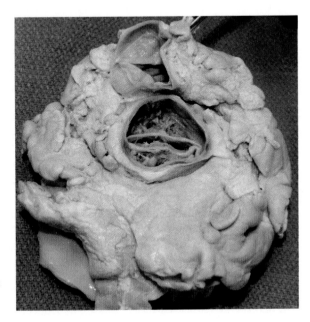

Fig. 6.32 An adult heart has a bicuspid aortic valve, which is stenotic and markedly calcified

Fig. 6.33 One leaflet of a
bicuspid aortic valve is
prolapsed (*asterisk*). The
raphe (*arrow*) deviates to the
right, adjacent to one of the
two developed commissures
(*arrowhead*)

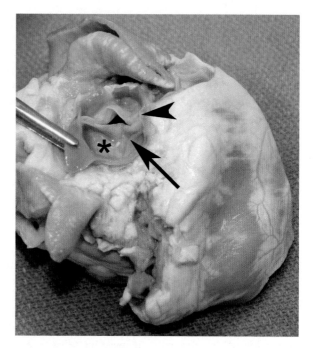

In another interesting heart (Fig. 6.33), one leaflet of a bicuspid aortic valve is prolapsed (asterisk). Note the raphe (arrow), which usually is seen in place of a third commissure that never develops. Instead of traversing the middle of one of the leaflets, the raphe here deviates to the right, adjacent to one of the two developed commissures (arrowhead). Such a deviant course appears to have resulted in a lack of support of the leaflet, leading to aortic regurgitation [31] instead of the more common scenario of aortic stenosis due to thickening and calcification of a congenitally abnormal aortic valve.

A remarkably aneurysmal ascending aorta in Fig. 6.34 is associated with a congenitally anomalous aortic valve, which appears to be unicuspid (arrowhead) with ill-formed raphes (arrows) replacing two absent commissures. In other words, the abnormal valve has the keyhole morphology of a unicuspid valve and lacks the typical two well-formed commissures of a bicuspid valve as were shown in the previous heart. Important here is the well-recognized association of ascending aortic dilatation and/or dissection with both types of congenital aortic valve disease [32]. Atherosclerosis in the ascending aorta (asterisk), although not surprising, is probably nonspecific in congenital aortic valve disease. Indeed, aortic dilatation and/or dissection associated with a unicuspid or bicuspid aortic valve is considered to be due to medial degeneration, which may be a result of long-standing, abnormally high level turbulence of blood ejected through a malformed valve or otherwise idiopathic [33]. Surgical treatment, nevertheless, is clearly indicated as definitive therapy, the "footprints" of which have been enumerated elsewhere in this manuscript.

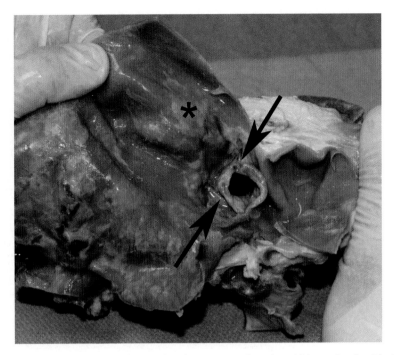

Fig. 6.34 A congenitally anomalous aortic valve appears to be unicuspid (*arrowhead*), with a key-hole morphology and ill-formed raphes (*arrows*) replacing two absent commissures. Atherosclerosis in the ascending aorta (*asterisk*) is probably an incidental finding

Atrial Septal Defect

What looks, at first glance, like another mildly atherosclerotic aortic aneurysm in Fig. 6.35 is in fact anterior to the ascending aorta (arrow). An aneurysm of the main pulmonary artery here is a finding which triggers in the mind of an astute patholo-gist the consideration of pulmonary hypertension. The next question is, why? Fur-ther assessment of the heart quickly answers the question (Fig. 6.36). A large ASD (asterisk) in an adult heart means a long-term left-to-right shunt, resulting in an ongoing "flooding" of the lungs to the point of development of progressive pul-monary hypertension, Eisenmenger's syndrome [34], and a surgically uncorrectable ASD short of a complex transplantation. . . .no easily interpretable "footprints" of a surgeon in this case!

Patent Ductus Arteriosus

How can a patent ductus arteriosus (PDA) lead to an irreparable hemodynamic insult? Figure 6.37 shows a probe passing through a PDA which has persisted for years into adulthood. Not appreciated in this image is calcification of the wall

Fig. 6.35 An atherosclerotic aneurysm of the main pulmonary artery here is anterior to the ascending aorta (*arrow*), a key relationship aiding interpretation of this heart

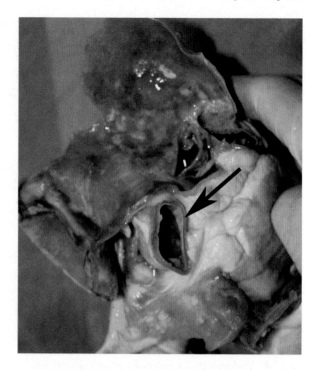

Fig. 6.36 A large ASD (*asterisk*) in an adult heart was associated with a long-term left-to-right shunt

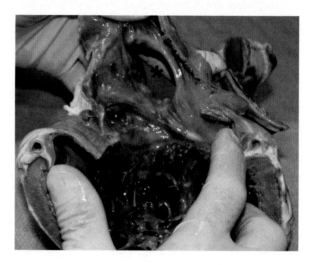

of a large "hole" communicating the descending thoracic aorta and the main pulmonary artery, which results in a left-to-right shunt (Fig. 6.38) which, over time, causes pulmonary hypertension and atherosclerosis and dilatation of the pulmonary artery (asterisk). Surgeons can't sew through calcium, making closure of the PDA

Fig. 6.37 A probe passes from an atherosclerotic (*asterisk*) aorta through a PDA, which persisted for years into adulthood

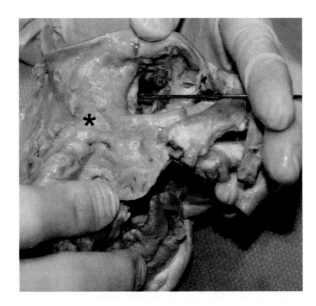

Fig. 6.38 The probe passes through the PDA into a pulmonary artery, which is severely atherosclerotic (*asterisk*) and dilated because of pulmonary hypertension resulting from the long-standing left-to-right shunt

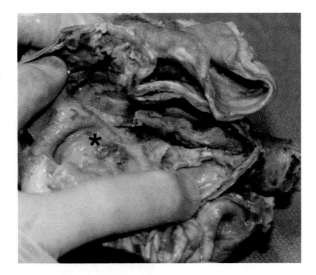

difficult at least. Consider what "footprints" might have been apparent in a failed attempt to repair such a congenital defect after long neglect or not knowing [35, 36]. Right. . .endovascular techniques may abbreviate the serious time needed for such consideration [34].

Transposition of the Great Vessels

Arterial switch became a revolutionary surgical approach to treating congenital transposition of the great vessels in the late 1970s [37–39]. The previously standard surgical approach was the fashioning of a baffle in the atria, as seen here in the right atrium (Fig. 6.39, asterisk; probe in SVC), in order to direct systemic venous return (Fig. 6.40, probe in SVC and LV) into the left ventricle and pulmonary venous return of oxygenated blood (Fig. 6.41, probe in PV) into the right atrium (Fig. 6.42, probe from PV into RA). This redirection of flow permitted the ejection of systemic venous return into the lungs and the pulmonary venous return into the systemic arterial tree via the transposed pulmonary artery and aorta, respectively. Complicating this surgical redirection of blood was heart block [40], in addition to technical mishaps following complex intracardiac surgical manipulation. Arterial switch (Fig. 6.43) eliminated these complications by correcting the direction of oxygenated and deoxygenated blood, "simply" by correcting the positions of the main pulmonary artery (PA) and ascending aorta (A) relative to the left (LV) and right (RV) ventricles. Even the necessitated reimplantation of the coronary arteries (Fig. 6.44) into the "new" ascending aorta was technically achievable (arrows) without significant anastomotic compromise of blood flow, although not entirely devoid of compromise of coronary flow [41].

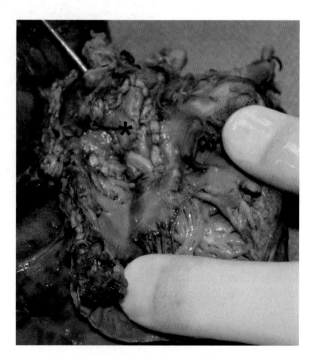

Fig. 6.39 A baffle (*asterisk*) seen from the right side of the heart directs systemic venous return (probe in SVC) to the left side of the heart

Fig. 6.40 Because of a surgically placed interatrial baffle, a probe passes from the SVC into the left ventricle (*asterisk*) through the mitral valve

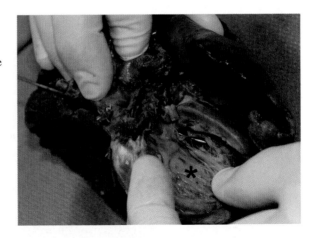

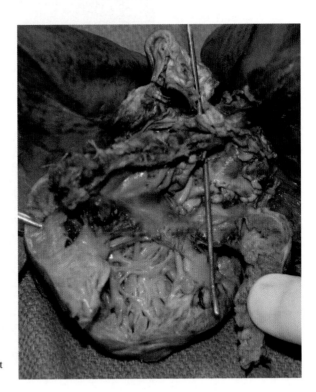

Fig. 6.41 Because of a surgically placed interatrial baffle, pulmonary venous return of oxygenated blood (probe) is directed to the right side of the heart

Fig. 6.42 Confluence of pulmonary vein and right atrium is opened to clarify diversion of blood by interatrial baffle

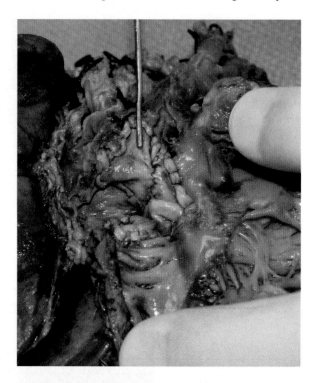

Fig. 6.43 Arterial switch corrects the direction of oxygenated and deoxygenated blood by correcting the positions of the main pulmonary artery (PA) and ascending aorta (A) relative to the left (LV) and right (RV) ventricles

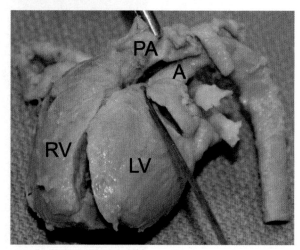

Aortic Coarctation

Figure 6.45 shows a probe in the main pulmonary artery, passing through a PDA, and into the descending thoracic aorta just distal to a coarctation of the aorta (arrow). Note the tight narrowing of the aortic lumen (arrow) compared to the lumen of the

Fig. 6.44 The coronary
arteries are reimplanted into
the "new" ascending aorta
(*arrows*)

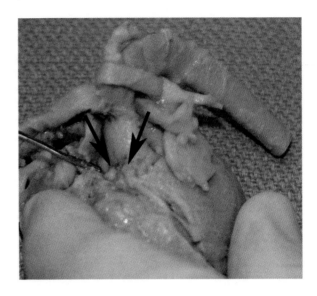

Fig. 6.45 A probe in the
main pulmonary artery passes
through a PDA and into the
descending thoracic aorta just
distal to a coarctation of the
aorta (*arrow*). There is a tight
narrowing of the aortic lumen
(*arrow*) compared to the
lumen of the aortic arch
(*asterisk*) and that of the
descending thoracic aorta
(*double asterisk*)

aortic arch (asterisk) and that of the descending thoracic aorta (double asterisk). A preductal coarctation can cause congestive heart failure in infancy because of an abnormal increase in left ventricular afterload [42]. Furthermore, it is known that in association with preductal coarctations, collateral circulation does not form during embryological development [43], adding to the stress on the left ventricle. With juxtaductal coarctations, collateral circulation off-loads the left ventricle, allowing comfortable survival into or beyond the teenage years before repair is indicated. Although the reason for this difference between the two types of aortic coarctation is unknown, the result can affect risk of surgical repair [44]. Open surgical repair of a coarctation of the aorta may involve interposition of a tube graft to open up the constriction to blood flow. Operative mortality is increased by concomitant cardiac anomalies [45]. The astute pathologist is familiar with the increased prevalence of bicuspid aortic valves in these patients [46] and, if at autopsy, should check for such an association of congenital anomalies and the possibility of two previous surgical procedures. There may be a need for an extraanatomic approach to surgical correction of aortic coarctation [47], unusual "footprints" to challenge awareness.

Sinus of Valsalva Aneurysm

In Fig. 6.46, a "balloon" of fragile tissue (below tip of probe) just above the posteroseptal leaflet of the tricuspid valve of the heart seen can be, at first glance, a puzzling finding. Figure 6.47 shows a probe passing into the right coronary cusp of the aortic valve, and Fig. 6.48 shows the tip of the probe inside that fragile balloon (arrow), adjacent to a high ventricular septal defect (arrowhead). A sinus of valsalva aneurysm, usually involving the right sinus, may be clinically silent until it ruptures, although a large aneurysm can be obstructive [48]. Rupture results in a

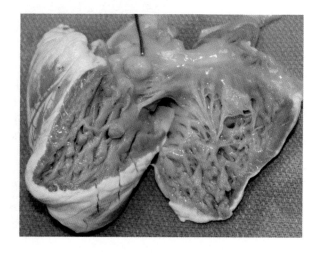

Fig. 6.46 A ballooning fragile tissue (below tip of probe) just above the posteroseptal leaflet of the tricuspid valve of the heart characterizes a sinus of Valsalva aneurysm

Fig. 6.47 A probe passes
into the right coronary cusp
of the aortic valve

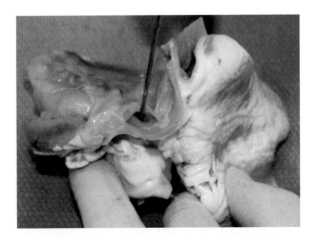

Fig. 6.48 The tip of a probe
from the right sinus of
Valsalva passes into the
aneurysm (*arrow*), which is
adjacent to a high ventricular
septal defect (*arrowhead*).
Associated with these defects
is an aneurysm of the
interatrial septum (*asterisk*)

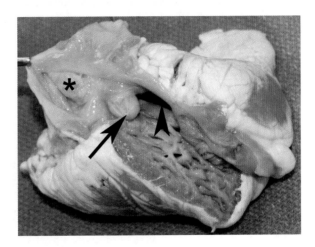

sudden, marked left to right shunt, usually into the right atrium and/or right ventricle [49]. Surgical repair, through an ascending aortotomy is straightforward, placing a patch (probably Dacron) over the entrance into the hole. Distortion of the
sinus, with postoperative aortic regurgitation, has been reported, however [50]. Certainly, a piece of cloth in the right coronary sinus at autopsy can be a meaningful
finding.

Also of interest in same heart (Fig. 6.48) is an aneurysm of the interatrial septum
(asterisk), comprised of a large patulous, translucent sac replacing the normal fossa
ovalis. Imaging modalities can lead to a misdiagnosis of an intracardiac tumor [51].
Here, rupture would not be expected to occur in a relatively low-pressure setting
in each atrium. However, clinical significance could arise if a thrombus developed
in the aneurysmal sac, particularly on the left side where an embolic event might
result in serious injury [52]. If this patient had undergone surgical closure of the

sinus of valsalva defect, concurrent coverage of the deformed fossa ovalis with a pericardial patch would have been prudent and would have added minimal risk to the surgery [53].

Endomyocardial Fibrosis

Figure 6.49 shows a view into both ventricles from the removed apex of the heart of a 19-year-old female with chronic heart failure due to endomyocardial fibrosis. In addition to mitral and tricuspid valve insufficiency, the markedly thickened, fibrotic endocardium (short arrow) resulted in a debilitating restrictive cardiomyopathy. Hypertrophy, involving the left ventricular wall (long arrow), right ventricular wall (double long arrow), and interventricular septum (arrowhead), is remarkable. Characteristic of hearts with this disease was a fibrotic obliteration of the left ventricular apex (Fig. 6.50, arrow), the so-called mushroom sign [54].

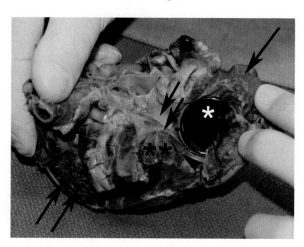

Fig. 6.49 A view into both ventricles from the removed apex of this heart shows a markedly thickened, fibrotic endocardium (*short arrows*) and hypertrophy involving the left ventricular wall (*long arrow*), right ventricular wall (*double long arrow*), and interventricular septum (*double asterisk*). The mitral valve was replaced by a St. Jude prosthesis (*asterisk*)

Because of the patient's intractable heart failure, surgical treatment was undertaken. The mitral valve (Fig. 6.49) was replaced by a St. Jude prosthesis (asterisk) to correct mitral regurgitation, and thickened endocardium was resected below the mitral annulus (double asterisk) in an effort to improve diastolic function of the left ventricle. A Carpentier-Edwards ring valvuloplasty was placed (Fig. 6.51, arrow) to correct tricuspid regurgitation resulting from annular dilatation. Note the heavily fibrotic endocardium (asterisk) lining the dilated right atrium.

A poor postoperative clinical outcome resulted in an autopsy which was rich in cardiac findings. At first glance, the thickened white endocardium would lead one to consider a congenital endocardial fibroelastosis (EFE), which can be associated with other left-sided anomalies, such as mitral valve disease [55]. Furthermore, one could attribute the pathology in the right side of the heart as part of a complex centered

Fig. 6.50 A fibrotic obliteration of the left ventricular apex (*arrow*) characterizes endomyocardial fibrosis

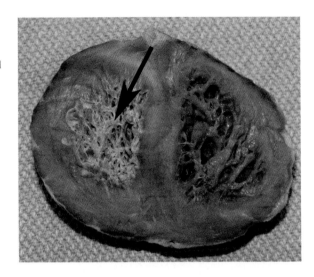

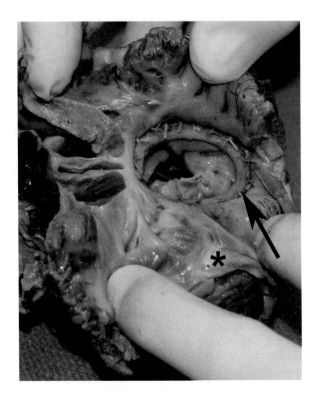

Fig. 6.51
A Carpentier-Edwards ring valvuloplasty was placed (*arrow*) to correct tricuspid regurgitation resulting from annular dilatation. A heavily fibrotic endocardium (*asterisk*) lines the dilated right atrium

physiologically on EFE, causing a restrictive cardiomyopathy and associated mitral insufficiency and left-sided heart failure. However, the fibrotic obliteration of the left ventricular apex would not be explained by a diagnosis of EFE. Histological examination of the endomyocardium would, of course, tell the story.

The patient was a 19-year-old Venezuelan female, with a history of idiopathic restrictive cardiomyopathy. Her history was compatible with endomyocardial fibrosis, a tropical disease that affects an estimated 10 million people worldwide [56]. The diagnosis was easily distinguished from EFE by microscopic examination of tongues of fibrous tissue extending from the thickened, fibrotic endocardium into the underlying myocardium. . .in contrast to the "clean" plane of separation between the two layers of tissue, which characterizes the histology of EFE. A point to be made here is that gross examination at autopsy, including postoperative findings, may seem to pull together in a complex scenario and lead even the astute observer astray. Recognition of the "footprints of a surgeon," the focus of attention in this monograph, is essential for intelligent assessment of the heart at autopsy, but, alas, it is still only part of the journey.

References

1. Gruber PJ, Epstein JA. Development gone awry. Congenital heart disease. Circ Res 2004;94:273–83.
2. Pierpont ME, Basson CT, Benson DW, Gelb BD, Giglia TM, Goldmuntz E, McGee G, Sable CA, Srivastava D, Webb CL. Genetic basis of congenital heart defects: current knowledge. Circulation 2007;115:1–24.
3. Fost CH, Connolly HM, Edwards WD, Hayes D, Warnes CA, Danielson GK. Ebstein's anomaly—review of a multifaceted congenital cardiac condition. Swiss Med Wkly 2005;135:269–81.
4. Carpentier A, Chauvaud S, Mace L, et al. A new reconstructive operation for Ebstein's anomaly of the tricuspid valve. J Thorac Cardiovasc Surg 1988;96:92–101.
5. Moodie DS, Ritter DG, Tajik AJ, O'Fallon WM. Long-term follow-up in the unoperated univentricular heart. Am J Cardiol 1984;53:1124–28.
6. Krishnan U. Univentricular heart: management options. Indian J Pediatr 2005;72:519–24.
7. Malhotra SP, Ivy DD, Mitchell MB, Campbell DN, Dines ML, Miyamoto S, Kay J, Clarke DR, Lacour-Gayet F. Performance of cavopulmonary palliation at elevated altitude: midterm outcomes and risk factors for failure. Circulation 2008;118:S177–81.
8. Margossian RE, Solowiejczyk D, Bourlon F, Apfel H, Gersony WM, Hordof AJ, Quaegebeur J. Septation of the single ventricle: revisited. J Thorac Cardiovasc Surg 2002;124:442–7.
9. Obler D, Juraszek AL, Smoot LB, Natowicz MR. Double outlet right ventricle: aetiologies and associations. J Med Genet 2008;45:481–97. Review.
10. Lacour-Gayet LF. Intracardiac repair of double outlet right ventricle. Semin Thorac Cardiovasc Surg Pediatr Card Surg Ann 2008; 39–43.
11. Rodefeld MD, Ruzmetov M, Vijay P, Fiore AC, Turrentine MW, Brown JW. Surgical results of arterial switch operation for Taussig-Bing anomaly: is position of the great arteries a risk factor? Ann Thorac Surg 2007 Apr;83(4):1451–7.
12. Bradley TJ, Karamlou T, Kulik A, Mitrovic B, Vigneswaran T, Jaffer S, Glasgow PD, Williams WG, Van Arsdell GS, McCrindle BW. Determinants of repair type, reintervention, and mortality in 393 children with double-outlet right ventricle. J Thorac Cardiovasc Surg 2007;134:967–73.

13. Rastelli G, Kirklin JW, Titus JL. Anatomic observations on complete form of persistent common atrioventricular canal with special reference to atrioventricular valves. Mayo Clin Proc 1966;41:296–308.

14. Squarcia U, Squarcia lA. Giancarlo Rastelli: the scientist, the man. Clin Cardiol 2007;30: 485–7.

15. Mavroudis C, Weinstein G, Turley K, Ebert PA. Surgical management of complete atrioventricular canal. J Thorac Cardiovasc Surg 1982;83:670–9.

16. Minette MS, Sahn DJ. Ventricular septal defects. Circulation 2006;114:2190–7.

17. Barratt-Boyes BG, Neutze JM, Clarkson PM, Shardey GC, Brandt PW. Repair of ventricular septal defect in the first two years of life using profound hypothermia-circulatory arrest techniques. Ann Surg 1976;184:376–90.

18. Schwerzmann M, Samman AM, Salehian O, Holm J, Provost Y, Webb GD, Therrien J, Siu SC, Silversides CK. Comparison of echocardiographic and cardiac magnetic resonance imaging for assessing right ventricular function in adults with repaired tetralogy of Fallot. Am J Cardiol 2007;99:1593–7.

19. Saleeb SF, Solowiejczyk DE, Glickstein JS, Korsin R, Gersony WM, Hsu DT. Frequency of development of aortic cuspal prolapse and aortic regurgitation in patients with subaortic ventricular septal defect diagnosed at <1 year of age. Am J Cardiol 2007;99:1588–92.

20. Verheugt CL, Uiterwaal CS, Grobbee DE, Mulder BJ, Verheugt CL, Uiterwaal CS, Grobbee DE, Mulder BJ. Long-term prognosis of congenital heart defects: a systematic review. Int J Cardiol 2008 Aug 5 [Epub ahead of print].

21. Bartz PJ, Cetta F, Cabalka AK, Reeder GS, Squarcia U, Agnetti A, Aurier E, Carano N, Tachana B, Hagler DJ. Paradoxical emboli in children and young adults: role of atrial septal defect and patent foramen ovale device closure. Mayo Clin Proc 2006;81:615–8.

22. Wechsler LR. PFO and stroke: what are the data? Cardiol Rev 2008;16 (1):53–7. Review.

23. Takenaka T, Horimoto M, Fujiwara M. Anomalous origin of the left anterior descending coronary artery from the right sinus of Valsalva associated with effort angina pectoris. Eur Heart J 1993;14:129–31.

24. Turkoglu S, Ozdemir M. Anomalous origin of the left circumflex coronary artery from the right coronary artery and the left anterior descending artery from the right coronary sinus. J Invasive Cardiol 2006;18:E214–6.

25. Kimbiris D. Anomalous origin of the left main coronary artery from the right sinus of Valsalva. Am J Cardiol 1985;55:765–9.

26. Shirani J, Roberts WC. Origin of the left main coronary artery from the right aortic sinus with retroaortic course of the anomalistically arising artery. Am Heart J 1992;124: 1077–8.

27. Rigatelli G, Rigatelli G. Coronary artery anomalies: what we know and what we have to learns. A proposal for a new clinical classification. Ital Heart J 2003;4:305–10.

28. Angelini P. Coronary artery anomalies. An entity in search of an identity. Circulation 2007;115:1296–305.

29. Frescura C, Basso C, Thiene G, Corrado D, Pennelli T, Angelini A, Daliento L. Anomalous origin of coronary arteries and risk of sudden death: a study based on an autopsy population of congenital heart disease. Hum Pathol 1998;29:689–95.

30. Goland S, Czer LS, De Robertis MA, Mirocha J, Kass RM, Fontana GP, Chang W, Trento A. Risk factors associated with reoperation and mortality in 252 patients after aortic valve replacement for congenitally bicuspid aortic valve disease. Ann Thorac Surg 2007;83: 931–7.

31. Cosgrove DM, Rosenkranz ER, Hendren WG, Bartlett JC, Stewart WJ. Valvuloplasty for aortic insufficiency. J Thorac Cardiovasc Surg 1991;102:571–6; discussion 576–7.

32. Guntheroth WG. A critical review of the American College of Cardiology/American Heart Association practice guidelines on bicuspid aortic valve with dilated ascending aorta. Am J Cardiol 2008;102:107–10. Review.

33. Della Corte A, De Santo LS, Montagnani S, Quarto C, Romano G, Amarelli C, Scardone M, De Feo M, Cotrufo M, Caianiello G. Spatial patterns of matrix protein expression in dilated

ascending aorta with aortic regurgitation: congenital bicuspid valve versus Marfan's syndrome. J Heart Valve Dis 2006;15:20–7; discussion 27.

34. Nascimento D, Nunes L, Oliveira F, Vencio E, Teixeira V, Reis M. Pulmonary atherosclerosis associated with an atrial septal defect in old age: Case report of an elderly autopsied patient. Pathol Res Pract 2008 Oct 21 [Epub ahead of print].

35. Giroud JM, Jacobs JP. Evolution of strategies for management of the patent arterial duct. Cardiol Young 2007;17 Suppl 2:68–74. Review.

36. Tekin Y, Ozer S, Murat B, Hulusi UM, Timucin ON. Closure of adult patent ductus arteriosus under cardiopulmonary bypass by using foley balloon catheter. J Card Surg 2007;22: 219–20.

37. Wong D, Golding F, Hess L, Caldarone CA, Van Arsdell G, Manlhiot C, McCrindle BW, Miner SE, Nield LE. Intraoperative coronary artery pulse Doppler patterns in patients with complete transposition of the great arteries undergoing the arterial switch operation. Am Heart J 2008;156:466–72.

38. Love BA, Mehta D, Foster VF. Medscape. Evaluation and management of the adult patient with transposition of the great arteries following atrial-level (Senning or Mustard) repair. Nat Clin Pract Cardiovasc Med 2008;5:454–67. Review.

39. Graham Jr TP, Markham L, Parra DA, Bichell D, Graham Jr TP, Markham L, Parra DA, Bichell D. Congenitally corrected transposition of the great arteries: an update. Curr Treat Options Cardiovasc Med 2007;9:407–13.

40. Reddy VM, McElhinney DB, Silverman NH, Hanley FL. The double switch procedure for anatomical repair of congenitally corrected transposition of the great arteries in infants and children. Eur Heart J 1997;18:1470–7.

41. Gagliardi MG, Adorisio R, Crea F, Versacci P, Di Donato R, Sanders SP. Abnormal vasomotor function of the epicardial coronary arteries in children five to eight years after arterial switch operation: an angiographic and intracoronary Doppler flow wire study. J Am Coll Cardiol 2005;46:1565–72.

42. Midgley FM, Scott LP, Perry LW, Shapiro SR, McClenathan JE. Subclavian flap aortoplasty for treatment of coarctation in early infancy. J Pediatr Surg 1978;13:264–8.

43. Caminos OW. Congenital heart diseases: their study and treatment. MCI Publications, Sønderborg, 1999.

44. Backer CL, Stewart RD, Kelle AM, Mavroudis C. Use of partial cardiopulmonary bypass for coarctation repair through a left thoracotomy in children without collaterals. Ann Thorac Surg 2006;82:964–72.

45. Uddin MJ, Haque AE, Salama AL, Uthman BC, Abushaban LA, Shuhaiber HJ. Surgical management of coarctation of the aorta in infants younger than five months: a study of fifty-one patients. Ann Thorac Cardiovasc Surg 2000;6:252–7.

46. Ciotti GR, Vlahos AP, Silverman NH. Morphology and function of the bicuspid aortic valve with and without coarctation of the aorta in the young. Am J Cardiol 2006;98: 1096–102.

47. Carvalho MV, Pereira WL, Gandra SM, Rivetti LA. Aortic coarctation in the adult: regarding a case and extra-anatomic bypass approaches. Rev Bras Cir Cardiovasc 2007;22:501–4.

48. Yang Y, Zhou Y, Ma L, Ni Y. Unruptured aneurysm of the sinus of Valsalva presenting with thrombosis and right ventricular outflow obstruction. J Card Surg 2008;23:782–4.

49. Moustafa S, Mookadam F, Cooper L, Adam G, Zehr K, Stulak J, Holmes D. Sinus of Valsalva aneurysms-47 years of a single center experience and systematic overview of published reports. Am J Cardiol 2007;99:1159–64.

50. Jung SH, Yun TJ, Im YM, Park JJ, Song H, Lee JW, Seo DM, Lee MS. Ruptured sinus of Valsalva aneurysm: transaortic repair may cause sinus of Valsalva distortion and aortic regurgitation. J Thorac Cardiovasc Surg 2008;135:1153–8.

51. Dodd JD, Aquino SL, Holmvang G, Cury RC, Hoffmann U, Brady TJ, Abbara S. Cardiac septal aneurysm mimicking pseudomass: appearance on ECG-gated cardiac MRI and MDCT. AJR Am J Roentgenol 2007;188:W550–3. Review.

52. Ossemann M, Laloux P, Marchandise B, Jamart J. Association between stroke and atrial septal aneurysm assessed by transesophageal echocardiography in a cardiologic population. Acta Neurol Belg 1995;95:170–7. Review.
53. Harkness JR, Fitton TP, Barreiro CJ, Alejo D, Gott VL, Baumgartner WA, Yuh DD. A 32-year experience with surgical repair of sinus of Valsalva aneurysms. J Card Surg 2005;20: 198–204.
54. Cury RC, Abbara S, Sandoval LJ, Houser S, Brady TJ, Palacios IF. Images in cardiovascular medicine. Visualization of endomyocardial fibrosis by delayed-enhancement magnetic resonance imaging. Circulation 2005;111:e115–7.
55. Boudoulas H. Etiology of valvular heart disease. Expert Rev Cardiovasc Ther 2003;1: 523–32. Review.
56. Mocumbi AO, Ferreira MB, Sidi D, Yacoub MH. A population study of endomyocardial fibrosis in a rural area of Mozambique. N Engl J Med 2008;359:43–9.

Chapter 7
A Matter of Mindset

Abstract The purpose of this monograph has been to address the need of pathologists in practice, and especially in training, to achieve a new level of competence in dealing, at the time of autopsy, with the anatomic complexity of a heart that has undergone previous surgical treatment, whether that treatment occurred in the recent or remote past. Ready identification of postoperative morphologic changes in the heart, the "footprints" of a surgeon, will greatly increase the comfort level of the pathologist as he takes on the challenge of the operated heart. However, at autopsy, the pathologist may still be challenged to understand what his or her careful observations are conveying regarding the underlying disease and effectiveness of one or more surgical operations. By applying a consistent mindset, the pathologist can understand the findings of the operated heart at autopsy and form an accurate interpretation relating those findings to their overall importance and to the cause of death.

Keywords Comfort level · Mindset · Competence · Understanding · Interpretation

The purpose of this monograph has not been to describe in an exhaustive fashion the normal anatomy of the heart or to provide another textbook and/or atlas of cardiovascular pathology. Other authors [1–5] have accomplished these tasks in a substantive manner. This author has attempted to address the need of pathologists in practice and, especially, in training to achieve a new level of competence in dealing, at the time of autopsy, with the anatomic complexity of a heart that has undergone previous surgical treatment, whether that treatment occurred in the recent or the remote past.

Exposure

Exposure to detail is of critical importance when it comes to dealing with postoperative morphologic changes in the heart. In the first four chapters of this monograph, the reader is exposed to anatomic landmarks, which have been fondly described as the "footprints" of a surgeon. Ready identification of these landmarks will greatly

S.L. Houser, *The Operated Heart at Autopsy*, DOI 10.1007/978-1-60327-808-9_7,   165
© Humana Press, a part of Springer Science+Bussiness Media, LLC 2009

increase the comfort level of the pathologist as he takes on the challenge of the operated heart. If one or more of the "usual" landmarks of routine cardiac surgery are missing in the postmortem examination, the pathologist must address the all-important question, why?. If the pathologist isn't familiar with the routine landmarks, that question may not arise, and details—perhaps important details—will be missed.

For a moment, let's consider the task at hand for a cardiac surgeon who has been requested to "fix" or improve the function or status of a sick heart of a patient who wants to live longer and/or feel better than he/she (probably) would without heart surgery. Armed with a detailed knowledge of the patient's overall condition and pathology, the surgeon decides on a strategy of action, the details of which will result in a series of anatomic landmarks, which can at autopsy "paint a picture" of how the surgeon's strategy was carried out. Consider key points of the surgeon's strategy once the goal of the operation on the heart is decided. The methodology of the operation will be multifaceted, and the details of these technical components of the operation will be based on either standard or modified techniques, the details of which have been described eariler in this manuscript and are outlined in the following table.

Method	Standard	Modified
1. Surgical approach		
–to the heart	Median sternotomy	Partial sternotomy; Thoracotomy; Subxiphoid
–to the pathology		
–CABG	Vein/arterial grafts	Variable use of conduits
–Valve	Repair/replacement	Variable use of prosthetics
–Aortic repair	Tube graft	Composite graft + coronary Reimplantation vs. CABG
–Anomalies	Direct repair	Palliative, stepwise approach
–Heart failure	Approved devices	Clinical trial-based devices
2. Use of CPB	Right atrial/ascending Aortic cannulation	Femoral vein/femoral Artery cannulation; other
3. Myocardial protection	Antegrade cardioplegia; Retrograde cardioplegia	Intermittent cross-clamping of ascending aorta [6]

The table above summarizes in essence the choices of technique which a surgeon has to make in order to get "the job" done despite the many challenges to be faced during cardiac surgery. Standard techniques apply well most of the time. However, based on numerous anatomic and physiologic variables, some of which have been reviewed in previous chapters of this manuscript, seldom are any two operations on the heart exactly alike, and the surgeon knows and adapts accordingly. Hence, the "footprints" at autopsy sometimes vary, and the pathologist who is familiar with which antomic landmarks of cardiac surgery to expect and how (and why) they vary is in an advantageous position while in the autopsy suite.

It is possible, and here recommended, that a pathologist go one step further in gaining exposure to the identification and meaning of anatomic landmarks of cardiac surgery. By setting aside some time to visit an operating room and observing the techniques of cardiac surgery first hand, a pathologist can gain valuable perspective in seeing these landmarks as they develop during an operation. Consider the value of actually seeing venous and arterial cannulas placed to establish cardiopulmonary bypass. Watching sutures placed with Teflon pledgets that buttress the suture material and prevent tissue from tearing under the tension will reinforce the concept of attention to detail on the part of the surgeon. Observing the administration of cardioplegic solution either antegrade (into coronary ostia or distally implanted vein bypass grafts) or retrograde (into the coronary sinus) to preserve the functional integrity of the myocardium while the aortic cross clamp is *visibly* in place brings to bear the critical importance of intraoperative myocardial preservation. Watching the surgeon gain access to intracardiac sites of resection and reconstruction will allow the pathologist easy recognition of the multiple suture lines on the heart at autopsy. Such first-hand observation will serve the pathologist well in gaining familiarity in identifying the "footprints." Grasping the reality of the cardiac surgeon's love of "being there" may be a little less intuitive, however.

Understanding

Understanding of autopsy findings relating to a heart that has previously undergone surgical treatment will follow proper exposure to the details of cardiac anatomy, pathophysiology, and surgical techniques. Only then can the pathologist fulfill his obligation of submitting an accurate and meaningful report of his findings. The underlying goal of most open-heart surgical procedures is to relieve symptoms of myocardial ischemia, improve cardiac output, or a combination of both. Myocardial ischemia may result from congenitally anomalous coronary anatomy [7, 8], hypertrophic cardiomyopathy [9, 10], or, most commonly, atherosclerotic coronary artery disease [11]. If surgical treatment is indicated, the surgeon's approach will be guided by the underlying morphologic abnormality. Most procedures performed to relieve myocardial ischemia will include the placement of coronary artery bypass grafts. The concept of bypass surgery is straightforward, viz., directing blood around a coronary obstruction to improve flow into the distal run-off, thereby increasing myocardial perfusion. However, as discussed in Chapter 2, there are multiple technical variations available to the surgeon to accomplish this goal. Bypass conduits can be constructed with veins harvested from multiple sites or with arteries, usually internal mammary or radial. Frequently, but not always, multiple-bypass procedures use a combination of arterial and venous conduits. One conduit may be used to bypass one or multiple coronary arteries. Re-do bypass procedures add yet another level of complexity to these operations, giving the surgeon still more technical options from which to choose. The pathologist at autopsy should be aware of these technical options in order to understand the gross findings. Furthermore, a thorough knowledge of normal coronary anatomy is obviously important [12]. Without these bits of knowledge, an understanding of the findings of a postmortem coronary injection, as discussed in Chapter 3, would be difficult at best to grasp.

Pathologists are well aware that the pathophysiology of an abnormally low cardiac output is multifactorial [13]. When surgical treatment is indicated, it logically follows that the selection of which operation to perform is based on the morphological cause of the low output. The cause may be ischemia, in which case, a coronary artery reconstruction is done. Ischemia may have resulted in ventricular dead space, requiring resection of an apical left ventricular aneurysm and closure by one of multiple alternative techniques [14]. Ischemia may also have resulted in a left-to-right shunt, requiring repair of a ventricular septal defect by one of multiple alternative techniques depending on the location of the hole in the septum [15]. Ischemia may have resulted in a ruptured papillary muscle, requiring placement of an intraaortic balloon pump because of cardiogenic shock and an emergent replacement of a flail mitral valve [16]. Ischemia may have resulted in a ventricular free wall rupture, requiring emergent repair and relief of pericardial tamponade [17] or repair of a pseudoaneurysm in the pericardial space [18].

After the first year following transplantation, most cardiac allografts are lost because of chronic rejection, which is characterized by a progressive intimal thickening and luminal narrowing, a vasculopathy that results in myocardial ischemia and loss of graft function [19]. The vasculopathy involves myocardial as well as epicardial coronary vessels to the point that bypass surgery is usually contraindicated. When an individual with a transplanted heart comes to autopsy, the postmortem coronary injection, as described in Chapter 3, can be very instructive. During the subsequent cardiac dissection, tissue sections that cross all lines of anastomosis between recipient and donor tissue should be put up to look for evidence of acute or chronic tissue damage. In addition, multiple (20–25) sections of myocardium serving as equal representations of each major area of coronary distribution should be taken so that a quantitative effort, such as morphometric analysis [20], can be made to characterize the prevalence and severity of allograft vasculopathy in the heart.

Let the reader be advised that longitudinally oriented cushions of smooth muscle have been characterized in human coronary arteries as normal [21] and as pathologic findings [22–27]. Whelan et al. [28] described these "coronary endocardial cushions" in humans as well as in seven additional mammalian species and suggested that these cushions may play a functional role in intramural coronary arterial blood flow and predispose to ischemic heart disease. Vessels with these muscular cushions, particularly if they produce a more or less concentric morphology in cross-section, could clearly mimic histological features of cardiac allograft vasculopathy (CAV). A very regular arrangement of smooth muscle cells inside internal elastic lamina is characteristic of longitudinal intimal cushions. Although intimal thickening of CAV is frequently concentric, lesions of CAV are not necessarily concentric. Longitudinally oriented smooth muscle cushions vary in morphology, and, depending on the manner in which a vessel with these cushions is cut in cross-section, an apparent intimal thickening might be concentric or eccentric. A study by this author and colleagues [29] indicates that muscular cushions in human coronary arteries can potentially affect one's assessment of the prevalence of CAV in human grafts.

Because of these mimics of CAV, a failure to quantify vascular lesions in allograft hearts at the time of autopsy may result in an erroneous diagnosis and assessment of the severity of CAV in clinical studies.

Low cardiac output may be a result of valvular heart disease. With rare exceptions, stenotic valvular disease is congenital, degenerative, or postinflammatory, and the treatment of choice is valve replacement [30]. In select cases of congenital valve stenosis and in an occasional case of acquired mitral stenosis, the surgeon may choose valve repair over replacement, which usually means an open commissurotomy [31]. A double valve replacement, usually aortic and mitral, suggests that the underlying disease is postinflammatory, i.e., rheumatic valvular heart disease, which commonly involves the mitral valve alone, both valves simultaneously, but rarely the aortic valve alone [32, 33]. As discussed in Chapter 4, the pathologist should note the type of valve prosthesis used in each case and try to understand the reasoning behind the surgeon's choice.

Valvular insufficiency, another cause of low cardiac output, may also be associated with multiple clinical scenarios. Like valve stenosis, the cause of valve regurgitation may be congenital, degenerative, or postinflammatory, and the treatment of choice is usually valve replacement. However, in mitral valve prolapse, a specific fibromyxomatous degenerative process, the valve can frequently be repaired by resection of the prolapsed leaflet tissue and placement of an annuloplasty ring for support of the repair [34, 35]. Mitral or tricuspid valve regurgitation because of annular dilatation, usually a consequence of ventricular wall remodeling, is usually repaired by suture or ring annuloplasty [36]. Aortic valve insufficiency due to prolapse following an acute aortic dissection can frequently be repaired by resuspending the prolapsed commissure with buttressed sutures [37]; however, when annular dilatation, as in association with an ascending aortic aneurysm, is the cause of aortic insufficiency, the valve must be replaced [38]. Mitral regurgitation resulting from ischemic papillary muscle dysfunction can be treated effectively by valvuloplasty as well as by valve replacement. Although preserving a patient's native valve tissue is generally preferred over valve replacement and potential complications related to prosthetic valves, patient follow-up has shown a significant recurrence of mitral regurgitation following valvuloplasty for treatment of ischemic valve disease [39], and valve replacement may be the treatment of choice.

A few other intracardiac lesions that limit stroke volume, hence cardiac output, can be treated surgically in a straightforward manner. Abnormal rings of tissue in the left atrium and left ventricular outflow tract, cor triatriatum [40] and diaphragmatic subaortic stenosis [41], respectively, are simply resected. Tunnel-like subaortic stenosis [40] and idiopathic hypertrophic subaortic stenosis (eccentric hypertrophic cardiomyopathy) can be relieved by a myomectomy done through the aortic valve [41], which opens up the outflow tract. Additional obstructive lesions, such as congenital valve atresia and hypoplastic left heart syndrome [42–44], usually challenge the surgeon in a single or multiple stages of treatment. Subsequently, at autopsy, the pathologist is similarly challenged to understand what his or her careful observations are conveying regarding the underlying disease and effectiveness of one or more surgical operations. Studying any clinical data available and timely communication with involved clinicians can be very helpful to the pathologist in these types of cases.

Interpretation

Finally, only after the pathologist understands the findings of the operated heart at autopsy is an accurate *interpretation* relating those findings to their overall importance and to the cause of death possible. In Chapter 5, the reader was confronted with a list of complex clinical scenarios consisting of cardiac surgery and subsequent autopsies done during the same hospitalization in each case. A consistent mindset was addressed in each case in order to offer a framework of reason and guidance that might help the reader prepare to face the detail and tedium of similar autopsies in the future.

Although not unique to cases involving cardiac surgery, the importance of the strength and accuracy of the pathologist's interpretation of this type of autopsy case is multifaceted. As indicated previously in this monograph, the surgeon has a driving need to understand why the operation had a bad outcome. Only after that level of understanding is achieved will peace of mind follow for the surgeon. Beyond this point, the next question that arises is whether or not postoperative mortality could have been prevented. If not, clinicians need to face the question of patient selection. If postoperative death could have been prevented, the questions of why and how arise. Was there an error committed intraoperatively, postoperatively, or in both aspects of patient care? In any case, issues of technique and judgment will need to be scrutinized. If this monograph contributes to reducing the need for similar scrutiny in the autopsy suite, then its author will consider his effort in writing it worthwhile.

References

1. Bonnett R, Ray R, Chopra P. Illustrated textbook of cardiovascular pathology. Taylor Francis, Abingdon, UK, 2004.
2. Silver MD, Gotlieb AI, Shoen FJ. Cardiovascular pathology (3rd ed.). Churchill Livingstone, New York, 2001.
3. Virmani, R, Burke A, Farb A. Atlas of cardiovascular pathology. W.B. Saunders, Philadelphia, 1996.
4. Rowse AL, McKay R, Smith A. A practical atlas of congenital heart disease. Springer-Verlag, London, 2003.
5. Bharati S, Lev M. The pathology of congenital heart disease: a personal experience with more than 6,300 congenitally malformed hearts. Armonk, Futura, New York, 1996.
6. Liu Z, Valencia O, Treasure T, Murday AJ. Cold blood cardioplegia or intermittent cross-clamping in coronary artery bypass grafting? Ann Thorac Surg 1998 Aug;66(2): 462–5.
7. Eckart RE, Jones SO 4th, Shry EA, Garrett PD, Scoville SL. Sudden death associated with anomalous coronary origin and obstructive coronary disease in the young. Cardiol Rev 2006;14:161–3.

8. Frommelt PC, Frommelt MA. Congenital coronary artery anomalies. Pediatr Clin North Am 2004;51:1273–88. Review.

9. Friehs I, del Nido PJ. Increased susceptibility of hypertrophied hearts to ischemic injury. Ann Thorac Surg 2003;75:S678–84. Review.

10. Rodriguez-Porcel M, Zhu XY, Chade AR, Amores-Arriaga B, Caplice NM, Ritman EL, Lerman A, Lerman LO. Functional and structural remodeling of the myocardial microvasculature in early experimental hypertension. Am J Physiol Heart Circ Physiol 2006;290:H978–84.

11. Reiss AB, Glass AD. Atherosclerosis: immune and inflammatory aspects. J Investig Med 2006;54:123–31. Review.

12. Baert AL, Oudkerk M. Coronary radiology (medical radiology/diagnostic imaging), Springer-Verlag, New York, 2004.

13. Gheorghiade M, Sopko G, De Luca L, Velazquez EJ, Parker JD, Binkley PF, Sadowski Z, Golba KS, Prior DL, Rouleau JL, Bonow RO. Navigating the crossroads of coronary artery disease and heart failure. Circulation 2006;114:1202–13. Review.

14. Trehan N, Kohli V, Meharwal ZS, Mishra Y, Sharma VK, Mishra M. Surgical treatment of post infarction left ventricular aneurysms: our experience with double breasting and Dor's repair. J Card Surg 2003;18:114–20.

15. Mantovani V, Mariscalco G, Leva C, Blanzola C, Sala A. Surgical repair of post-infarction ventricular septal defect: 19 years of experience. Int J Cardiol 2006;108:202–6.

16. Chen Q, Darlymple-Hay MJ, Alexiou C, Ohri SK, Haw MP, Livesey SA, Monro JL. Mitral valve surgery for acute papillary muscle rupture following myocardial infarction. J Heart Valve Dis 2002;11:27–31.

17. Vohra HA, Chaudhry S, Satur CM, Heber M, Butler R, Ridley PD. Sutureless off-pump repair of post-infarction left ventricular free wall rupture. J Cardiothorac Surg 2006;1:11–13.

18. Perek B, Jemielity M, Dyszkiewicz W. Clinical profile and outcome of patients with chronic postinfarction left ventricular false aneurysm treated surgically. Heart Surg Forum 2004;7:E132–5.

19. Rahmani M, Cruz RP, Granville DJ, McManus BM. Allograft vasculopathy versus atherosclerosis. Circ Res 2006;99:801–15.

20. Houser SL, McMorrow IM, LeGuern C, Schwarze ML, Fuchimoto Y, Sachs DH, Madsen JC. Histomorphometric comparison of cardiac allograft vasculopathy in miniature swine. J Heart Lung Transplant 2004;23:50–60.

21. Amenta PS. Elias-Pauly's histology & human micro-anatomy (5th ed.). John Wiley and Sons, New York, 1987, pp.198–200.

22. Gross L, Epstein EZ, Kugel MA. Histology of the coronary arteries and their branches in the human heart. Am M Pathol 1934;10:253–74.

23. Dock W. The predilection of atherosclerosis for the coronary arteries. JAMA 1946;131:875–8.

24. Velican C, Velican D. Intimal thickening in developing coronary arteries and its relevance to atherosclerotic involvement. Atherosclerosis 1976;23:345–55.

25. Velican D, Velican C. Study of fibrous plaques occurring in the coronary arteries of children. Atherosclerosis 1979;33:201–15.

26. Velican C, Velican D. The precursors of coronary atherosclerotic plaques in subjects up to 40 years old. Atherosclerosis 1980;37:33–46.

27. Rahlf G. Intramyocardial microarteriopathy. Virchows Arch Path Anat Histol 1980;388: 289–311.

28. Whelan NL, Subramanian R, Jin J, Keith IM. Intramyocardial arterial cushions of coronary vessels in animals and humans: morphology, occurrence and relation to heart disease. J Vasc Res 1996;33:209–24.

29. Houser SL, Muniappan A, Allan J, Sachs D, Madsen J. Cardiac allograft vasculopathy: real or a normal variant? J Heart Lung Transplant 2007;26:167–73.

30. Resnekov L. Aortic valve stenosis. Management in children and adults. Postgrad Med 1993;93:107–10, 113–14, 117–22. Review.

31. Halseth WL, Elliott DP, Walker EL, Smith EA. Open mitral commissurotomy. A modern re-evaluation. J Thorac Cardiovasc Surg 1980;80:842–8.

32. Vaturi M, Porter A, Adler Y, Shapira Y, Sahar G, Vidne B, Sagie A. The natural history of aortic valve disease after mitral valve surgery. J Am Coll Cardiol 1999;33:2003–8.

33. Chockalingam A, Gnanavelu G, Elangovan S, Chockalingam V. Clinical spectrum of chronic rheumatic heart disease in India. J Heart Valve Dis 2003;12:577–81.

34. Oliveira JM, Antunes MJ. Mitral valve repair: better than replacement. Heart 2006;92:275–81. Review.

35. Gogbashian A, Sepic J, Soltesz EG, Nascimben L, Cohn LH. Operative and long-term survival of elderly is significantly improved by mitral valve repair. Am Heart J 2006;151:1325–33.

36. Matsuyama K, Matsumoto M, Sugita T, Nishizawa J, Tokuda Y, Matsuo T, Ueda Y. De Vega annuloplasty and Carpentier-Edwards ring annuloplasty for secondary tricuspid regurgitation. J Heart Valve Dis 2001;10:520–4.

37. Albes JM, Stock UA, Hartrumpf M. Restitution of the aortic valve: what is new, what is proven, and what is obsolete? Ann Thorac Surg 2005;80:1540–9. Review.

38. Fleck TM, Koinig H, Czerny M, Hutschala D, Wolner E, Ehrlich M, Grabenwoger M. Impact of surgical era on outcomes of patients undergoing elective atherosclerotic ascending aortic aneurysm operations. Eur J Cardiothorac Surg 2004;26:342–7.

39. Hung J, Papakostas L, Tahta SA, Hardy BG, Bollen BA, Duran CM, Levine RA. Mechanism of recurrent ischemic mitral regurgitation after annuloplasty: continued LV remodeling as a moving target. Circulation 2004;110(11 Suppl 1):II85–90. Review.

40. Slight RD, Nzewi OC, Buell R, Mankad PS. Cor-triatriatum sinister presenting in the adult as mitral stenosis: an analysis of factors which may be relevant in late presentation. Heart Lung Circ 2005;14:8–12. Review.

41. Newfeld EA, Muster AJ, Paul MH, Idriss FS, Riker WL. Discrete subvalvular aortic stenosis in childhood. Study of 51 patients. Am J Cardiol 1976;38:53–61.

42. Singh GK. Subvalvular aortic stenosis. Curr Treat Options Cardiovasc Med 2000;2:529–35.

43. Reinhartz O, Reddy VM, Petrossian E, MacDonald M, Lamberti JJ, Roth SJ, Wright GE, Perry SB, Suleman S, Hanley FL. Homograft valved right ventricle to pulmonary artery conduit as a modification of the Norwood procedure. Circulation 2006;114(1 Suppl):I594–9.

44. Hannan RL, Ybarra MA, Ojito JW, Alonso FA, Rossi AF, Burke RP. Complex neonatal single ventricle palliation using antegrade cerebral perfusion. Ann Thorac Surg 2006;82:1278–84; discussion 1284–5.

Abbreviations

AICD: automatic implantable cardiac defibrillator

ARDS: acute respiratory distress syndrome

ASD: atrial septal defect

AV: atrioventricular

Ber-EP4: a specific clone of an antibody to an epithelial antigen

BIVAD: biventricular assist device

BP: blood pressure

BT: Blalock-Taussig

C4d: a fragment of C4 released during activation of the classic complementpathway by the antigen-antibody complex

CABG: coronary artery bypass grafting/graft(s)

CAV: cardiac allograft vasculopathy

CHD: congenital heart disease

CI: cardiac index

CK: cytokeratin

cm: centimeter(s)

CO2: carbon dioxide

CPB: cardiopulmonary bypass

CPR: cardiopulmonary resuscitation

CT: computed tomography

CVP: central venous pressure

DIC: disseminated intravascular coagulation

DKS: Damus-Kaye-Stansel

DLP: dual-lumen perfusion (a proprietary acronym)

DORV: double-outlet right ventricle

ECG: electrocardiogram

ECMO: extracorporeal membrane oxygenation

EFE: endocardial fibroelastosis

EMA: epithelial membrane antigen

FIO2: fraction of inspired oxygen (in arterial blood)

GI: gastrointestinal

g: gram(s)

He: helium

HIT: heparin-induced thrombocytopenia

ICU: intensive care unit

IABP: intra-aortic balloon pump

IVC: inferior vena cava

kg: kilogram(s)

LAD: left anterior descending coronary artery

LIMA: left internal mammary artery

LV: left ventricular or left ventricle

LVAD: left ventricular assist device

ml: milliliter(s)

mm: millimeter(s)

NBT: nitro-blue tetrazolium

OPCAB: off-pump coronary artery bypass

PA: pulmonary artery

PDA: posterior descending coronary artery

PFO: patent foramen ovale

PICC: peripherally inserted central catheter

PV: pulmonary vein

RA: right atrium

RCA: right coronary artery

RVAD: right ventricular assist device

RVH: right ventricular hypertrophy

RVOT: right ventricular outflow tract

SAM: systolic anterior motion

SVC: superior vena cava

SVG: saphenous vein graft(s)

SVR: systemic vascular resistance

TEE: transesophageal echocardiography

TOF: tetralogy of Fallot

TTC: 2,3,5-triphenyltetrazolium chloride

TTF: thyroid transcription factor

VSD: ventricular septal defect

WT-1: Wilms tumor 1

XVE: extended lead vented electric (a proprietary acronym)

Glossary

Annular circumference (normal adult): tricuspid (10–12.5 cm); pulmonary (7–9 cm); mitral (8–10.5 cm); aortic (6–7.5 cm)(autopsy protocol used at Massachusetts General Hospital)

Annuloplasty: (see valvuloplasty)

AV canal defect: anomalous development of the embryonic endocardial cushions of tissue, which line the canal-like opening between the atrial and ventricular chambers of the heart

Baffle: a Dacron patch used to create an interatrial tunnel in transposition of the great vessels; used to redirect systemic venous return into the left atrium and pulmonary venous return into the right atrium

Blunt dissection: separating tissues or mobilizing tissue planes without using a sharp cutting edge of an instrument, i.e., knife or scissors

Broviac line: a type of central venous catheter, which can be used to draw blood for testing and to administer therapeutic agents intravenously

Cardiomegaly: enlarged heart due either to myocardial hypertrophy, chamber dilatation or both; a heart weight more than 350 g in women and more than 400 g in men (Waller BF, Roberts WC. Cardiovascular disease in the very elderly. Analysis of 40 necropsy patients of 90 years or older. Am J Cardiol 1983;51:403–21)

Cardiopulmonary bypass: resting the heart by draining venous blood into an external machine, in which the blood is filtered, oxygenated, heated, or cooled, and then pumped back into the body's arterial circulation, allowing a surgeon to operate on a non-beating heart

Chiari complex: a membranous, fenestrated network of tissue in the right atrium at the confluence of inferior vena cava and area of the coronary sinus during embryologic development of the heart; normally becomes atretic in the neonate

Crista supraventricularis: a saddle-shaped muscular crest in the right ventricular outflow tract situated between the tricuspid valve and the pulmonary valve; consists of septal and parietal components and demarcates the junction between the outlet septum and the pulmonary infundibulum

Destination therapy: permanent treatment, as opposed to treatment used as a step, or bridge, to definitive therapy

Double-outlet right ventricle: a congenital anomaly of the heart in which the right ventricle empties into both the aorta and pulmonary artery, supplying total systemic and pulmonary circulation

Ebstein's anomaly: a downward displacement of part or all of the effective ring of the tricuspid valve, with associated abnormality of the valvular apparatus and architecture of the right ventricle

Endocardial cushion: thickened tissue that lines the primitive atrioventricular canal and normally engages the interatrial septum primum and interventricular septum during embryologic development of the heart

Free style porcine root replacement: use of a stentless bioprosthesis

Hemashield graft: a type of Dacron tube used for arterial reconstructive surgery

Homograft aortic valve: harvested from a human cadaver or the native heart of a human heart transplant recipient and cryopreserved for later selective implantation in a patient needing an aortic valve replacement

Intraaortic balloon pump: a mechanical device inserted into the aorta to improve left ventricular failure and/or myocardial ischemia when medical therapy alone is insufficient

Isthmus of aorta: segment of descending thoracic aorta between the take-off of the left subclavian artery and the ligamentum arteriosum; common site of aortic coarctation

Juxtaductal: adjacent to the ductus, or ligamentum, arteriosus, as a juxtaductal (or periductal) coarctation of the aorta

Left ventricular preload: left ventricular circumferential wall stress at end diastole; quantified by left ventricular end-diastolic (filling) pressure, normally 5–12 mmHg; a low value suggests a deficit in blood volume in the body; a high value suggests an overload in blood volume and/or left ventricular failure

Low cardiac output state: an overall biochemical, hemodynamic, and clinical picture reflecting a low cardiac index (<2.4 L/m2); may also be called low flow state

Left ventricular afterload: left ventricular wall stress (load) against which a stroke volume of blood is ejected; a function of mean arterial pressure, radius of left ventricle, and left ventricular wall thickness; approximated quantitatively by the systemic vascular resistance

Left ventricular hypertrophy: myocardial thickness >1.2 cm, measured 1.0 cm below the mitral valve annulus (autopsy protocol used at Massachusetts General Hospital)

Median sternotomy: a vertical (in a cephalocaudal plane) incision through the middle of the sternum; usually performed with a mechanical saw

Minimally invasive surgery: operating through a surgical incision which is significantly smaller than one used in a previously standard approach for a given operation; surgical procedures done with minimal trauma to the patient

Myocardial preservation: preventing excessive depletion of ATP in the sarcomeres of the heart during periods of intra-operative myocardial ischemia, particularly during the time in which the ascending aorta is cross-clamped;usually achieved by rapid cooling and/or arresting the heart with a cardioplegic solution given antegrade (into the coronary ostia) and/or retrograde (into the coronary sinus)

Pledget: a small (usually <1 cm) square or rectangular piece of Teflon used surgically to buttress sutures to prevent their tearing tissue as they are tied down

Preductal: proximal to the ductus, or ligamentum, arteriosus, as a preductal coarctation of the aorta

Pseudoarthrosis: a false joint, or non-union, resulting from incomplete healing of bone that has been surgically severed or fractured

Restrictive cardiomyopathy: a failure of diastolic relaxation of the heart because of stiffness of the ventricular free wall, resulting in inadequate filling and decreased cardiac output

Right ventricular hypertrophy: myocardial thickness >0.3 cm, measured 1.0 cm below the tricuspid valve annulus (autopsy protocol used at Massachusetts General Hospital)

Sharp dissection: separating tissues or mobilizing tissue planes by using a sharp cutting edge of an instrument, i.e., a knife or scissors

Single ventricle: see univentricular heart

Stent: a wire mesh cylinder placed into an artery or vein graft to retain the effect of angioplasty, viz., the dilated lumen of a previously stenotic segment of the vessel

Systemic vascular resistance: a function of peripheral vasomotor tone and calculated to equal 80x (MAP-CVP)/CO, where MAP is mean arterial pressure, CVP is central venous pressure, and CO is cardiac output; left ventricular afterload

Tetralogy of Fallot: a congenital anomaly of the heart characterized by right ventricular hypertrophy, a ventricular septal defect, right ventricular outflow tract obstruction (infundibular and/or valvular), and an overriding aorta

Transposition of the great vessels: congenital reversal of the aorta and pulmonary artery such that the aorta carries unoxygenated blood (systemic venous return) to the body and the pulmonary artery carries oxygenated blood (pulmonary venous return) to the lungs

Trendelenburg procedure: an emergent pulmonary artery embolectomy done (usually) through a median sternotomy, using cardiopulmonary bypass for circulatory support

Truncus arteriosus: a congenital anomaly characterized by a single vessel arising from the heart and giving off the coronary circulation, systemic circulation, and pulmonary circulation; usually overrides a ventricular septal defect with atrophy of the right ventricular outflow tract

Univentricular heart: a congenital anomaly in which the ventricular structure, instead of a normal left and right ventricle separated by a septum of myocardium, is a single chamber with the morphology of a normal right ventricle, normal left ventricle, or neither

Valvuloplasty: repair (not replacement) of a heart valve;may involve tightening the annulus (annuloplasty) with suture technique alone or by sewing the annulus to a ring device;may include resection of part of a valve leaflet, closure of the defect with suture, and seating a ring device to support the repair

Ventricular assist device (VAD):   mechanical apparatus that diverts atrial blood away from a failing ventricle and pumps the diverted blood into the aorta (LVAD), pulmonary artery (RVAD), or both (BIVAD)

Index

Printed in the United States of America